FACES OF
HOLINESS II
MODERN SAINTS IN PHOTOS AND WORDS

FACES OF HOLINESS II

MODERN SAINTS IN PHOTOS AND WORDS

ANN BALL

Our Sunday Visitor Publishing Division
Our Sunday Visitor, Inc.
Huntington, Indiana 46750

ISBN: 0-87973-409-4
LCCCN: 2001-130328

Cover design: Monica Haneline
Interior design: Sherri L. Hoffman

Printed in the United States of America

DEDICATION

This book is lovingly dedicated to our Holy Father Pope John Paul II, who has shown great courage in carrying out the wishes of the fathers at our last council in giving to the Catholic world holy and exemplary models from all countries and all walks of life, and by doing so has greatly encouraged us all in the knowledge that we, too, should strive for sanctity.

It is also dedicated to the next generation of my family: Courtney, Jeremy, Jaycie, Little Courtney, Dalton, Austin, Max, Victoria, Brenden, Christian, Michael, and the twins. May the saints lead them ever closer to God.

And to my friend Johannes Zheng; may he enjoy the company of the saints he loved and served on this earth.

DECLARATION OF OBEDIENCE

In loyal and loving obedience to the decrees of several Roman Pontiffs, in particular those of Pope Urban VIII, I declare that I in no way intend to pre-judge Holy Mother Church in the matter of saints, sanctity, miracles, and so forth. Final authority in such matters rests with the See of Rome, to whose judgment I willingly submit.

The Author

TABLE OF CONTENTS

INTRODUCTION

Saints come in clumps. When I first began researching the lives of the saints, I noticed that if there was one saint, there were more. I suppose I noticed it most clearly when I investigated the life of St. John Bosco. So many of his peers, his students, the members of his religious orders were already being thought of for the honors of the altar.

When I pointed this out to a priest friend, he laughed and said, "Yes, saints come in clumps." There is, of course, a logical reason for this pattern of sanctity. Many saints of Europe began important religious works as founders of religious orders after the time of the French Revolution.

They began works to combat the evils of their day. In our own century, the blood of martyrs worldwide has caused an explosion of holiness in many places. The Church is thriving in precisely those countries where the Faith has been the most persecuted. Countries which only a few decades ago were classified mission lands are now sending forth apostles of their own. When I was a young girl, my mother used to warn me away from bad companions, saying, "When you play with dirt, you will get dirty." The reverse also holds true, "When you play with light, you yourself will begin to shine." Those who would be saintly can benefit by being around the saints.

In this volume alone you will see the influence of some saints such as St. Thérèse on others, often those whom they never met in person but only touched through the written word. It is my hope that the reader of this book will find new heavenly friends and that their lights will cover the reader, causing him or her to shine more brightly in the Faith.

Alexia Gonzalez-Barros
Spain, 1971-1985

Smiling Teen on the Cancer Ward

The patient in the crisp white hospital bed was obviously very ill. A large metal device was fitted to her head and neck with screws, and she had been given a medication that turned her mouth purple. She turned to her visitor and said, "First, they made me look like Frankenstein; now, I look more like Dracula!" In spite of the horror of Alexia's condition, the friend had no option but to laugh at the young teen's comment. Earlier, Alexia's mother had brought her a woolen cap to keep her head warm since all her hair had fallen out from the chemotherapy. Alexia had a keen sense of humor and asked her mother to embroider "I am bald" on the cap.

To visitors, Alexia always presented a cheerful demeanor, turning the conversation to them and away from her own problems. One of her doctors brought his students to see her, telling them "I want you to see how it is to be joyful, despite pain and suffering."

Alexia Gonzalez-Barros died of cancer in 1985 at the age of 14. This Spanish teenager accepted her fatal illness, kept a cheerful sense of humor, offered her suffering for others and faithfully lived her motto and constant prayer, "Jesus, may I always do what you want."

Alexia was born March 7, 1971, the youngest of five surviving children of Francisco Gonzalez-Barros and his wife Ramona. She was basically a cheerful and serene child who infected others with her sunny disposition. Her birth came after

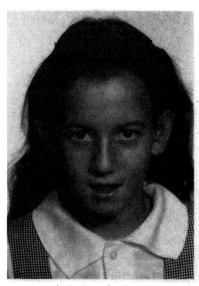

Alexia Gonzalez-Barros
PHOTOS COURTESY OF THE GONZALEZ-BARROS FAMILY

Alexia imitating Charlie Chaplin

the death of two infant sons, and she quickly became the apple of the eyes of everyone in the warm and loving family. She never abused this fact, and she was never spoiled or allowed to be a tiny tyrant. Her parents would tell her, "You have to behave like a lady. We are all ordinary people in this house, but ill-mannered, never!"

Although Alexia's sister and three brothers were quite a lot older than she, the siblings enjoyed a close and loving relationship. Their happiest times were the ones spent with the family.

As a small child, Alexia was happy and mischievous, getting into many of the same types of scrapes most normal children do. Her family vividly remembers the time she got a toasted corn kernel stuck in her nose. When her mother came to fetch her from school, Alexia had a very grave expression on her face because she was scared. Halfway home, she finally blurted out, "Mother, I have a corn kernel inside my nose. Will somebody have to cut me open to get it out?" Although her mother assured her that they could remove it at home, the task was difficult and Alexia began to panic. When she was finally able to remove it, she tearfully embraced her mother and promised never to put corn in her nose again.

Alexia made her first confession at the age of six at the parish church of El Santissimo Cristo de la Victoria, near the family's home. One day shortly thereafter she made a double genuflection before the Tabernacle as she and her mother were leaving the church. Her mother thought to ask her if she had ever mentioned that Alexia could give our Lord a greeting as she genuflected before the Blessed Sacrament. Giving her mother a wide-eyed stare, Alexia responded, "Of course I tell Him things, Mommy. I say, Jesus, may I always do what you want." Startled, the mother reflected that she had never taught these words to her child.

Alexia's father suffered a heart attack when she was seven, and after he came home from the hospital she would come home from school and spend long hours with him in silence. For a time, the family's financial picture was not good because the doctor had advised Francisco to take a complete rest for six months, which was hard on his business.

Alexia loved picnics, playing with her friends, and taking vacations with her family. In the summers, the family often visited the grandparents at their homes in Galicia and the outskirts of Madrid. One special family trip was to Rome where she made her first Communion. Her parents were to celebrate their 25th wedding anniversary and decided to allow Alexia to receive her first Holy Communion at the same time. They decided to go to Rome and hold their thanksgiving and Alexia's reception of the sacrament at the Mass said over the relics of Blessed Josemaria Escrivá, founder of Opus Dei. The following day, the family attended a general audience with the Pope at St. Peter's Square. After his talk, Alexia suddenly let go of her mother's hand and ran as fast as she could to a cordoned area that held well-wishers at bay. A lady lifted Alexia over the blockage and a Swiss guard on the other side caught her and set her on the floor. Alexia ran to the Pope along with the other children and handed him a letter which she had written. The Pope smilingly took the letter, traced the sign of the cross on her forehead, and gave

Alexia presenting her letter to Pope John Paul II

Alexia with the family dogs

her a kiss. Returning to her mother, Alexia smiled in triumph and said, "I gave it to him, didn't I?" The letter had been Alexia's own idea and she was determined to give it to the Pope herself, disregarding her parents' suggestion to hand it to one of his bodyguards or one of the Swiss guards.

Later, shopping, listening to music, and reading were favorite occupations. Alexia loved fashionable clothes, and she was often given hand-me-downs from her first cousins who were good dressers. The rest of the time, her mother made her clothes, following Alexia's own designs. Alexia had good taste and could draw well. When it came to reading, Alexia was made in the mold of the rest of her family — all were bookworms. One of the favorite family outings was to attend a nearby bookfair and to search the various stalls for an interesting book.

From the time she was young, Alexia had a great devotion to her guardian angel. She named him Hugo, telling her mother that she didn't just want to call him "guardian angel" as other people did. She never explained why she picked that name, but in a book her family found, St. Hugo was described as a French bishop who fought the devil all his life. They guessed that Alexia named her guardian angel after this saint.

Alexia loved school and did well there. She loved her teachers and fellow students and they, in turn, loved the happy and good-natured little girl. She learned to dance at the Alcalá Girls Club where she also took cooking and flamenco lessons and attended talks on Christian formation. Once during her long illness she had the happiness of visiting her school. One of her last letters, dictated to her father, was addressed to her fellow students.

At twelve, Alexia developed a crush on a boy named Alfonso whom she saw on her way to visit her cousins in Palamos. They never really met because they didn't have mutual friends to introduce them, so all she knew of him was what little she saw of him. A few days before her death she said, "What a pity! Now Alfonso will never know how much I love him."

In the spring of 1984, Alexia began to complain about back pains. X-rays were taken but nothing unusual was found. She took some back-strengthening exercises at a rehabilitation center but in the fall, the pain seemed to get worse. In February 1985, she went to the doctor again and at first he felt it was simply a painful but harmless muscle contraction. As they were about to leave, Alexia confessed that she couldn't move her hand. The doctor had more x-rays taken and to his horror he found damage to her spinal cord. She had developed a malignant tumor that left her paralyzed. As the doctor immediately admitted her to the hospital, Alexia freely confessed to her mother that she was frightened. She also prayed, "Jesus, I want to get well, I want to be cured, but if you do not want it, I want whatever you want." With simplicity and without show, Alexia had offered her life to God. Later, she told her mother, "Mommy, please be calm. I am not afraid any more. I'm happy."

Alexia had once begun a school paper with the words, "To serve is to live joyfully." In her suffering, she attempted to serve God always with joy. She said, "Believe it or not, God sends the strength you need and even makes you smile about it."

Eventually, Alexia underwent four lengthy surgeries and an uninterrupted series of painful treatments, including chemotherapy, which made the last ten months of her life a true way of the cross. She suffered from Ewing's sarcoma, a grave but sometimes curable cancer. She never lost her sense of humor. At

Alexia as "Dr. Frankenstein"

one point she was lying completely immobile, able only to move her eyes and speak. She told her family, "I feel like a talking head!" She kept a joyful serenity in the midst of torture. Where did this young teen get the strength to suffer? From her youth, she had prayed always to do what Jesus wanted. To her last moments she had the happiness of doing just that.

Alexia disliked any show of weakness in herself and took pains to hide it from her visitors. Sometimes when visitors left, she would tell her mother, "I am so tired of smiling." Once when her father was in the room she became very depressed and asked him to leave because she knew it hurt him to see her that way. Later, she recanted and called him back, once more putting on her smiling face. Toward the end, she often talked about going to Heaven and once she told her mother she was very tired. When her mother said how sad they would be if she left them, Alexia exclaimed, "Sad? Of course not, Mom! You would be very happy because I will be very happy myself in Heaven. Don't you think I deserve it with all that I'm going through?"

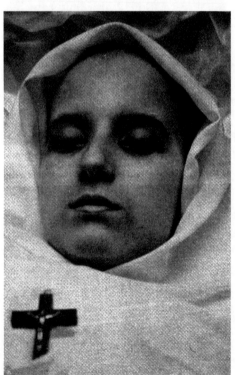

A beautiful child in her simple shroud

Alexia was grateful for all the many kindnesses shown to her. Daily, she prayed, "Lord, for all who pray for me, return their prayers a hundredfold; for all those who do favors for me, pay them back a hundredfold as well." One of the nurses brought her a pair of earrings. Since she had lost her hair, they made her seem a bit more feminine. Although they bothered Alexia a little, she wore them constantly so the nurse would see how much she liked them. Daily she offered her sufferings to God and confided to a family friend that she thanked Him for them.

When one of her nurses complimented her on her bravery, she responded, "No, Sister, it is God who is helping me."

Alexia died peacefully on the morning of December 5, 1985. Her simplicity extended even to her burial clothes. She was dressed in a white nurse's gown and in a simple white shroud.

Alexia's cause for beatification has been entered at Rome. ✢

2

Anacleto Gonzalez Flores and Companions
Eight Lay Martyrs of the Cristiada
Mexican Martyrs killed in 1927 and 1928

The government of Mexico under the dictatorship of Plutarco Elias Calles (1924-1928) was anti-clerical and Calles himself aimed to eradicate the Catholic Church. In 1925 he attempted to establish a national church. He kicked foreign clergy out of the country and closed and confiscated the property of church schools and other charitable works. In 1926 the onerous "Ley Calles" was passed with 33 articles against the Church. After consulting with Pope Pius XI, the bishops closed the churches and suspended the public cult in protest. For the first time in more than 400 years the churches of Mexico were closed. A petition containing over two million signatures was ignored and the Catholics could stand no more. Numbers of the faithful took up arms to defend their religious liberty. They began to fight with insufficient munitions and virtually no military experience; their main weapon the belief that God was with them. The Cristero Rebellion officially began New Year's Day 1927. The conflict began in Jalisco and spread rapidly to Nayarit, Colima, Michoacan and Zacatecas. The rebellion ended not in the field but at the bargaining table and with strong assistance from international diplomacy. A majority of the Catholic bishops of the country opposed the Cristero uprising. From exile, Bishop Pascual Diaz of Tabasco and other detente-minded prelates worked ceaselessly, trying to reach an accommodation with the government. A key figure in the peace process was the American ambassador, Dwight Whitney Morrow, who wanted to end the religious conflict for both humanitarian and practical reasons. Morrow's chief ally in attempting to end the fighting was Father John J. Burke, head of the U.S. National Catholic Welfare Conference. The Vatican was also anxious for a peaceful solution. Calles' successor, Alvaro Obregón, was assassinated two weeks after his election, and Emilio Portes Gil was named interim president. Portes Gil was more flexible in his policy toward the Church than Calles, and an agreement, known as the *arreglos* (arrangements) was reached on June 21, 1929. Most of the Catholic Cristeros went home, thinking that the fight for freedom of worship had been won. On June 27, for the first time in almost three years, church bells pealed joyously. Although short-lived and not completely successful in its aims, the Cristiada made a mark on Mexican history and its battle cry *"Viva Cristo Rey"* still re-sounds today in the lives and heroism of its glorious martyrs and saints.

Anacleto Gonzalez Flores

Anacleto Gonzalez Flores was born in Tepatitlan, Jalisco, on July 13, 1888, and baptized the following day in the church of San Francisco. He was the second of twelve children of Valentin Gonzalez Sanitize and Marie Floors Navaho.

Although the family was poor, his father taught Anacleto strength of will, hard work, discipline, patriotism, and the love of learning. As a boy, Anacleto helped his father in his work of making rebozos (shawls), enjoyed memorizing long discourses, and played in the town band. He had

Anacleto as a young man; notice the ACJM lapel pin

PHOTOS (EXCEPT PAGES 42, 44, AND 46) COURTESY OF THE ARCHDIOCESE OF GUADALAJARA, MEXICO

the aptitude of a leader from an early age, inspiring respect and not allowing the others to take advantage of the weak. At the age of seventeen, he attended spiritual exercises given by a missionary and became more serious and reflective. He determined to use his art of oratory to serve God and his country and began to gather the local youth to teach them catechism.

A priest who was a friend of the family suggested that Anacleto enter the auxiliary seminary of San Juan de los Lagos, and helped pay the tuition. Anacleto began his studies with the strength of will he had learned from his father and in just a few months he was able to have a conversation in Latin with his professor. For this, he gained the nickname of "Maestro" (Teacher) or, more familiarly, "El Maestro Cleto." Later, Anacleto studied theology at the conciliar seminary of Guadalajara. Although he gained a strong humanistic formation, he realized that his vocation was not to the priesthood.

In 1912, Anacleto went to Mexico City where he joined the Catholic National party. His free time was spent campaigning in Los Altos de Jalisco. In 1913 he entered the Escuela Libre de Derecho in Guadalajara. At 26, Anacleto had studied the encyclical *Rerum Novarum*, the great directive for Catholic social works written by Pope Leo XII. He formed a circle of fellow students dedicated to this pope, and began to study the initiatives of the Spanish writer and politician Donoso Cortes, the Frenchman Frederick Ozanam and the German Winhorst.

In 1914, the Carrancistas troops of General Alvaro Obregón entered Guadalajara and ravaged and plundered the city. The cathedral, the conciliar seminary, the hospital of St. Martin and other church property was confiscated. The inhabitants of the city, furious because of so much violence, asked the help of the northern general Francisco "Pancho" Villa. Anacleto took refuge in the town of Concepción de Buenos Aires, Jalisco, where his brother Severiano lived. He stayed there for several months helping his brother in a small food store. Then Villa's troops passed through town going to the aid of Guadalajara. Anacleto joined the troops as a secretary. However, once among the Villista officers, his illusions faded and he returned to Guadalajara to resume his study of law.

In Guadalajara, Anacleto was involved in much social and religious activity. He became an enthusiastic member of the ACJM (Catholic Association of Young Mexicans). Anacleto loved teaching catechism and worked hard to attract boys and girls to his classes. Later as a member of the conferences of San Vícente, he began to visit the poor, the sick, and the prisoners.

Anacleto gave conferences in the circles of the ACJM, wrote articles in magazines and newspapers, and founded the periodical La Palabra, with the objective of refuting the antireligious articles of the Constitution of 1917.

Anacleto displayed his tenacity in the matter of his education. In 1917 a federal law nullified the validity of many of his previous studies; they were not recognized by the state. All of the classes in philosophy, theology and some other sciences that he took in the seminary were now worthless. The poor Maestro had to re-take all of his studies in order to gain his bachelor's degree. This took five years, but he finished in April of 1922 and passed the test to receive the designation "attorney superando."

In addition to his almost superhuman activities and studies, Analeto cultivated a deep interior life. He was a daily communicant, dedicated time each morning to prayer and became a third-order Franciscan. His spiritual director was the saintly Archbishop of Guadalajara, Francisco Orozco y Jiménez.

July 22, 1918, Guadalajara saw the first violent conflict between government forces and the Catholics. Anacleto defended the rights of the people and did not rest until some unpopular decrees were revoked. He elaborated a philosophy of resistance based on the non-violent principals of Mahatma Gandhi. In July of 1919 he was jailed briefly because of his ideas. In 1922, he was a coordinator of the first Congress of the National Catholic Workers celebrated in Guadalajara. At the conference, the National Confederation of Catholic Workers was organized and soon spread throughout Mexico.

November 17, 1922, Anacleto married Maria Concepción Guerrero Flores in the chapel of the ACJM, blessed by Archbishop Francisco Orozco y Jiménez. The previous year in a conference in Guadalajara, Anacleto had said "The family is the true unifier, energetic and vigorous, in which rests all the good of society." With Maria Concepcion, he planned to begin his own family.

In 1924, the governor of Guadalajara closed the conciliar seminary and the church run orphanage and hospital. Anacleto organized the Union Popular, in order to revive the flagging spirits of the Catholics. He was named its chief and Luis Padilla was elected secretary. They founded the periodical Gladium as the official voice of the movement. In one of the first editions they wrote: "We are in the vespers of an infamous problem ... the country is a jail for the Catholic Church. In order to be logical, a revolution must gain the entire soul of a nation. They will have to open a jail for each home, and they

Anacleto at age 18

don't have enough handcuffs or hangmen to bind up the hands and cut off the heads of the martyrs. We are not worried about defending our material interests, because these come and go; but our spiritual interests, these we will defend because they are necessary to obtain our salvation. We are not able to accept the churches being profaned. We cannot accept that our bishops and the priests who baptized our children, gave us the Eucharist, and helped us at the hour of our death with the sacraments that bring eternal life, are being thrown out of the country."

In creating the Union Popular, Anacleto dreamed of his martyrdom. His writings of this time, his preparations, the flag with its colors of red and white, the words on this same flag "Viva Cristo Rey" and on the back side, "Queen of the Martyrs" at the foot of the image of Guadalupe, the prayer that daily the members of the Union were to repeat ("Humbly we ask that you confound the enemies of the Church, we pray, hear our prayer. Queen of martyrs, pray for us and for the Union Popular") all pertained to and were part of the mystique of martyrdom.

The Union rapidly gained strength throughout the diocese of Guadalajara with the blessing and approval of Archbishop Orozco y Jiménez, while the Holy See awarded Anacleto with the cross Pro Ecclesia et Pontifice.

Anacleto Gonzalez Flores as a young attorney

The National League for the Defense of Religious Liberty was formed in Mexico City in May of 1925.[1] It favored recourse to arms, against the pacifist doctrine of the Union Popular. Anacleto was not in agreement with armed battle and insisted that only by means of moral strength could they gain their aims. He and his archbishop were committed to this.

After the sacrilege on August 3, 1926 in the sanctuary of Our Lady of Guadalupe in Guadalajara, the cry of rebellion resonated throughout the State of Jalisco. August 15 in Zacatecas, Father Luis Batis and three members of the ACJM—Manuel Morales, Salvador Lara and David Roldan—determined supporters of religious liberty were murdered. In October, Jalisco, called by President Calles "The Henhouse of the Republic" rose up in arms in Tlajomulco, Ameca, Cocula, Ciudad Guzman, Chapala, Atengo, Ayutla and Tecolotlan to Calles' surprise. He considered religion only a thing for women and children.

Front page of the Gladium

Anacleto was between a rock and a hard place. Until this moment he had been obedient to his archbishop and advocated passive, non-violent resistance. But now, in conscience, could he accept a government that used its strength to squash his brothers who were armed only because of their idealism? Why insist on a vain pacifism and put down to death like canon fodder thousands of enthusiastic Catholics? He made up his mind during the last days of December 1926 when some delegates of the League came from Mexico City and presented an ultimatum to the Union Popular, basing his decision on the legitimacy of the defense, the same that some bishops accepted tacitly and others openly, and the notification to the Holy See.

In December 1926 the chiefs of the Union Popular were convoked by "El Maestro," who said: "The League has begun a revolutionary adventure with a determination that may be one of the true heart. For my part, my personal position is that I may not be other than that demanded of my post. I will be with the League and I will throw on the scale all that I am and all that I have. This remains clear: the Union Popular was not made to be an instrument of civil war. Today, however, without doubt we are driven to the mountain."

His die was cast. Before, he was dominated by indecision and incertitude; now he was ready to launch himself into the active insurgence. Anacleto was named the moral chief of the resistance. Miguel Gómez Loza was the treasurer and Heriberto Navarette the secretary. In January of 1927 the guerrilla war began in all of Jalisco. The periodical Gladium was the bulletin of war that carried notices of the camps of combat at the same time that it exhorted the Catholics to help the Cristeros with money, shelter, food and clothing.

The Catholic women were among the first to be animated by the Cristero ideal. The feminine Brigade of St. Joan of Arc was formed to assist the troops in getting provisions and in carrying information from the chiefs.

From his various hiding places, Anacleto studied the major strategies, wrote and sent bulletins, and gave speeches. He seemed to long for martyrdom and on various occasions mentioned that if God gave him this grace it would complete his greatest desires.

In the capitol, the feeling was that the rebellion of the Catholics must be severely crushed. General Jesús Maria Ferreira felt that the most expeditious plan would be to capture the chiefs of the Union Popular and the ACJM, and set the time for this as the morning of April 1, 1927.

At this time, Anacleto was staying in the home of the Vargas Gonzalez family. Ferreira's agents knew the probable whereabouts of the chiefs and they moved in two directions: the homes of Luis Padilla and Vargas Gonzalez. At the Vargas home, they found Anacleto, who quickly destroyed compromising documents. Frustrated at not finding all they were seeking, the agents arrested the entire Vargas family. The young brothers Florentino, Jorge and Ramón were carried to the Colorado jail, while Anacleto was taken to the headquarters of the military. Mrs. Elvira Vargas and her daughter Maria Luisa were jailed at the city hall, but were set free that afternoon along with the mother and sister of Luis Padilla.

General Ferreira ordered Anacleto's torture in an effort to learn more about the Cristeros. He was hung by his thumbs until his fingers were dislocated and the bottom of his feet were slashed. He steadfastly refused to give them any information.

The notice of his capture ran rampant throughout the city, and many supporters gathered in front of the Colorado jail. General Ferrerira did not want public demonstrations and had the sense to stop the assault. He improvised a summary court and condemned the prisoners to death, accusing them of causing the assassination of the North American Edgar Wilkens. Because they mistakenly thought that Florentino Vargas was younger than he was, he was freed.

The first Friday of April 1927 (dedicated to the Heart of Jesus) at three in the afternoon they were taken out to be shot. A short while afterwards, the attorney Francisco Gonzalez Nunez, a cousin of the Vargas family, arrived with an *amparo*, or stay of execution, which he had obtained from the competent authorities. He was too late. The four bodies were thrown out on the patio of the inspector of police at the Colorado Jail.

That night, the bodies of the martyrs were waked in the homes of Luis Padilla, of the Vargas family and in that of Anacleto Gonzalez Flores. Hundreds of friends, relatives and admirers passed by the body of the Maestro, touching his remains with veneration. The house became a veritable garden of flowers.

Anacleto's young widow brought her sons into the room. "Look," she said to her oldest, "This is your father. He has died defending the

Bier of Anacleto, his wife and sons

Funeral of Anacleto

Faith. Promise me on his body that you will do the same when you are older if God asks it of you."

The following day, thousands defied the presence of the police and accompanied the bodies to the cemetery of Mezquitan, reciting prayers and singing to Christ the King and the Virgin of Guadalupe. The mourners risked their lives to make public their admiration for the moral chief of the Cristero movement. A loud voice was heard saying that although they were enslaved, they were not conquered and that they had been consecrated by the blood of their dead hero. A voice called out, "Humbly we pray that you confound the enemies of your Church," and the multitude replied with strength "This we pray, hear us!"

The following day, General Ferreira gave an official statement that after his investigation he had determined that Anacleto was "the brains" behind the shooting of Edgar Wilkins, an American citizen, and that Anacleto and his group of "fanatics" were trying to cause trouble with the United States and acting against Mexico's interests. The general pressured the periodical El Informador to publish his statement. The newspapers of Jalisco and of Mexico City reproduced this official version in their columns, in spite of the fact that Anacleto's own writings had been published many times in the same publications. The American ambassador thanked the General for informing him of this conspiracy, but Mr. Wilkens's widow was not satisfied with the lie. She wrote a protest to Washington saying that it was well known that her husband's murderer was one Guadalupe Zuno who had killed her husband in order to rob him.

Jorge and Ramón Vargas Gonzalez

Jorge and Ramón were the sons of doctor Antonio M. Vargas and Elvira Gonzalez, sturdy Catholics who had eleven children. They were born in Ahualuco de Mercado, Jalisco. Jorge was born September 28, 1899 and Ramón was born January 22, 1905.

After their university studies, Jorge began working at the Hydroelectric company while Ramón pursued the study of medicine. The brothers both became active members of the ACJM and were admirers of "Maestro" Anacleto Gonzalez Flores.

During the persecution of religious, the Vargas family gave refuge to a number of priests and seminarians. Father Lino Aguirre, the future bishop of Culiacia, was one who was sheltered and the young Jorge shared his room. He told the priest, "Father Lino, it is not good for you to go about alone. I am going to be your bodyguard." After work Jorge, dressed in overalls and riding his bicycle, accompanied the priest on the rounds of his hidden ministry.

Jorge's sister Maria Louisa recalls when Anacleto came to their house. "We had already had in our house various priests and a group of young seminarians, but never the chief of the Cristeros. The responsibility of lodging him was enormous but it was impossible to close the doors against him — this, never."

Ramón Vargas was nicknamed "el Colorado" because of his red hair. Anacleto enjoyed talking with this

Ramón and Jorge Vargas Gonzalez

idealistic young medical student. He asked him if he did not want to work with the wounded Cristeros, but Ramón responded by saying that he was a man of peace.

The afternoon of March 31, 1927, Ramón told a school friend that he had a premonition that he should not go home that evening. Although the friend suggested that he could sleep at the hospital, Ramón went home late and went to sleep.

At five in the morning, there was a tapping on the window and later on the door. The Vargases had a drugstore attached to their house, and a voice from outside insisted, "We need a medicine." The secret police had scaled the walls and completely surrounded the house and began knocking at the entrance with more force and shouting "Open the door in the name of the law." Calling out that she was getting her key, Mrs. Vargas went to warn her sons. Florentino went to the door and asked to see their orders. "Here it is," said one of the policemen, showing his pistol. Immediately the house was flooded with secret police.

The agents took as prisoners Anacleto and the three Vargas brothers, Feliciano Estrada, a friend of the family, and Bernardino Vega, a servant, and transported them to the Colorado Jail. In vain Anacleto attempted to intercede for the others. As the police van left, like the strong woman of the scriptures Dona Elvira called out to her boys, "My sons, until Heaven!"

Because of the position of his room, Ramón could have escaped. In jail, Florentino asked him why he had not. Ramón replied, "I told myself, my mother and my brothers are prisoners, am I to run away?"

At the jail, Anacleto and the brothers Vargas encountered Luis Padilla who had also been taken prisoner that morning. All five were put in the same room for an interrogation. Anacleto accepted the responsibility of his own actions but would not tell any information about the Cristeros. The police demanded, "Didn't you tear into a thousand pieces a letter in the moment you were taken prisoner in order not to compromise them?"

In answer to his silence, Anacleto was horribly tortured. At the end, he was taken down and one of the policemen hit him on the shoulder with the butt of his gun so hard that it fractured the shoulder. The questioning and beatings continued with the others but following Anacleto's heroic example they remained steadfast and silent.

Finally, the torments were suspended and General Ferreira condemned four of the five to death for supporting the rebels. Florentino Vargas was set free because they thought, erroneously, that he was under age.

The general ordered that they be executed simultaneously, but Anacleto asked that he be the last to be shot in order to be a comfort to the others until the last moment. The four recited the act of contrition in a loud voice, and a hail of bullets ended their final cry of "*Viva Cristo Rey!*" The bodies were taken to the police station, where they were thrown on the patio.

During the morning arrests, the mothers and sisters of the prisoners had also been taken as prisoners and were held in the municipal presidio. The were released about five in the afternoon. A rumor was going around that the youth were going to be taken to Mexico City to be shot. Three of the Vargas sisters determined to go there and took a car as far as Las Juntas where they would get the train for the capital. On arriving at the train, the sisters ran up to the windows looking for their brothers with vain hope. Just then their cousins Pancho and Carolina Gonzales arrived by car to give the sisters the sad news that their brothers had already been killed.

The sisters returned home and found their mother in the family chapel. "Weren't you able to catch the train?" she asked anxiously.

The funeral of Anacleto and the Vargas Gonzalez brothers

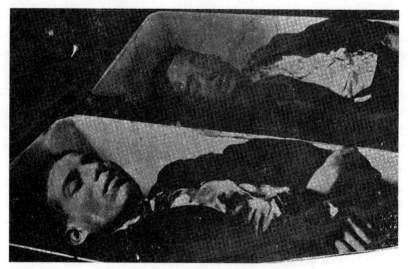

Jorge and Ramón Vargas in their caskets

From their faces she read the truth. The girls began to sob. Holding Maria, she told her daughter not to cry and the heroic mother said, "I already was afraid of this and because of it I have offered them to Our Lord. They are already in Heaven. We are going to make preparations to receive them as martyrs."

The notice of the executions flashed like gunpowder through the city of Guadalajara. The homes of the martyrs were rapidly filled with mourners. At eight that evening the bodies of Jorge and Ramón were returned to their family. Surprisingly, Florentino's body did not arrive with the others.

A relative in the house began to cry loudly. Calmly, Doña Elvira quieted her saying, "You know that our mission as mothers is to raise our children to heaven. And I, already I have three saints."

At ten o'clock that night, the family and friends were surprised and overjoyed when Florentino arrived. His mother ran to embrace this son she had thought was dead. And then she said these beautiful and inimitable words: "Ay, my son, how close you were to the crown of martyrdom. Now it is your obligation to live so as to merit it."

During the night hundreds of people passed near the mortal remains of the two martyrs, piously touching medals and rosaries to the bodies. The following day a multitude accompanied the martyrs to the cemetery.

Luis Padilla Gómez

Luis Padilla Gómez, son of Dionisio Padilla and Mercedes Gómez de Padilla, was born in Guadalajara on December 9,1899. His father died when Luis was very young. His mother and two sisters formed a close and loving family with Luis, the only surviving son. They clung to their strong Catholic faith. After attending primary school and the Jesuit-run San José institute, Luis entered the Conciliar Seminary of Guadalajara. Although in the seminary he had profound religious feelings, he left in November of 1921, feeling he did not have a true vocation to the priesthood.

Luis had the natural inclinations of a writer, although he destroyed the diary in which he had written his first literary efforts. A succeeding diary he called "Remembrances and Impressions." While in the seminary, he wrote what he called Misticas. These writings show his love and devotion to the Sacred Heart and to the Virgin Mary, and speak of his admiration of the priesthood and yet of his doubts of his own vocation. They also show his constant desire to give himself to God: "Oh, my Jesus, most perfect symbol of love and pain, You have loved me always, from the manger, from Calvary and on the altar. I want to love You and make You my only delight. Only you, my Jesus, for always. I will follow you in forgetfulness of all the scorn and pain I may receive. You say, 'If someone wants to follow me, he picks up his cross and follows.' Yes, Jesus, I will follow you, forgetting the world and even if hell passes over me. In the meantime, Lord, hide me in your wounds."

After making the spiritual exercises in the city of León, he wrote in his diary about their impact on him and the decision he had come to. He wanted to immolate his life to

Luis Padilla Gómez, 1926

an ideal. He wrote, "Jesus, my life has no value, but I want to make it of value by offering it to You. What do you say? Will you accept it?" At the age of twenty-four, he wrote about himself in his diary. "My motto: God with me and for me. How I want to live: without fear of life. How I want to die: With great hope in the future life."

In 1920, Luis finished the philosophy course at the seminary with such high marks that his superiors proposed to send him to Rome for further studies. However, since he was still uncertain of his vocation, he did not accept the opportunity and left the seminary. He returned home and dedicated himself to an apostolate as a catechist and of social action. He transformed his room into an oratory dedicated to the Sacred Heart. He passed hours daily praying before the Blessed Sacrament. His love of the Virgin of Guadalupe was such that he seemed like a young man in love. His daily life was based on a solid mercy that he practiced not only in church but in his own home.

His Marian devotion is shown in his prayer: "Mary, before the world was completed, you were already in the mind of the Most High, pure like the moon. You, in your Immaculate Conception overcame the snake. You in your birth are the hope of the Messiah. You in the temple are the model of the hidden life. You, in the Incarnation are the point of union between the divine humanity and the human God.

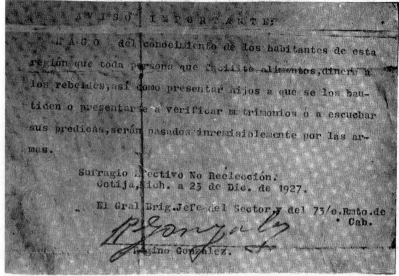

Scare tactics of the times. The poster warns people not to aid the rebels, have their children baptized, or their marriages solemnized, under pain of being shot

You, in Bethlehem, are the first altar of the Child God. You at Calvary are the supreme priest that offers your Divine Child. You, in Heaven, are our Hope. You, forever Mother."

Luis had been a member of the ACJM since it was founded in Guadalajara, and he became the Archdiocesan President of the group. Later, he was selected as the secretary of the Union Popular, the regional delegation of the National League of the Defense of Religious Freedom. When the religious persecution broke out again in 1926, Luis worked diligently with his companions in the ACJM to make a financial boycott effective, and he worked closely with Anacleto in the activities of the League. Unlike Anacleto who wrote articles for many publications, Luis wrote letters, poetry, and gave a class in literature at the seminary. Just as Anacleto had a legal air about him, Luis had the heart of a pastor, wise and holy. His spirit awoke again with the vibrant feeling of a priestly vocation and in August of 1926, he wanted to return to the seminary. But now he couldn't; the churches were closed and the seminaries were dispersed.

In his diary for 1925, Luis had mentioned martyrdom, and had prophetically written, "I will not scrimp on giving my blood to God." On the day of his apprehension, he had written of pardon: "I pardon them, I humbly pardon them, thinking of You, Lord! And I pardon all. It is so good, so sweet to pardon."

"Lord, when men turn against me to torment me or treat me with cruelty, I will bless the wounds they inflict on me . . . thinking of You. And if among them (my brothers) there is one that turns to me with love, I will forgive him, I forgive him with humility . . . thinking of You, Lord! And I will forgive all of them. . . . It is so good and sweet to forgive while my wounds are still open and bleeding!"

On the morning of April 1, 1927, Luis was apprehended by the secret police at his home. They took him to the Colorado jail where, along with Anacleto and the Vargas brothers, he was beaten and insulted before being sentenced to execution. He wanted to go to confession, but Anacleto told him, "No, brother, now is not the hour to confess, but to request pardon and to pardon our enemies. God is a Father and not a judge, the one that gives you hope. Your own blood will purify you."

The four stood with their arms in the form of a cross. Immediately, the brothers Vargas, Jorge and Ramon, were shot. Luis knelt down and, engrossed in prayer, received the bullets that opened the doors of Heaven to him.

That night, his body was waked in his home. Hundreds came to give homage to the sturdy martyr of Christ. In 1952, his mortal remains were translated to the crypt of the church of San Agustin and in 1981 they were translated to the church of San José in Analco.

Ezequiel Huerta Gutierrez

The brothers Ezequiel and Salvador Huerta, sons of Isaac Huerta and Florencia Guiterrez Oliva, came from a family with a long history in the mining industry. After their marriage, Isaac and Florencia settled in Magdalena where Isaac ran a store and Florencia raised their five children: José, Ezequiel, Eduardo, Salvador and Maria del Carmen.

José and Eduardo became priests and worked in various parishes in Guadalajara. Father José is especially remembered for founding two large orphanages; Father Eduardo founded a school that still exists today. Carmen assisted her priestly brothers in their parishes.

Ezequiel was born January 7, 1876, and baptized in the parochial church of Magdalena in 1877. As a boy, he was idealistic, pleasant, generous and very sociable.

From a young age he wanted to visit Guadalajara and at last he was allowed to ride with his father in the back of a wagon filled with barrels of tequila. On the way, Isaac, as was his custom, invited all to recite the rosary. One of the workers with him grumbled about this. After a few miles, one of the wagon wheels came loose, spilling all into the ditch. As he rose, Isaac called out with anguish for his son. Immediately Ezequiel answered, "Here I am, Papa. I am OK." The boy had not suffered so much as a scratch. On the other hand, the worker who had grumbled and refused to say the rosary was covered with blood and half dead with fright. From that time it became a family custom to recite the rosary before leaving on any trip, and in future accidents none had been hurt.

After completing their primary education in their hometown, Ezequiel and Salvador went to Guadalajara to finish their education. With all her sons in the city, Doña Florencia convinced her husband to sell their house and store and move to Guadalajara.

Ezequiel had a beautiful tenor voice and in school he studied music and singing. He studied with an Italian master and learned the main parts of various classic operas. He formed a large chorus and the group sang in the religious festivals in the churches of Guadalajara. Once, while he was singing in a church where he sang daily, a jealous companion attempted to kill him and stabbed him in the stomach but Ezequiel quickly recovered. He then defended the man, excusing him on the grounds that he was the poor father of a family.

An Italian opera company came to town and their star became ill. Ezequiel was selected to replace him and was so successful he was offered a contract to continue with the company. He refused on the grounds that his voice was dedicated to the service of God. He rode from church to church on his bicycle to sing in praise of the Lord at many services.

Ezequiel Huerta

Ezequiel married Maria Eugenia Garcia on September 17, 1904. Energetic and authoritative, the couple were a happy pair. They had ten children. Ezequiel was a dedicated family man and loved his wife and children enormously and was generous and affectionate with them. Their home life was tranquil and happy. While Ezequiel sang, Maria cared for the children and the home, spending many hours in the kitchen preparing the food for so many mouths. In 1914, the family consecrated their home to the Sacred Heart; Father Eduardo made the enthronement.

His daughter recalls that her father rose early each day. He sang as he bathed and then watered the flowers before leaving for Mass with one or more of the older children. She says he received Communion fervently and said the rosary daily.

The idealistic Ezequiel did not like to charge for his services, so his priest brothers often made the contracts with the churches to ensure that he was paid fairly.

In 1925, Ezequiel was professed as a third-order Franciscan.

In 1926, when the temples were closed because of the religious persecution, Ezequiel was left without work and he became the custodian of the temple of San Felipe Neri. His two oldest boys, Manuel and José de Jesus, were already members of the Union Popular and joined the resistance. Both participated in a number of battles in Jalisco. At the end of 1927, Jose took refuge in the United States.

General Ferreira considered the two Huerta brothers who were priests instigators of the rebellion. He also felt that Ezequiel's wife was a part of the Cristeros. In one battle, Manuel had been wounded so his mother dressed as a countrywoman and went to look for her son. She spent some time nursing some of the wounded.

In March of 1927, Ezequiel's wife took two of her daughters, Maria Carmen, age 16, and Teresa, age 9, to one of the hidden Masses. The gospel of the day mentioned the necessity of having the disposition to defend the faith with blood. She offered God whatever he designated for her loved ones, her two sons in battle and her husband valiantly guarding the church of San Felipe. Just as she was reflecting in prayer on her offering, a boy burst into the room and told the assembled Catholics that the police were in front of the house. The priest consumed the sacrament and escaped through the garden. Maria took the chalice from the little table which was serving as an altar and hid it in Teresa's coat telling the child to hide and not to give the chalice to anyone but her father.

The police burst in and arrested a number of the faithful including Maria and two nuns. Maria del Carmen literally ran under the legs of the po-

Ezequiel Huerta and his wife and son

liceman and seeing her mother in the Julia (the police van) she ran home to tell her father. Immediately, Ezequiel advised an attorney friend of his who went to the commissioner to release his wife and the other people detained. Then he went to get little Teresa who had not moved from her hiding place with her treasure.

Maria was released at eight that evening and the family rejoiced together. Ezequiel and Maria hugged and cried with happiness, giving thanks to God that nothing had happened. That night they determined that what had happened was only a prelude to something worse.

Ezequiel attended the wake for Anacleto on the night of April 1 and the next day he stayed with his children while his wife went to pay her respects. About nine in the morning, police arrived, telling Ezequiel that he had been denounced as having Cristero priests hidden in his house. At that moment, a young seminarian friend of the family, Juan Bernal, arrived. He later was able to give testimony about the ultimate hours of the Huerta martyrs.

Roughly, the police began to search the house. Maria came home about this time. Finding nothing, the police told Maria that they were taking Ezequiel to headquarters to make a declaration.

The loving couple looked into each other's eyes and their faces were bathed with tears. The two young daughters ran to their father and gave him a kiss but when Maria attempted to approach him she was rudely pushed aside by the police. As the agents left with Ezequiel and young Bernal, Maria called, "Don't worry, Ezequiel, if you don't return to see us in this life we will see you in Heaven."

The agents added insult to injury. In addition to taking the breadwinner of this loving family, they also took their food: beans, corn and rice that Ezequiel had provided for his family.

Maria and friends of the family went to find where Ezequiel had been taken, looking at all the police stations in the area and in the military zone with no result. That night, the forlorn children dragged their mattresses to their mother's room and they all said the rosary together before they lay down and attempted to sleep.

What happened to Ezequiel during his tragic journey is known through the testimony of two witnesses, the youth Bernal and the watchman of the municipal palace.

Sergeant Felipe Velazquez questioned Ezequiel about the whereabouts of his two priest brothers, about his two oldest sons and the

Cristero movement. Ezequiel didn't open his mouth, so he was beaten until the blood began to run down in his face.

"We are going to hang your brother Salvador by the thumbs — and you, if you don't talk, we will hang you by your hind legs," furiously cried the sergeant. For his answer, Ezequiel began to sing with all the strength of his soul "My Christ lives, my King lives." Other bestial beatings and slaps interrupted his song until he couldn't make another sound. Two men carried him to the jail and dropped him in the room with Bernal.

Shocked at his appearance, Bernal asked him what had happened.

Painfully, in a low voice, the tortured one was able to say, "Nothing much. Listen, when they carry my body to my house tell Maria that in the purse under my belt I have a hundred pesos in gold; it is all that I have to give her."

On the morning of April 3 the two brothers were carried in the Julia to the cemetery of Mezquitan and shot. The families were not able to claim the bodies because General Ferreria demanded the sum of six thousand pesos to release them. Therefore, they were buried in a single grave. Later their remains were exhumed and reburied in the family plot of the same cemetery until they were translated to the Church of the Sweet Name of Jesus by order of Jose Garibi Rivera, archbishop of Guadalajara. Finally, in 1980, they were translated to the chapel of the seminary of the Missionary Xaverians in Carmen de Arandas, Jalisco.

Salvador Huerta Gutierrez

Salvador Huerta was born March 18, 1880, in Magdalena, Jalisco and baptized March 22 in the railroad church. As a child he was serious, yet cheerful, obedient and loving. The last of four boys, he seemed to be his mother's pet. He was quiet like his father and energetic like his mother.

After attending primary school, he studied in Guadalajara. Here he enjoyed attending the opera with his brother Ezequiel. After secondary school, he didn't want to go to college and went to work as a mechanic in the shop of some Germans where he learned a great deal. Later, he went to Zacatecas and worked as an explosives technician in the mines. He was noted for his carefulness, responsibility and competence. In spite of his care, in one terrible mining accident he was saved almost miraculously. Later he suffered a number of other accidents including cutting off a finger in his workshop. He suffered his misfortunes with good humor, feeling that God had reserved another form of death for him.

From Zacatecas, Salvador went to work in Aguascalientes in the round house where the train locomotives were made and repaired. Here he was able to leave for frequent visits to Atotonilco to visit his mother and sister who were there attending their priest uncle, Father José Huerta. It was on one of these trips that he met Adelina Jiménez, a child of twelve years who was an orphan living with her uncle. Salvador waited a few years to declare himself, and even then had to overcome difficulties with her family. They told her this worker, eight years older than her, would not be able to give her the good life that she had always been accustomed to. Love triumphed, however, and they were married April 20, 1907.

Against all the arguments by her family, Salvador and Adelina had a wonderful marriage. They had twelve children. Salvador loved his wife and did everything to make her happy. The couple moved to Guadalajara in order to be closer to Salvador's parents. Adelina came down with a liver disease which was very painful. Once, Salvador told her, "When I am dead, ask our Lord to stop your pain." At this, she responded, "I prefer to live all my life in pain rather than that you die!"

Salvador Huerta

Salvador's children recall that they were educated with firmness but were also given their father's confidence. They also recall how he always sacrificed himself for his family. Once, during the war between the Carrancistas and the Villistas Salvador went to find some food for his family. He returned through the lines of the combatants, riding his bicycle and balancing a sack of rice on the handlebars. The children say they never lacked anything to the point where they thought they were rich. On Sundays after Mass the family would go to the country around Lake Chapala for a festive time of family fun.

Salvador opened a workshop to repair cars and soon became known as the best mechanic in Guadalajara. He was called the "Magician of Cars" and was well respected for his work. Eventually the shop grew large enough that he had eight workers. In addition to teaching them mechanic's skills, Salvador also taught them responsibility and respect for the things of God.

On his way to work, Salvador always passed by the church of Calvary for a visit to the holy Sacrament. He was a member of Night Adoration and was devoted to Divine Providence, the Sacred Heart and the Holy Spirit.

One Christmas, Salvador was sad because he didn't have enough money to buy gifts for his children. The afternoon of the 24th, a client came and paid a bill that was long overdue. Happily, Salvador told his children, "The Child Jesus has brought us this money." Then he joyfully left to buy the children some toys.

His children say that Salvador taught them piety more with his example than with his words. Confession, Communion, spiritual exercises, visits to church and prayers were taught by his own actions. His regular blessing at meals was, "Divine Providence I ask in each instant and moment that never we lack a house, clothes, work and sustenance."

On the afternoon of April 1, 1927, Ezequiel came to Salvador's house to discuss the execution of their friend Anacleto. Prudently, they decided that it was very important to stop their sons who were planning on leaving the Cristero front for a visit to their families. The next morning, Adelina left with her daughter and a baby to warn the boys.

Salvador with some of his workers

That same morning, Salvador was at work when the secret police came and said, "Maestro, the chief wants you to come and fix a car at the commandancia of police."

Salvador was flooded with sadness as he thought "perhaps my hour has come." Without showing his emotion, he answered, "Bring it here, please, where I have all my tools."

"That isn't possible, maestro. It is necessary that you come." Without losing his habitual serenity, he got his tools and began walking toward the commissariat.

Salvador was taken to the office of the chief who questioned him about his two priest brothers, the hiding place of the archbishop, and about the Cristero movement. His only response was silence. He was tortured and finally thrown in jail with his brother Ezequiel. While he was being questioned, the agents went to his house and searched through everything. They found some rosaries and religious articles and a revolver that his son had left there.

"What is this?" the official demanded of the Huerta children.

The oldest responded, "Aren't we allowed to have a gun in order to defend ourselves against crooks?"

The official pointed to the butt of the gun where it was inscribed, "And the word was made flesh and lives among us," words emblematic of the Cristeros.

That night, a foul and humid cell sheltered the Huerta brothers. The cold wind punished their tortured bodies. Two guards entered and invited them to follow. In spite of their injuries, the two arose and entered the Julia to be carried to the cemetery of Mezquitan. At the cemetery, they were led to the wall on the right side.

Turning to his brother, Ezequiel said, "We pardon them, right? Then his beautiful voice was stilled by the sound of the bullets. Salvador, then turned to his brother and said, "Brother, you are already a martyr." Then taking a candle in his hand, he held it in front of himself, telling his executioners, "I put this light on my chest so you won't fail to hit my heart. I am ready to die for Christ." The shots covered his final words.

Monday April 4 the magazine Excelsior ran an editorial announcing the shooting of the brothers, protesting that they were killed without any justice, without investigation, and without the right of defending themselves.

Divine Providence cared splendidly for the numerous orphans left by the Huerta brothers. Many people came to visit the two families bringing congratulations for the two martyrs and also bringing material aid for the families. After the Cristero war, the Jesuits and the Salesians allowed the children to study at their colleges and all 22 of the children carried out good careers in medicine, engineering, music and vocations to the priesthood and to religious life.

Luis Magana Servin

Luis was born August 24, 1920, the oldest of three children of Raymundo Magana Zuniga and Mari Concepción Servin Gómez. He was baptized in his parochial church. He was confirmed in 1905 and received his First Communion on Christmas Day, 1909.

Luis began attending parochial school at the age of six. He was a well behaved child both at home and in school. Although of a tranquil nature, he enjoyed the play and the playthings of childhood. Baseball was his preferred sport. Along with a fair complexion, Luis had beautiful eyes. When a painter of Arandas began to paint a picture of the Virgin of Refuge, he looked for a model for the Christ child among the children of the catechism classes. He painted the eyes of Luis. The picture still hangs today in the church at Arandas.

His days followed a regular routine. He rose early and attended Mass with his father. After breakfast, he attended school. In the after-

Luis Magana at the beach with friends (lower right)
PHOTO COURTESY OF FATHER TIBERIO MUNARI, MISSIONERO XAVERIANO

noon, he helped his father with his work in a tannery. At the tannery, Luis was his father's "right hand man," helping with enthusiasm and cheerfulness. In the evenings, the family prayed the rosary together before bedtime. Twice a week, Luis attended catechism classes.

As a young man, Luis became interested in the social questions and studied the encyclical *Rerum Novarum* by Pope Leo XIII that had been published in 1891. He joined the Association of St. Mary of Guadalupe, a group that united worker artisans. He put social justice into practice in humane treatment and kindness with his workers. For Luis there was no distinction between poor and rich; he treated all as if they were the same. Luis followed the counsel of Monsignor José Mora y del Rio, bishop of Mexico City, "Treat your workers with love and they will never leave you."

Luis loved his church, his parish, and his priests. From a young age he had been a member of the ACJM,[2] and was one of the founders of the group in Arandas.

In January of 1922, the ACJM hosted a meeting where Luis heard and met the great defender of religious liberty, Anacleto Gonzalez Flores. Anacleto had worked with word and pen to renovate Mexican society.

Luis was among the group that founded Nocturnal Adoration in Arandas in 1922. They pledged to guard and pray before Jesus in the Sacrament during the hours of the night. Luis was faithful to his turn at adoration. From Christ in the Blessed Sacrament, Luis gained his strength and enthusiasm for the defense of the Church. For him, God came first and then everything else.

Luis was also devoted to the Virgin Mary, especially under her title of Our Lady of Guadalupe. A dynamite attack had been made on the image at the basilica in Mexico City and Luis was among those in Arandas who made a special act of reparation for that attack. He took a solemn vow to defend the sacred image.

Luis was active in his parish and helped the pastor in many ways. He used his organizational skills for the Church and organized youth groups to go and help the poorest families.

In spite of his activity for the church, Luis did not ignore his work or his family. A man who worked in the same area for many years remembers that Luis was sincere, a good salesman, and generous to his workers and to the poor. He was held in high regard by his clients.

All that was said of Luis was good, and this in a small town where gossip runs faster than truth.

Luis was well established financially and had already bought a house when he met his future wife, a young orphan named Elvira. His aunt introduced them, and they married when she was eighteen and he was twenty-four in January of 1926. From the beginning, the marriage was a happy one. Their first child, Gilberto, was born in April of 1927. Five months after Luis's death, Elvira gave birth to a daughter whom she named Luisa in memory of him.

Arandas, primarily a rural area, was peaceful during the years from 1910 to 1917. But during the Cristero conflict of 1926-1929, the town was one of the strong points of resistance to the government. From January of 1927 the priests went into hiding, exercising a secret ministry and going about in disguise. Many of the men joined in the fighting and the old women and children served as messengers and transported provisions to the Cristeros. Luis Magana was a pacifist and didn't enlist as did many of his companions, but he proposed to help spiritually and materially as did most of the Catholics of the area.

Luis Magana Servin
PHOTO COURTESY OF FATHER TIBERIO MUNARI,
MISSIONERO XAVERIANO

Well aware of the danger, Luis organized backing and sent arms, food and other necessities to those in the Cerro Gordo.

All knew of the murder in August 1926 of Father Luis Batis and three young members of the ACJM on the road to Zacatecas. Then in January came news of the execution of Anacleto Gonzalez Flores and three more ACJM members in Guadalajara. Miguel Gómez Loza, the moral chief of the Cristeros and the civil governor of Jalisco, established his headquarters on a rancho near Arandas about the middle of 1927 after the federales had burned the center of operations in Cerro Gordo. In order to frighten the people the bodies of the Cristeros shot in Arandas were hung in some trees at the south of the town near the bank of the river. Then the military authorities demanded that the farmers bring their corn harvest to a designated center in order to prohibit them from using it to aid the Cristeros. Many countrymen had to abandon their fields and their homes. Luis's parents generously lodged some of these farmers in their own home. The government of Jalisco had demanded that the municipal president of Los Altos provide a list of all who were suspected of aiding the Cristeros. Luis's name appeared on this list. He may also have been reported for his work done with the ACJM by a woman who served as a "stool pigeon" for General Miguel Martínez.

On the morning of February 9, 1928, federal soldiers sent by General Martínez came to the Magana home to arrest Luis. Not finding him at home, they took his younger brother Delfino, telling Don Raymundo that if Luis didn't turn himself in that day, they would shoot their prisoner.

When Luis returned home for lunch, he found his wife and parents in tears. They told him what had happened and with his usual serenity he told them, "Be calm, I will speak with General Martínez to find out what is going on and I promise you to bring Delfino here. At the most, they will take me to Guadalajara where they are taking everyone."

Luis bathed, shaved, and dressed in a new suit. He ate lunch tranquilly with his family. On finishing, he knelt in front of his parents and asked their blessing. Then he hugged them all, kissed his little son, and left.

A friend saw him walking and asked where he was going so dressed up. On learning what was going on, he told Luis, "Don't go, they will shoot you!" Then Luis, opening his arms and looking at the sky replied, "What happiness! Within an hour I will be in the arms of God."

Luis made his way to the military office which had been established in the church and asked for General Martínez. He was immediately arrested and conducted under escort to the hotel where the general was staying.

On entering the room, the general demanded, "Who are you?"

"My General, I am Luis Magana, whom you are looking for, " he said without a tremble, looking the general in the face. "The one you have detained is my brother and he hasn't done anything. Now that you have me, turn him loose."

General Martínez saw before him a valiant man, dressed for a fiesta, calm and serene as if he were going to be given an award. Rising from his seat, he passed a few words with his lieutenant and said, "Well, young man, we are going to see if in truth you are as valiant as you seem." Then he ordered, "Let the other go and shoot this one immediately in the patio of the church."

It was nearly four in the afternoon and the streets were almost deserted. The firing squad of eight soldiers left with Luis and with Pancho Muerte who had also been arrested. Crossing the town plaza, the group entered the atrium of the church. Luis refused the traditional blindfold and asked to say two words. Two witnesses in nearby hiding places have given solemn testimony as to what happened. Luis said, "I am neither a Cristero nor a rebel. But if you accuse me of being a Christian, that I am. Soldiers that are going to shoot me, I want to tell you that from this moment I pardon you and I promise you that on arriving in the presence of God you are the first ones I will intercede for. Viva Cristo Rey, Viva Santa Maria de Guadalupe."

A sacrilegious satire by the Federales

PHOTO COURTESY OF FATHER TIBERIO MUNARI, MISSIONERO XAVERIANO

The sounds of the bullets carried throughout the still town on this sad afternoon. At their home, the Magana family could hear the sounds, knowing in their hearts that it was their own martyr who was executed.

A number of curious people gathered at the church. A soldier posted a letter on the front door that said, "Here die the Cristeros!" General Martínez wanted to make an example to the entire town of Arandas.

Don Raymundo went to ask General Martínez's permission to take the body of his son home. At the temple, he noticed the sign and tore it down. Later, the loving father placed a small wooden cross on the wall where the young martyr was shot. Wrapping the corpse in a white sheet, he carried it home on a small ladder. The family removed Luis's bloody shirt and guarded it as a precious relic.

That night in the home of the martyr, friends and relatives gathered for the wake. People collected the martyr's blood, which did not coagulate normally, on small pieces of cotton. The next afternoon, the martyr was buried in Carmen cemetery. In 1980 the mortal remains of Luis were exhumed and translated to the chapel of the Xaverian seminary of Arandas where they were placed next to the remains of the Huerta brothers.

Miguel Gómez Loza

Miguel Gómez Loza was born in Paredones, a suburb of Tepatitlan, Jalisco, August 11, 1888. He was the son of Petronilo Loza and Victoriana Gómez. His father died when he was only two years old, so he and his older brother were raised by the young widow, who had a profound faith. Later the brothers reversed their last names to reflect their appreciation of their strong and loving mother.

From childhood Miguel had a strong love of God and a great devotion to the Virgin. In the public school the teachers had adorned the main room with a picture of Benito Juarez at the same height as the image of Our Lady. Young Miguel felt this was desecration, so he pulled the picture of Juarez off the wall and ran away with it to the sound of loud applause from his companions.

Even as a youth his talent for leadership was evident. He was a friend to all and earned the respect and admiration of his peers. He was an acolyte and became a sacristan and a catechist. He gathered the signatures from his town and petitioned to change the name from Paredones to El Refugio in honor of the Virgin.

At twenty-two, Miguel took part enthusiastically in the Catholic National Party and was its representative at the voting booths in his home town. Once when he heard that the political adversaries were planning an electoral fraud, he organized a group of friends to carry the urns to Tepatitlan in order to ensure a fair count of the vote. He resolved to study law in order to defend the interests of the Catholics.

Miguel moved to Guadalajara and entered the prepatory of the conciliar seminary, but soon realized he did not have a vocation to the priesthood so he enrolled in the Institute of the Sacred Heart of Jesus. In Guadalajara he met the main Catholic leaders of his day including Anacleto Gonzalez Flores. In 1913, he and El Maestro were the candidates from Tepatitlan at the convention of the Catholic National Party.

At home, he established a number of cooperative ventures and with Anacleto formed the student group La Girondia. At twenty-six he entered the University of Morelos, but his school work didn't take away from his social work. He created other cooperatives and a study circle for the workers.

In 1914, the Carrancistas invaded Guadalajara and took over the church properties, expelling the priests and foreign religious and closing the private schools and universities. Miguel returned to El Refugio until 1915 when he returned to resume his studies. He became a member of the ACJM in 1915 and in 1917 founded various circles of workers. In 1919 he established a national congress of Catholic workers called the Catholic Confederation of Work to unify industry workers, commercial employees and agricultural laborers.

His spiritual director, Father Vicente Maria Camacho, said that Miguel was jailed no fewer than fifty-eight times for organizing protests against the government. He was often beaten and several times at the point of being shot for his faith. He told Father Camacho, "It doesn't get me excited." While in jail, he remained serene and composed, leading his fellow prisoners in prayer and singing. He had an image of the Virgin of Refuge on a pin which he always wore over his heart until the day of his death.

In 1922, Miguel completed the final exam for a degree in jurisprudence and received the approval of the synodal judges. He was, however, unable to obtain the signature of the governor. In December of that year he married Maria Guadalupe Sanchez Barragan in the small chapel of the ACJM. At breakfast that morning, one of his friends jokingly told Miguel that the first thing he should buy his wife was a lunch kit so that she could bring him his food in jail.

Although he had gone to the Secretary of the Governor in order to obtain the official title of his profession, he had gotten no results. He moved to Arrandas and opened an office as an attorney. Here he put himself at the disposal of the priest for all that referred to the social question and the works of the apostolate in the parish. Soon he was known and appreciated throughout the town for his honesty, his interest, and his religiosity.

In January of 1923, Miguel was present with a group of Arandenses at the mountain of Cubilete for the blessing of the first stone of the monument to Christ the King, which was given by the Vatican's Apostolic Delegate Monsignor Ernesto Filippi. For the generous gift, Monsignor Filippi was rewarded by the government with immediate expulsion from Mexico.

The authorities in Arandas, learning that Miguel lacked the official professional title, expelled him from town without any judicial order. After three months of exile in Guanajuato, he returned to Guadalajara where he was reunited with his family.

In 1924 during Calles' regime, Miguel became one of the leading organizers of the Union

Miguel Gómez with his little daughter

Popular in Guadalajara. The Union protested the arbitrary actions of the government and attempted to unite the Catholics. Pope Pius XI, acting according to the petition of the Archbishop of Guadalajara, presented the cross Pro Ecclesia et Pontifice to three of the most outstanding Catholic defenders of Mexican Catholicism: Anacleto Gonzalez Flores, Miguel Gómez Loza and Maximino Reyes.

In June of 1925 there were massive arrests of student protesters. Miguel worked hard in their defense, soliciting and obtaining amparos from the federal authorities. He was jailed in February of 1926, released in April and re-arrested by agents of the secret police. Again, friends obtained his release.

In protest of the Calles laws against the church, the Union Popular declared an economic boycott. Miguel, treasurer of the Union, campaigned strongly in favor of the boycott and sent the youth of Catholic Action to spread the word in all the towns of Jalisco. In July, the churches were closed. The faithful gathered in houses, holding Mass secretly at night. Problems escalated and in December, delegates of the League came to persuade the Union Popular to leave its neutrality and opt for armed conflict.

After a visit to his home town, Miguel returned to find that the Union Popular had accepted to enter the conflict and he was assigned as the civil chief of the zone of Los Altos de Jalisco. He accepted his new obligation and from that time he traveled from one Cristero camp to the other, wherever he was needed. From his places of hiding, he maintained contact with Anacleto who was in Guadalajara coordinating the strategies of the Cristeros in arms. He did not take arms himself; rather, his mission was one of animating the combatants. He solicited the ecclesiastical authorities to provide chaplains to give spiritual assistance to the troops.

Miguel Gómez Loza

After the death of Anacleto and some others on April 1, 1927, Miguel was named as the civil chief and governor of Jalisco. Although saddened by the loss of his friend, Miguel gained in faith and in his enthusiasm for the Cristero cause.

On October 30, 1927, the Cristeros solemnly celebrated the feast of Christ the King. Miguel reported to Father Camacho, "Help me to give thanks to God today, the feast of Christ the King. We are making a general Communion of more than a thousand men."

By March of 1928, Miguel was established on a ranch near Atotonilco called El Lindero. His hiding place was discovered and on the 21st a contingent of federales was posted at the rancho where Miguel was with his faithful secretary Dionisio Vazquez. He was killed and his body was translated to Atontonilco and later to Guadalajara.

Thousands gathered for the funeral of Miguel Gómez Loza, and attended his burial in the cemetery of Mezquitan. In 1947 his remains were translated to the sanctuary of Our Lady of Guadalupe in Guadalajara where they joined those of his friend and fellow martyr Anacleto Gonzalez Flores. ✣

Notes

1. Liga Defensora de la Libertad Religiosa was begun in Mexico City in 1925 to work in favor of the right of the Catholic Church.

2. The Association Catolica de la Juventud Merxicana was founded in the archdiocese of Guadalajara in 1913 by the Jesuit Father Bernardo Bergoend. It coordinated the young Mexican Catholics to work for the restoration the Christian social order in Mexico.

3

André Bessette, C.S.C.
Alfred Bessette
Canada, 1845-1937

Miracle Man of the Mountain

There are many different kinds of saints. There are great saints who have done big things. There are also great saints who have done small things so faithfully and well that they, too, share in the heavenly reward. Blessed Brother André Bessette was one of these "small" saints.

"I am only a man, just like you," time after time Blessed André reminded petitioners who came to him for a cure. Known as a thaumaturge of healing during his lifetime, this humble lay brother gave all the credit to God, through the intercession of St. Joseph and the faith of the persons healed. Then, quietly, he said, "I will pray for you." And time after time, healing came.

At his birth, Alfred Bessette was so weak and frail that the midwife baptized him immediately. Throughout life his health remained poor,

and no one would have predicted that he would live to the ripe old age of ninety-one. His parish priest introduced him to the brothers of the Holy Cross and suggested he apply for admission, although Alfred demurred at first because of his lack of education. The priest persisted although the Brothers, aware of Alfred's poor health, gave him little encouragement. In his letter of reference, Father Provençal wrote, "I am sending you a saint." After his novitiate, the Holy Cross superiors hesitated

First Communion photo, age 12
PHOTOS COURTESY OF REV. BERNARD LAFRENIERE, C.S.C.

to admit him to final orders. Montreal's saintly Bishop Ignace Bourget visited Nortre Dame and André, overcoming his customary humility sought the opportunity to speak privately with him, pleading for the bishop's help as "I do so want to be a brother." The Bishop told him, "Do not fear, my dear son, you will be allowed to make your religious profession." No doubt the Bishop's intercession helped in the final decision, but his novice master also pleaded his case before the Holy Cross authorities, saying, "If this young man becomes unable to work, he will at least be able to pray for us. Dear confreres, we are all dedicated to teaching people to pray. This man teaches mainly by his example."

In spite of his poor health, he lived a long and full life. Someone once asked him how he managed to live so long. Laughing, Brother André replied, "By eating as little as possible and by working as much as possible."

Alfred was born in 1845 in a small town near Montreal, the sixth of ten children of a carpenter and woodcutter. His father was killed in an accident when he was nine. His mother died a few years later of tuberculosis. The children were all parceled out to relatives and Alfred, orphaned and nearly illiterate, was forced to find some form of work. Although he had been an apprentice at several skills, he never completed any as his health always failed him. He never attended school. His mother attempted to teach him the little she herself knew, but his letter of application to Holy Cross was written by his parish priest as he could barely write his name. Later the brothers taught him to read, and his favorite book was a copy of the Gospels. He said, "It is not necessary to have been well educated, to have spent many years in college, to love the good God. It is sufficient to want to do so generously."

Prayer, however, was a part of Alfred's early education. Before the death of his parents, the large and loving family gathered nightly to say the rosary. Alfred and his mother shared a rosary and the beads were pulled along by her work-worn hands after they had passed through the tiny hands of her son, kneeling beside her. Even as a child, he had already begun to meditate daily on the Passion.

He loved to assist at Mass in the parish church and the pastor became his friend and patron. He made his First Holy Communion shortly after his mother's death. Alfred's father, a carpenter himself, introduced his son to devotion to the great carpenter of Nazareth.

Alfred put himself under the saint's special protection when he was only a child. Later, in his travels and his work experience, his devotion to St. Joseph the laborer, who knew both exile and poverty, deepened and took firm root in Alfred's heart.

Young Alfred worked at a number of unskilled jobs in Canada and the United States until his entrance to Holy Cross in 1870. Once professed as a lay brother of the Holy Cross, for forty years he humbly, joyfully and uncomplainingly washed floors and windows, cleaned lamps, carried firewood and worked as a porter and messenger. Afterwards, he served as a doorkeeper at the order's college in Montreal. He once commented wryly, "When I joined this community, the superiors showed me the door and I remained there for forty years."

Brother André learned the love of God as a child. He knew how to speak of this love with such intensity that he inspired hope in all those who met him. He showed God as a loving father, gave people common-sense advice, and had empathy with those he counseled.

Young Brother André at his profession as a Holy Cross Brother

These traits, along with his warm sense of humor, drew people to him. He said, "You mustn't be sad; it is good to laugh a little." Especially with the poor and the unfortunate the good brother was merry, and his own inner happiness communicated itself to others. Brother André's appointment to the porter's job was no accident. His gentleness of manner and his pleasant disposition became evident to all who knew him. He had a positive knack for putting people at ease. His knowledge of English, which he had learned while in the United States, also proved most helpful.

After his work for the day was finished, he visited the sick and the elderly in their homes or in the hospital. He put all of his good nature and good humor into the daily outings, and some began to criticize him and say he just liked to travel around in a friend's car. Brother André responded, "There are some who say that it is for pleasure that I visit the sick, but after a day's work it is far from being a pleasure. . . . It is not sufficient to give money, one must offer his sympathy and open his heart." He pointed out, "There are homes for the poor filled with men and women who often are abandoned, without relatives or friends. When one is poor, friends are rather scarce. Among these people are found some who had relatives and many friends when they were living in wealth. . . . It would do healthy men good to visit the sick. This could provide them with good subjects for meditation."

Thousands of the poor, the hurt, and the unhappy visited him. In his little office he counseled them, cried with them, and prayed for them. He had high principals and could be quick or sharp at times, especially when fatigue made him nervous or cross. When he realized that he had spoken sharply, he was contrite and consoled himself with the thought, "Well, at least they know that I am nothing but a poor sinner." He did not distinguish among those who asked for his help and he prayed for all, no matter what their race or religion. "Our Lord is our big Brother, and we are the little brothers. Consequently, we should love one another as members of the same family." He often counseled people to pray more. "You are not far from the good God. When you whisper 'Our Father who art in heaven,' He has His ear to your lips." He also told them, "The earth is a temporary stopping place, heaven is our real home."

Brother André had a particular love for the Eucharist and encouraged people to go to Communion more often. Sadly, he would say, "If you ate only one meal a week would you survive? It is the same for your soul. Nourish it with the Blessed Sacrament." Although he had a deep devotion to St. Joseph, his primary love was the Passion of Our Lord on which he often meditated, a practice begun in his childhood. He saw it as the supreme act of God's love for man. He saw in the cross not a cross which depresses but a victorious cross, a cross which brings resurrection into full daylight.

Brother André spent long hours in prayer. He prayed simply, without trying to use grandiose phrases. He addressed himself to God, to Our Lady, St. Joseph and other saints. Prayer was so important in his eyes that he made it his life's work. Later, in his work for the building of St. Joseph's Oratory, he saw it as an immense place of prayer, accessible to all believers.

Brother had been porter for about five years when his extraordinary powers began to manifest themselves at the college itself. He visited a student who was ill with a severe fever in the infirmary and told him, "You are in perfect health. Go outside and play." The young man followed his order and when a doctor came to check him he was perfectly well. Soon after this, a smallpox epidemic broke out at the nearby Holy Cross College in St. Laurent. Both religious and students became ill and some died. Brother André volunteered to nurse the sick and when he arrived he knelt and prayed to St. Joseph to protect the sick. Not another person died. Reports of André's healing powers began to circulate throughout Montreal and the trickle of early visitors developed into a flood of sick people who began to come to the college. The afflicted spread their sufferings before Brother André and Brother André spread before them his hope and his faith.

As a young man, he had a dream in which he saw a church in an unfamiliar setting. Later he recognized the place as the top of beautiful Mount Royale and he believed a shrine in honor of his patron, St. Joseph, should be built here. Through his initiative and efforts, such a church was begun, enlarged and rebuilt. The oratory that stands there today is the largest church in the world dedicated to St. Joseph. Throughout the time of its construction, he never referred to it as "my" project. Instead, he said, "God choose the most ignorant one. If there was anyone more ignorant than I am, the good God would have chosen him."

The first shrine on Mount Royale was a simple wooden chapel. The flood of sick people coming to the college had disturbed the parents of the students who did not like their children being so close to potential contamination. For a while the sick were received at a small trolley station near the college. Then the passengers began to complain. André found himself in the eye of a hurricane. Some doctors charged him with being a quack and the board of health and even the Archbishop's office were drawn into the controversy. He was cleared by the health authorities as being "harmless." The Archbishop called for the provincial and demanded, "Will André stop this work if you order him to?" The provincial testified as to his obedience. Then the

Archbishop said, "Then let him alone. If the work is from God, it will continue; if not, it will crumble." In 1904 when Brother André asked permission to build the small chapel, he told the superiors, "We will be able to receive the sick there and finally relieve the pressure on the school." At first his request was refused, but his superiors allowed him to put a statue of St. Joseph in a niche on the mountain and told him to save the alms he received and the few pennies he earned as a barber for a future project. Soon he had collected two hundred dollars and he was given permission to construct a small chapel.

Brother André was one of the first to count on St. Joseph as a realtor, and appealed to him about property many times. For several years Holy Cross authorities had attempted to buy land on Mount Royale but the owners refused to sell. Brother, along with several other of the brothers and students, began planting medals of the saint on the property. Suddenly, in 1896, the owners yielded. Later, a mason with a serious stomach ailment asked Brother for his prayers. Brother responded by asking him, "If St. Joseph cured you, would you come and work with me on the mountain? If you are willing, I shall count on you tomorrow morning." The mason obeyed and for the first time in months put in a full day's work.

Brother André as an old man

The first chapel afforded little shelter from the elements and the sick still came to the college. The chorus of complaints also continued and his superiors considered transferring him. A group of religious interceded for him with the provincial telling him to enlarge, enclose and heat the chapel and the pilgrims would then come. The renovations were completed in 1908 and Brother André was made custodian of the shrine and he took up residence there.

Pilgrims came by the hundreds and then by the thousands. Brother André spent eight to ten hours each day in his new office, welcoming

the sick. Some were cured, some were not, but all felt better for having met him. People began to leave crutches, braces and little plaques
of gratitude to St. Joseph. The provincial felt that the plaques were
not in good taste, but Brother André pleaded with him saying they
were signs that the people could understand.

Soon after the oratory was opened, Brother André realized that a
priest was needed there. To his joy a young priest was sent and André
told him "St. Joseph sends souls who are troubled as well as bodies that
are ill to see us." The priest confessed that he had been allowed to stop
his teaching duties and go to assist Brother only because his eyesight
was failing and he couldn't keep up with his teaching. Brother André
simply told him that since St. Joseph had sent him, St. Joseph would
help him. After a few weeks the priest told Brother André that he couldn't
see any longer and that therefore he would have to quit. Distressed by
his inability to help, he said, "I feel that I have failed you." André just
whispered, "Wait until the morning." The following day, the young
priest came to him with joy and dramatically improved sight.

More renovations were needed and during the depression, the
project stalled for lack of funds. Brother André told his superiors, "Put
a statue of St. Joseph in the middle of the building. If he wants a roof
over his head, he'll get it." Perhaps in desperation, the brothers did as
he had suggested and within two months they had enough money to
resume construction. Brother's use of these sacramentals was far from
superstition, however, and he said, "Such things are acts of love and
faith, of confidence and humility. Can one bargain with the good God?
The best way . . . is to submit to His Will."

Brother André died peacefully in a Montreal hospital in January
of 1937. An estimated one million people climbed the slope of Mount
Royale through rain, sleet and snow during the seven days following
his death to pay their final respects to this humble little brother whom
many thought of as the tiny "Miracle Man of the Mountain." In addition to the visits of half of Montreal, special trains were scheduled
from Maine, Massachusetts, Connecticut, Rhode Island, New Hamp-
shire and Vermont. Even doubtful intellectuals paid their respects.
One journalist confessed, "I was of the number of those who thought
themselves too intelligent to give credence to Brother André. And
now, if I had not gone to his tomb, I would regret it all my life." Thousands petitioned for his beatification and the first steps, the informal

investigation of his bishop, were taken almost immediately after his death. The Diocesan Process was opened within three years. Pope John Paul II beatified Brother André on May 23, 1982.

Today, many still come to ask his help. Over two million people visit the shrine annually. His life inspires us who remember his words "I am only a man just like you," to imitate his faithful service and his love of God. ✝

4

Annie Zelikova
Czechoslovakia, 1924-1941

Young Apostle of the Smile

Lying on her bed of pain, young Annie Zelikova told her visitor, "I must smile to my last breath. Ah, all I can give God now are my heartbeats and my smile. Nothing is left to me except love and trust."

A short time later on the night of September 10, 1941, Annie's mother realized that the end was near. She, along with the priest's housekeeper, kept vigil with her teenage daughter, praying the rosary as the last vestiges of life slipped from the body of the seventeen-year-old tuberculosis patient. Just before dawn in the age-old custom of the Moravian people, she placed the Candlemas candle in her daughter's hands, supporting both her girl and the candle. Annie's beloved Jesus had granted all that she asked of him, to do only with her as He willed, surely he would not deny her last wish — to die with a smile. Her face broke out with one of her beautiful smiles and slowly she spoke, "How beautiful . . . it all is. . . I wouldn't . . . trade places . . . with anyone. My heart . . . is beating . . . for Jesus. I love Him so much. " Her last audible statement was a weak but definitive "I trust." As the Angelus began to chime, Annie's head fell back upon her pillow. The smiling eyes which in life sought only to give pleasure to Jesus and to gain souls, fluttered gently and closed.

Annie was born July 19, 1924, the oldest of two daughters of Alois Zelik and his wife. The couple owned a small farm. The family was solidly Catholic, and the faith practiced was of the traditional kind. Religious pictures adorned the walls. The family often visited the nearby Marian sanctuaries and the rosary was a common devotion. The children were given religious instruction by the Sisters of the Holy Cross whose convent and school were near the Zelik property.

When Annie was three her mother came down with pneumonia and was near death. Annie was taken to her aunt's home but the young child had intuited the seriousness of the situation. Normally sparkling and energetic, the three-year-old sat motionless on a kitchen chair.

Finally, the aunt noticed and asked her why she wasn't playing. Annie looked up and said, "My mom will be healthy again; yes, auntie, she will! God is going to heal her."

As a young child, Annie was often headstrong, bossy, obstinate and sometimes even jealous. Once she purposefully led her sister along a stony garden path which she knew would hurt the younger girl's feet. From the time of her First Communion, however, she seemed to gain a spiritual maturity which was far in advance of the norm for her age. Her spiritual growth was rapid, possibly because she was to have so little time in this world.

The smiling Annie Zelikova
PHOTO COURTESY OF REV. REDEMPTUS VALABEK, O.CARM.

Daily Mass became the highlight of her day. Once her father wanted his girls to come and help him in the family fields farthest from town as they did not have school that day. They would have to leave at a very early hour. Annie begged to be allowed to attend Mass first, but her father grumbled that she would then have little time for work in the fields. She finally won him over with the promise "I'll run, I'll get there real fast, and I'll make up for everything, every little thing."

One of the sisters had a way of explaining great mysteries of the faith in such a simple way that even the youngest child could understand them. Annie quickly grasped the meaning of the Real Presence in the Eucharist. Sister Milada also explained penance as a cleansing of the heart to be presented to the great guest we receive in Communion. The Eucharist and penance became the cornerstones of Annie's life.

Annie was a good student. Her favorite subject was art. She loved the beautiful and artistic rituals of the church, and delighted in spending time with Jesus, kneeling before the tabernacle. She took extra Latin lessons voluntarily in order to better follow the prayers of the liturgy. She read some of the spiritual classics and the Autobiography of St. Thérèse made a lasting impression on her. At school, she was popular, well liked by her teachers and her classmates. She was elected the president of her class. Often she would stay after school to help another student with a difficult problem.

At ten she was allowed to make three days of recollection with the neighboring Sisters. Later, she wrote of the ideals she had identified at this and a subsequent retreat. "I spent three days in the company of the good Jesus. The approaching Christmas season forcefully drove me to sacrifice. Of all the gifts, I wished to prepare as many flowers of love as possible. I slowly began to understand that there is another kind of life than that which we see around us. A life that is great, pure, holy. Up to now I loved Jesus, but now my desire grew to do something, to sacrifice for him. In school I often went to visit him and I tried to provide him with as much joy as possible. All this was done in a hidden way so that no one knew about it, because I confided it to no one. I [childishly] thought that I could be robbed of all that happiness, hidden in my heart. The second retreat caused many changes. My love was anxious to surrender everything, just so I could be closer to Jesus. My desire began to fly to the very heights of Carmel, in which I perceived that highest union with Jesus. Up to now I don't know why I yearned for Carmel right from my childhood years, especially since I never knew a Carmel. I just knew the Little Thérèse, Carmelite; I loved her and I wanted to imitate her virtuous life. My love was growing up. I knew what the word perfection meant. While learning, I stayed with Jesus. Many times I looked amazed at the marks I got for my work. But they really belonged to Jesus; I did everything with him. I ran to him with everything, even with the most ordinary things."

In Moravia when a new priest is ordained, the entire town is decorated and the young priest is brought to his local church in a festive and triumphant procession. In July of 1937, Annie and her sister, dressed in their white First Communion dresses, were in the procession for the First Mass of Father Joseph Zavadil at their parish. The celebration made such an impression on Annie that for the rest of the summer she and a little friend prayed the rosary in church daily for priests, and for the rest of her life, Annie imitated St. Thérèse in offering herself to Jesus in a special way for priests.

On Holy Thursday of 1938, Annie was doing housework at home when someone came to the door. Annie heard her mother answer the door and begin crying, telling the visitor "But that's a sin against heaven and against the infant — you can't kill it!" (In fact, a relative had had an abortion.) Resolutely, Annie went to her Jesus in the Blessed Sacrament.

The following day, Annie told her friend and mentor Sister Ludmilla that she had a secret to share with her. She began talking about sacrifice. Then she told her, "How much the world benefited when Jesus hung on the cross. We too can give much to the world if we let ourselves be nailed to the cross out of love. I wanted to give everything. When this year, before Holy Week, the flu hit me with high temperatures, coughing with great discomfort, I begged Jesus to tell me more clearly what he wishes of me. [Yesterday] I begged Jesus earnestly to tell me what kind of sacrifice he asks of me. . . . My demand remained without an answer. On Good Friday I was again at the Lord's tomb. And again I saw that there were so few people in church. I became aware that people simply do not react to God's immense love, and on top of that, so many sins are committed. . . . Again I begged Jesus that he compensate for all this in me as his property, that he take my body, my soul, my health, my life and simply everything that I have. Here I was overcome by an attack of coughing and my handkerchief became red with blood. I was overwhelmed with great happiness; I could do nothing else except to thank him."

Sister Ludmilla explained that the sin that Annie had asked to make reparation for was that of abortion. Then she asked the young teenager if she had spoken to her family about her feelings and about what was happening to her. She had not. Although the sister felt that Annie's family would not understand her spiritual offering of suffering in reparation, she did go to Annie's mother and suggest that she have some X-rays taken, saying that Annie seemed to look haggard. The mother did not grasp the sister's premonition. Annie seemed the picture of health. A hefty girl, she weighed more than most of her peers. So she continued her chores and her schooling. Some of the other sisters began to notice that Annie was obviously losing weight and that she looked a bit pallid, so Sister Ludmilla again went to Mrs. Zelik and pleaded for medical attention for Annie. Mrs. Zelikova asked Sister Ludmilla to take Annie to the sisters' hospital in Uherske

Annie, still smiling on her bed of pain
PHOTO COURTESY OF ROBERT NEMEC, CHRISTNET

Hradiste. On May 31, 1938, the head doctor sorrowfully read the diagnosis, "I'd give her three months, I wouldn't count on more. . . ."

Sister Ludmilla was crushed at the devastating news, but Annie happily led her to the train for home saying, "Christ is soon going to take me to himself!" Although the doctor's prediction, and Annie's hope, was for an immediate death, she lived with the crippling disease for another four years.

The stricken parents immediately offered the best of care, including a trip to the mountains for her health. Annie pleaded to be allowed to stay at home, telling her parents that she was in the hands of Jesus and if he willed her to get better she would do so at home as well as in the mountains. The future bishop Joseph Hlouch visited Annie at the request of the sisters and he was so overwhelmed with the spiritual depths of this fourteen-year-old that he became her spiritual guide for the rest of her days. He also became the first biographer of this holy teenager.

Annie tried to alleviate the anxieties of her parents by applying herself diligently to her schoolwork and to her tasks at home, constantly smiling. By the beginning of 1939, however, she coughed up blood for an entire week and her parents decided to keep her home from school. She continued her household chores and she determined to keep Jesus company at all times in an interior dialog. She wrote down some of her conversations with Christ and twenty of these have survived. At fifteen she wrote, "Dear Jesus, let my love for you be ever greater, and let that love make me forget myself completely. Everything — whether sorrow or joy — comes from your love. May everything that I am and that I have sing you a song of praise."

Annie developed a deep spirituality that was an incarnational one; she would not miss a single touch of God's love in all that happened. Hers was a practical love and in many ways it was based on the Little Way of her beloved St. Thérèse. She wrote, "Every instant it's possible to give him [Jesus] much — all of one's work, every movement, every word can be uttered with great love. Let us do as much as we can, and when we are unsuccessful in something, let us remain peaceful. It's not so much dependent on the fruit of our work and effort, but rather on the love which led us to that task." She explained how we are called to make our surroundings better: "In the midst of the world we can live like in heaven. Everything around us always mirrors God. And the less the world thinks of him, so much greater is our duty to let our thoughts be attentive only to him. To let resound the words: I am God's, I belong to heaven. How our neighborhood is depends on us — always. We have to change it, at least where we are; we have to produce heaven."

Her relationship with Jesus was very simple and very personal. "I am always united to him. In everything I am aware that Jesus, too, did this. I get up — Jesus used to get up. I get dressed — he certainly took his clothes in his hands in a holy way. I pray — he prayed, and how he prayed! Everywhere I go Jesus is with me. Everything I do, he does with me. Every day brings me new beautiful things. Every day I can come closer to Christ the Lord." Her words give us the key to her happy heart, "We will show him our love best if we wish only what he wishes, and are attentive to what makes him happiest."

Annie would have preferred to be in school. Throughout her illness she did manage to visit from time to time and she took a great interest in all that was going on there. She began writing letters to her friends as a sort of apostolate. A number of these have been preserved as well as her spiritual journal and the record of her spiritual exercises and retreats. Annie's writings highlight the amazing wisdom and spiritual maturity of this ever-smiling teenager. Through her letters, she kept reaching out to others until the end; her last letter was written just three days before her death. Her letter writing was one way she had of reaching out to those for whom she had offered her life — with a smile. In this final letter she admitted, "I can't write much more, my hands are too shaky."

Annie wanted to become a cloistered Carmelite, but it was obvious that this dream could never be realized. Her spiritual director, Father Hlouch, obtained permission, with a special dispensation from the canonical age, to admit her to the Third Order Secular of Carmel. She made private vows on February 7, 1941. Always a realist, Annie pointed out that nothing had changed since she had already been living out the spirituality of the Carmelite commitment.

As the disease which eventually killed her progressed, Annie was forced more and more to remain in bed. Even then she retained her cheerful acceptance. "Now I can show but one manifestation of my love — to will just what he wills. Everything else depends on this self-offering. Before I used to hand over my sacrifices to him; now Jesus does everything by himself. As for me I just eagerly lend myself to him. No — not that I lend myself to him — I give myself to him."

Just as in the lives of many saints, Annie Zelikova passed through a dark night of the soul. A week before her death she wrote, "Is it enough that God sees that everything that happens to me I accept with a smile?"

The Communists took over Moravia in 1939. Although those who knew her already considered her a saint, her story was not known outside her region for over twenty years. It was not possible to initiate the process of her beatification until the breakdown of the Communist regime. The diocesan process was completed in 1995. If one day she is accorded the honors of the altar, it will provide a resounding "yes" to her question, and will prove that teenage holiness is possible as shown in the life of the ever-smiling Annie Zelikova. ✢

Even in death, she smiled for Jesus
PHOTO COURTESY OF JAN PETKOV

5

Anthony Kowalczyk, O.M.I.
Poland-Canada, 1866-1947

One-Armed Blacksmith for God

On a warm July day in 1897, the shrill whine of the saw was joined by a shriek of pain. Working in the Oblates' sawmill at the mission of Lac La Biche, Sylvester Borque saw the blade still whirring and Brother Anthony lying on the ground, his arm mangled in the fast moving power belt. Between the crushed fingers, Brother clutched his rosary. Slowly he struggled to his feet and told Borque, "It is God's will."

Fortunately, a visiting Grey nun was a trained nurse and she treated the arm with the few medical supplies available. One of the fathers left immediately for Lac LaDelle to bring a doctor who arrived two days later. Then the silently suffering Polish handyman was transported by wagon to Edmonton. By the time they arrived, gangrene had set in and only amputation would save the brother's life. Lacking anesthetic, the doctors prepared to strap him to the operating table. "Don't do that," he said. "Give me my crucifix; that will be enough." Clutching his Oblate cross, Brother Anthony remained conscious during the operation, enduring it without a cry of pain.

The operation was successful, but during the convalescent period the mental agony of the young brother superseded the physical pain. Fear of the future in which he would have only one good arm preyed on his mind. Would the accident prevent him from taking final vows? "What good is a one-armed brother?" he thought.

Although assured by Bishop Grandin that he would be able to take his vows, the humble brother wrote to the Superior General:

"Permit the poor Brother Anthony to write you a word before returning to Lac La Biche. You have heard of my accident. Father Grandin and the sisters took me to Edmonton where the doctors cut off my hand on July twenty-second. I am well now and I have come to St. Albert for a rest. I shall return to Lac La Biche soon.

"I was afraid when the accident happened that I would not remain an Oblate. Father Grandin told me, 'It does not matter, you will be an Oblate.' Father Grandin is happy, the bishops are happy and I am happy. I hope you are happy too, my good Father.

"I will never be able to say thank you enough to everyone. I pray the good God will bless them and pray for me. Please give me your blessing."

A re-education was necessary. Like a small child, Brother Anthony had to learn the most simple of tasks, using his left hand instead of his right one. If he could not be as good a worker, he determined to be a better religious. His fears were put to rest in January of 1899 when he knelt before Bishop Legal and took life-long vows as an Oblate of Mary Immaculate.

For the rest of his life, Brother Anthony labored in Western Canada, structuring his life on love, patience and service. In 1912, Brother was fitted with an artificial limb with a hook replacing his hand. Disabled in the eyes of the world, this sturdy Polish brother did the work of four men, spending himself in the service of God, faithfully performing the monotonous tasks of his daily routine. From 1911 he labored at the college of St. John. He was the blacksmith, furnace stoker, laundryman, gardener, keeper of the animals, bell-ringer and sacristan. He had made a bargain with God to become a servant and he fulfilled that promise completely.

Anthony Kowalczyk was born June 4, 1866, at Dzierzanow, Poland. He was the sixth of twelve children of Ignatius and Lucy Kowalczyk, although only six of the twelve lived to adulthood. His parents were sturdy Catholics and it was at the shrine of his baptism, Lutogniew, where he learned the great love of the Virgin, which inspired his nickname, "Ave," in later life. He completed his elementary education at the village school where he also prepared for his First Communion, which he made at the age of twelve. He did not pursue a secondary education because his parents needed his help on their small farm. At fourteen, he was apprenticed to a blacksmith at Krotoszyn where he learned a trade that would serve him in good stead later in the Canadian missions. At seventeen, he left home to seek his fortune in the industrial centers of Westphalia and the Rhineland in Germany.

While working in Hamburg, he finally received the sacrament of confirmation at the age of twenty-four. In Hamburg, he worked among many rough workmen who were unbelievers and who jeered and taunted him because of his Catholic faith. One day he felt a searing pain in his eyes and a doctor diagnosed his condition as very serious with total blindness a probable consequence. On his way home, Anthony stopped in a church and knelt before Our Lady's altar, praying that he might be resigned to God's will. He then began to make the way of the cross and at the sixth station, he begged Veronica's help when he felt a physical change. Removing the bandage, he found that he could see again. This event plus learning the inspiring story of Father Adolph Kolping, Apostle of the Workers, led Anthony to the thought of serving God in a special way, but he still didn't know in what form he could best do this. He found a job in Mulheim and located a Catholic family with a room for rent. His landlady, whose son was studying with the Oblate fathers, suggested he consider the vocation of a lay brother. She spoke of the Oblates' need for workers on their Canadian missions, and encouraged him in many ways, including paying his way for a pilgrimage visit to the

shrine at Kevelaer. Anthony's mind was made up, so he was crushed when his father refused to give his permission for him to become a religious and volunteer for the missions. He confided his heartbreak to his confessor who told him, "God comes before your parents." At last his father accepted the priest's word and gave Anthony his blessing. Along with another Polish blacksmith he had met at the boarding house, James Ciesielski, Anthony traveled to St. Gerlach in Holland to apply to enter the Congregation of Missionary Oblates of Mary Immaculate.

At St. Gerlach, the novice master asked Anthony, "Well, my friend, are you taking up the religious life because you are out

Brother Anthony, God's blacksmith
PHOTOS COURTESY OF REV. SLAWOMIR TRZASKO, O.M.I.

of work? Do you think we should support you?" Anthony responded, "I have a job. That is not my reason. I have come because I was told that here I could serve God. I am afraid to die and have God say to me, 'Did you love the world more than you loved me?' " With that, the priest welcomed him to begin his postulancy.

Anthony made a final trip home, his first in five years. He realized that this visit meant a final goodbye, perhaps forever. He prayed for strength to persevere in his religious vocation, knowing that his family would offer strong temptations against it. Indeed his father made final arguments for Anthony to remain home before capitulating in the face of the boy's determination. It was a bittersweet parting and Anthony dared not look back. His heart ached with both joy and sadness as he left to become God's blacksmith.

Anthony began his novitiate on September 21, 1891. Excerpts from his record read: "He is in good health. He has a rugged constitution and is fitted for various kinds of work. He seems especially talented as a blacksmith. He is intelligent enough and his education meets the requirements for the life of a coadjutor brother. His energy and virtues point toward a life of piety, with every promise that he will become a good religious. He appears to be devout and seems well suited for community life." He made his first vows on October 2, 1892, and was appointed mechanic at St. Charles Juniorate in Holland. Brother Anthony's one great wish was to serve in the missions, but his request was initially refused. At last he received an appointment to Ceylon, but the appointment was canceled almost immediately. Finally, he was appointed to the missions of western Canada in the area which later became the province of Alberta. His superior wrote to his new superior in Canada: "He is the best among our coadjutor brothers, a saint in the making." How prophetic these words proved to be.

He sailed for Canada in May of 1896, arriving at Quebec City on June 1st. He was the first Polish Oblate to work in Canada. He continued his trip by rail to Edmonton and then by wagon to the mission of Lac La Biche. On the last leg of the trip, torrential rains had created large areas of swampy mud. The lead wagon became stuck and Father Grandin asked Anthony's help. The young brother first knelt on his knees in the mud to say a prayer and then rising he indicated the way by probing with a stick. At Lac La Biche, Brother Anthony spent many hours at prayer in addition to keeping all the machinery in excellent working condition. His example was an inspiration to the entire community.

In 1897, Brother Anthony was sent to the mission at St. Paul des Metis, where for ten years he was engineer, mechanic and gardener for the struggling mission. In addition, he was put in charge of a herd of swine which the superior hoped to use to ease the chronic food shortage. One year the hail destroyed the crops and the pigs were in danger of starving. There was a field of turnips set aside for just such an emergency but to reach it the pigs would have to pass through a field of oats. The superior commanded Brother Anthony to take the pigs to the turnip field but cautioned him not to let the pigs eat the oats. When Anthony protested that that would be impossible, the superior told him that there was no such word in the French language. After his usual *Ave*, he led the pigs single file behind him through the field in front of a crowd who gathered to watch. Not a single pig touched the oats. This and a number of other startling incidents such as finding lost items and making machinery work without the use of tools are related to show the power of Brother Anthony's prayer. The brothers teased him about his "little miracles."

About Brother Anthony himself, however, no claims are made for extraordinary supernatural occurrences. He did not perform excessive and highly publicized penances. He merely performed his daily tasks with a fidelity and love that were outstanding, combined with constant prayer and a gentle sense of humor. Outwardly his life appeared simple, dull and monotonous, but all that he did he did well out of love for God. A priest who knew the humble brother recalls that Brother Anthony was always happy and wanted those around him to be happy as well. He says, "One day I was working with him and I was in bad humor, grouchy and cranky. Brother Anthony said to me, 'Go away, the Lord doesn't want people who are unhappy working for him.'" Father McMahon says this was a good lesson in patience.

Though Brother Anthony's road was a simple one, it was not necessarily an easy one. Love and patience were its hallmarks. Who knows what struggles the humble brother endured to control his natural quick temper and discipline his body for the heavy labor he performed. He once told a friend, "You say the rule is hard. That is true, my brother.

I am 72. I find the rule difficult. You must bend and break your will." Even at this advanced age he could confess that the rule was difficult.

In 1911, Brother Anthony was transferred to St. John's College in Edmonton where he would work for the rest of his life. He obtained special permission to rise at 4 a.m. in order to have time to complete all his daily chores. The students were the center of his interest and they soon recognized in him a true friend. He was always ready to help in little ways such as repairing a watch, cutting a key for a locker, or mending eyeglass frames, and he was particularly kind to new students who were homesick. He encouraged the students to persevere in their calling to the priesthood. His superior recognized his insight into character and often asked Brother's opinion about the various candidates.

To symbolize his love for Mary, Brother Anthony obtained permission to build a replica of the Lourdes Grotto at the college. Although it would win no architectural prizes, the grotto still stands as a monument of the Polish brother's love and gratitude. The stones came from a river at the edge of the college property; the labor was his and that of volunteers. With his superior's permission, he dictated letters which the students wrote and which were sent to their families and to former students and friends to raise the necessary money to complete the construction of the grotto and to place the statue there.

By 1945, Brother Anthony's health began to fail and his age began to show. Loss of vision, rheumatism, failing memory and other ailments resulted in some time in the hospital for a while. He was given a new room near the chapel, but when his strength returned he asked to return to his old room and resumed doing what work he was capable of. He felt better when he was working at his cutomary tasks.

Brother Anthony in front of his grotto

Although there was little phenomenal or striking in Brother Anthony's life, one incident may have a supernatural origin. On September 17, 1945, Brother failed to appear in chapel and when he did not show up for dinner a confrere investigated. He found Brother Anthony sitting on the edge of his bed in his room. His face was bruised and swollen and his eyes blackened and bloodshot. He mumbled incoherently in reply to the brother's questions. He was rushed to the hospital where he was given the last rites. When his condition improved he asked to see a Polish friend, the mother of one of the Oblates. In answer to her question as to who had beaten him, Brother Anthony replied, "I don't know. I think it was the devil. He fought with me all night." That night haunted him for many days after his return from the hospital and he felt his death was approaching.

Brother's last day at the college was spent on his hands and knees, weeding the garden. That same day he went to St. Albert for his annual retreat. Two days later he was found fully dressed on his bed, paralyzed and unable to speak. After receiving the last rites, he passed peacefully into eternity on July 10, 1947.

Brother Anthony's cause for beatification was opened in 1952. In 1969, Karol Cardinal Wojtyla visited Canada and prayed at Brother Anthony's grave at the Oblate Cemetery at St. Albert. As Pope John Paul II, Wojtyla recommended the process be introduced in the Sacred Congregation for Canonizations on June 1, 1979. ✠

6

Antoni Gaudi
Spain, 1852-1926

God's Architect

The haughty young man in his dandified clothing loved fine cuisine, society life, and visiting the grand theater, the Liceu, where fancy costumed balls alternated with the performances of all the fashionable operas, plays and musical innovations of the day A lion of the architecture world, Antoni Gaudi began to make plans. With original form, unique sculptured decorations, his practical knowledge of the use of metal and his near-genius mathematical ability in constructions, he began to make plans — many and detailed — for modernistic, whimsical buildings the likes of which have never been seen before or since. But God, the Master Builder also had made plans. And his plans combined with the genius of the young architect to produce works that can never be fully understood outside of the Faith. As the life of the young architect entwined with his master work — the church of the Holy Family[1] in Barcelona — the architect himself grew in devotion and austerity. This church is the only modern church built in the slow, painstaking method with which the great cathedrals were built in medieval times. Just as Gaudi never hesitated to modify a design if he believed the changes would produce a better result, God did not hesitate to modify the soul of this artist. Gaudi's works were conceived with profound and habitual contemplation of the mysteries of faith, and, even incomplete, they move us. Gaudi said, "Beauty is the image of truth. The image is not the same thing as truth, but it opens the possibility to bring man closer to God."

When people asked Gaudi how he could continue for all the years needed for the construction of Sagrada Familia, he would answer "Don't hurry — St. Joseph is a saint with many resources." Or, again, "He who asked me to do it is not in a hurry."

As Barcelona's most famous architect, Gaudi could have lived a life of wealth and privilege surrounded by adoring patrons. Instead, he chose to live much as a monk would live, in very humble circumstances. Part of his philosophy was that all artists had to make personal sacrifices in order to create great art. For the last fourteen years of his life, Gaudi devoted himself to prayer and to the work at the Holy Family. He practiced an austere lifestyle. Penance and a detachment from material goods were hallmarks of this time of his life. He dressed in workmen's clothes of the poorest kind and ate only the simplest of foods, taking his lunch at his drafting table. Daily, he arose before dawn and walked to the cathedral for Mass. On returning to the Sagrada Familia, he supervised the construction until five-thirty in the evening. He then walked to the Church of St. Philip Neri where he prayed and sometimes visited with his spiritual advisor. Suffering from rheumatism, he felt the physical exertion of these long walks relieved the constant pain. On the eve of his death, Gaudi told a priest friend, "I am a battler by temperament. I have always fought and I have always got what I wanted, except in one thing; in the fight with my temper. I have not been able to defeat it." This soul who had grown close to God and who aimed, through his art, to draw others to God, recognized that man's struggle against his own nature is a bitter, difficult, and life-long task. Earlier, he had told an interviewer for La Razon, "Like everything human, I am incomplete."

Monday evening June 7, 1926, Gaudi had completed his work for the day and left for his daily walk to pray at St. Philip Neri. While crossing the Gran Via at Bailen Street, he was run down by a streetcar. Unconscious and dressed in his humble workmen's clothing, the pedestrians did not recognize Barcelona's most famous architect. Thinking him simply another poverty case, they took him to the charity ward of the Hospital of the Holy Cross.

During his life, Gaudi had expressed the wish to die unknown, received only by the love of God. This wish was partially fulfilled. The day after the accident, two men from Holy Family found him in the charity ward and had him moved to a private room. He recovered consciousness and,

Gaudi in 1888
PHOTOS COURTESY OF REV. I. SEGARRA

surrounded by a few intimate friends, he received the Last Rites and was able to speak a few words. He died on June 10 after speaking his last words, "Amen. My God! My God!"

Antoni Gaudi was born June 25, 1852 and baptized the following day in the parish church of Reus, Tarragona. He was given the name Antonio Placido Guillermo Gaudi i Cornet. His father, Francesco Gaudi, was a coppersmith. His mother, Antonia Cornet i Bertran, came from a long line of potters. The family was a pious one, and his mother was devoted to Our Lady of Mercy. While still a boy, he worked in his father's boiler making shop in Reus where he became fascinated by the inter-relationship of shapes and volumes and the artistic potential of wrought iron.

As a child, he suffered several bouts of rheumatic fever that undermined his health the rest of his life. His childhood vacations and periods of recuperation from his illnesses were spent in the Tarragona countryside at the family's farm in Riudoma. He loved the images and forms of nature and for him nature was the essence of God's design. This love of nature imprinted all his future works.

Gaudi attended grammar school in Reus, and later studied at the high school run by the Piarist Fathers. After high school, he moved to

Gaudi at the beginning of his career

Barcelona to begin his study of architecture. While in college, Gaudi developed a strong interest in all the humanities and took classes in philosophy, history and esthetics. He attended musical concerts and for a time was a member of an amateur theatrical group. He enjoyed his studies and read poetry and the classics. During his free time he traveled throughout the provinces, investigating the beauty of the landscapes and Spain's architectural monuments as well as studying the medieval buildings.

He also began to study the social problems of the day. He was particularly concerned with the living conditions of factory workers, which in many places were deplorable. He designed the buildings of the Workers' Cooperative of Mataro, the first employee-owned factory in Spain. At first an idealist, Gaudi came to believe that the ultimate solution was for people to put Christian social doctrine into practice.

While continuing his university studies, Gaudi did his military service in the infantry. Although he was deployed several times during the Third Carlist Wars, he was never engaged in combat.

Gaudi's parents supported both him and his older brother Francisco during their university education. Because of his modest means, Gaudi worked as a draftsman and designer for a number of architects and artisans, gaining much practical experience as well as completing his formal studies. He fell in love with Miss Pepita Moreu, but due to his timidity, by the time he gathered enough courage to propose to her she was already engaged to someone else. From that time he seems to have dedicated himself only to his studies and later his work. Although he did not score high marks, he was graduated as a master architect in 1878.

Gaudi left very few writings of his own and, contrary to the custom of the day, gave no lectures. He did, however, guide many visitors around the construction site of Holy Family and in so doing explained his philosophy of design and gave advice to his disciples and collaborators. After his death, some of his adherents gathered and published a collection of his comments that provide a valuable record of Gaudi's philosophy.

As a young man, Gaudi developed a reputation for being somewhat of a *bon vivant*. He enjoyed elegant clothes, expensive and exotic food, and fashionable society events. A cultural and political renaissance known as the Renaixenca was in full swing in Barcelona at this time. There was economic prosperity and the middle classes wanted to be in tune with the latest European styles. The 1888 World Fair was held in the city, and the Catalan movement, similar to Art Nouveau, came to the forefront of the art and architecture world. Gaudi formed a strong, lifelong friendship with Eduard Toda Guell, and the wealthy industrialist Guell family commissioned him for a number of works, which helped him gain much prestige. At the same time, he began to demonstrate his affinity for the political struggle of the workers.

In the space of a single year, his brother, mother, and sister died. He moved with his father and a chronically ill niece into an apartment in Barcelona.

Gaudi began work on Sagrada Familia in 1884. Determined to resolve the problems which arose in putting his own architecture into practice, by 1908, he stopped accepting other work and devoted himself exclusively to this project until his death. The last eight months of his life he slept on a cot in his workroom at the church. This church, like no other, is built in such a way as to show Gaudi's immense knowledge of the liturgy.

The pious owner of a religious bookshop and author of Christian publications, Jose Maria Bocabella y Verdaguer, formed a spiritual association dedicated to St. Joseph and the Holy Family. This association initiated the idea to build a monumental votive church in honor of the Holy Family. Impressed by the beauty and grandeur of the Italian churches he had seen on his travels, Bocabella intended the temple of Sagrada Familia to be built without financial support from the diocese. It was intended to be completed through private donations alone. The project was initially given to the diocese's architect, Francisco del Villar, and its cornerstone was set in 1882 on the feast of St. Joseph. Villar's plans were conventional. A year after construction began, Villar disagreed with the administration and resigned. Bocabella suggested Juan Martorell, technical councilor and supervisor of the entire project, as a successor. Martorell declined the commission and recommended his young assistant, thirty-one-year-old Antoni Gaudi. Bocabella trusted the reference, but was saddened at the elegant young man's seeming lack of religious interest. Officially, Gaudi took over in November of 1883.

In the course of his forty-three-year work on the holy temple, Gaudi's purely vocational interest changed into a deep passion. Gradually, as he united religion and art into a great concept, Gaudi metamorphosed into an artist obligated only to God. He grew ever closer to the One he called the "greatest master builder." Needless to say, he did not follow the plans of Villar. He took what had already been constructed and modified it into the unique work it has become today. Only the crypt retains the original design. The first service in the church was held in 1891.

In his work, Gaudi always intended to include the work of other artists. He saw architecture as the "mother of the arts." He insisted on many details and decorations in the work on Holy Family. Naturally when there is more than one creative genius at work, tensions arise; pleasant surprises happened also. The Japanese sculptor Etsuro Sotoo had been working on the church for twenty years, and after becoming acquainted with Gaudi's work became a convert to Catholicism. The Japanese architect Kenji Imai arrived in Barcelona two months after Gaudi's death. Gaudi's work made such an impression on him that he returned to Japan and gave a number of lectures on Gaudi. Then he, too, converted to Catholicism.

The stone carvings of the Flight into Egypt were made using real persons and animals as models. Gaudi looked for suitable representatives and copied them using plaster casts and models. Gaudi told Albert Schweitzer that the donkey was a difficult job. When word went out that he was looking for a model for the donkey, people brought him all the finest donkeys in Barcelona, but he could not use them because he felt that Mary and the Christ child would have been mounted on a poor, old, weary donkey which had something kindly in its face and seemed to know what was going on. He found his model at the cart of a woman selling scouring sand. He finally persuaded the owner to bring it to him and, while he copied it bit by bit in plaster, she cried, thinking it would kill the donkey. "That is the ass of the 'Flight into Egypt' and it has made an impression on you because it is not imagined, but is from actual life."

At age 72, procession of Christ the King in 1924

During the decade of 1910-20, a number of Gaudi's

friends died. He entered a dark and depressive time. He had previously suffered occasionally from bouts of depression. He began to close in on himself and separate himself from the world.

In 1911, Gaudi became ill and spent some months with his friend Dr. Santalo in the Pyrenees. He accompanied Josep Dalmases on a number of trips asking for donations for the work at Holy Family. With his love of detail, Gaudi was not always economical in his use of funds for the project. Some parts of it, however, were constructed under economic guidelines. The curved areas are one example of this. They were easy to manufacture by bricklayers and low-priced because of the use of the even steel bar reinforcing. In many ways, they anticipate the reinforced concrete bowls of our modern times.

During the last third of his life, Gaudi began to develop a deep spirit of penance. In 1894, his self-imposed Easter fast almost cost him his life. Afterwards, he designed the Nativity front of the Sagrada Familia. Mosen Gil Pares, the custodian chaplain of the Templo de la Sagrada Familia from 1907 to 1930, knew Gaudi for over twenty years. Of Gaudi's spirit of penance Gil Pares says Gaudi's life changed from that of a career man to that of a penitent and a mystic. "He did not live to eat and rest, but rather he ate and rested as necessary not to die. He heard the holy Mass and received holy Communion daily, and also visited the Eucharist daily. He never missed the grandiose collective religious celebrations of the city or the temple and the rest of the hours of the day he spent between prayer and work. From this life of faith sprang an extremely firm hope in God, which gave him an absolute spiritual tranquillity in moments of tribulation."

In front of his masterwork — Holy Family

When the news went out to Barcelona that Gaudi had died, people flocked to pay him homage. Masses of people attended his funeral on June 12, 1926, and followed the cortege to Holy Family where he was buried in the crypt of the church. During the Spanish Civil War, his tomb was opened during a police search, and it remained open until

1939 when a number of his friends gathered and identified his remains and the coffin was re-sealed.

Gaudi's work continues. After his death, three remaining towers were completed, according to his design, by Domingo Sugranes. This man was killed during the Spanish Civil War and work was stopped until 1952 when construction was taken up again. The church was inaugurated as a basilica on the feast of the Holy Family in 1999. Most of the world's great cathedrals have taken centuries to complete and Holy Family is no exception. The current architect in charge of the project, José Maria Bonet, estimated an additional forty years of work at a minimum, depending on the amount and number of donations available. In 1996, Toni Meca, an advertising agent in Barcelona began work on a movie entitled Glory Day. The movie will present Sagrada Familia as a finished work, "virtually," digitized in three dimensions.

In 1992, Father Ignatius Segarra motivated a group of five friends led by a young architect and professor, Jose Manuel Almuzara, to establish the Association for the Beatification of Antoni Gaudi. In 1998, the Bishops of Tarragona petitioned to open Gaudi's cause for beatification. The current parish priest of Sagrada Familia who is also the brother of the current architect for the continued construction of the temple was appointed as the vice postulator of the cause by the Association with the approval of the Cardinal-Archbishop of Barcelona. The cause was officially opened on April 12, 2000. ✝

Notes

1. In Spanish, El Templo Expiatorio de la Sagrada Familia.

7

Ceferino Jiménez Malla
Spain, 1861-1936

El Pelé – Heroic Gypsy

On the hot evening of July 25, 1936, a group of Spanish militiamen were roughly manhandling a priest in the dusty street of Barbastro. They were going to arrest him for the "crime" of being a priest. An elderly Gypsy horse trader saw what was happening and attempted to intervene, crying out, "Bullies! Mother of God! So many people against one innocent person!" With that, some of the soldiers turned and leapt on the Gypsy. Blows rained down on his head and shoulders. Then he was searched. In his pocket, the soldiers found a rosary and a fleme, a rasp for cleaning horse's teeth. Then the militiamen hauled the Gypsy, along with the priest, to the convent of the Capuchin Clarissan Sisters, which they had already turned into a temporary jail, and threw them in among the other 350 detainees.

A young anarchist leader, Eugenio Sopena, came to see the Gypsy, Ceferino Malla, in jail. Although he knew Ceferino was a Catholic, the anarchist, like so many others in the town, respected him, this honest Gypsy nicknamed "El Pelé." Sopena advised him, "Don't let them see you praying so much. Give me your rosary to hide and I'll set you free." The valiant Gypsy refused. To him, his rosary signified his faith. Resigned and calm, he spent the next fifteen days in a small room, three by four meters, with some others. Some who escaped death later testified to his constant praying.

In the early hours of August 9, Ceferino along with his Bishop Florentino Asensio Barroso[1] and eleven others were taken from their

Ceferino Jiménez Malla
PHOTOS COURTESY OF REV. MARIO RIBOLDI

temporary jail, thrown on the back of a truck, and carried to the cemetery. On the way, the driver of the lorry says that the seventy-five-year-old Ceferino never stopped shouting out "Long Live Christ the King." In the darkness, the headlights of the lorry illuminated the cemetery wall. The prisoners were lined against the wall and shot. As Ceferino gave his final cry of "Long Live Christ the King," he held up his hands, displaying his treasured rosary.

Those who shot him stripped Ceferino of his shoes and trousers and threw his body in a common grave, covering it with quick-lime and earth. His remains were never identified. Today, a photograph of him is displayed in the same cemetery, enclosed in the headstone over the mortal remains of his beloved wife, Teresa, in tomb number thirty-five.

The victims of August 9 were condemned to death for being Christians. In spite of the fact that Gypsies have been persecuted world wide, Cerefino was killed because he was a Catholic, not because he was a Gypsy. Through his life of faith and his death for the faith, Ceferino Jiménez Malla proves that Christ is present in all peoples and ethnic groups and that holiness can grow anywhere.

Ceferino Jiménez Malla was born in Benavent de Segria, Catalonia, in August of 1861. His baptismal certificate was ruined by dampness and the exact date is no longer legible. He was baptized in Fraga, where his nomadic parents, Giocanni and Giuseppa, made a brief stop. They were Catholic Kalos who traveled about Catalonia and Aragon with their three children.

As a child Ceferino knew what it was to be poor. He told his nieces and nephews, "As a child I sometimes suffered hunger; if I could see smoke when I got back from my roaming around, I knew there would be something to eat. If there was no smoke, it meant that the women had nothing to cook. During the winter I washed myself in the mornings with snow. I would be as red as a tomato, but then I no longer felt the cold." Some days he went around begging, as did many of the Gypsy children. Other days, he went with one of his uncles, selling wicker baskets. He collected snails, both for food and to sell. He never attended school and remained illiterate all of his life. He spoke Kalo, a Catalan dialect, as did the others of his tribe.

In the mountains, he met the bandit known as "Cucaracha" (the Cockroach), who took a liking to the young Gypsy boy. The criminal, the scourge of the region of Los Monegros, often came among the tents and carts of the Gypsies, bringing Ceferino something to eat. When Ceferino was fourteen, however, the bandit was captured and executed by the Civil Guard.

At eighteen, Ceferino married Teresa Jiménez Castro according to the customary Gypsy ceremony. The tall, handsome young husband with somewhat protruding ears loved to dance, clapping his hands or striking the castanets and shouting "Olé." He whirled his petite young wife, in her brightly colored clothes with her engagement necklace of dangling gold coins happily about in time to the rhythmic Gypsy tunes.

A wanderer like his parents before him, Ceferino traveled about the towns and cities of Aragon with his wife until he reached the age

An older Ceferino

of forty. He attended all the local fairs and especially enjoyed the annual Fair of St. Andrew in Huesca. So illiterate that he could not even write his own name, he became an expert salesman. He presented customers with a printed visiting card, which showed his name and the words "horse dealer" on it.

A former mayor of Barbastro had contracted tuberculosis and began to cough up blood one day in the Piazza San Grancesco. Others around fled for fear of contagion, but overcoming his own fear, Ceferino approached the man, picked him up in his strong arms, and carried him home.

In 1918, Ceferino went to France with some money borrowed from the brother of the man he had carried home. He returned with several young mules which had been auctioned off by the French government. He sold these and offered half of his profit to the man who had loaned him the money, but the man declined. Ceferino used his profits to purchase and sell other mules and horses. He cared for his animals well, carefully grooming and shoeing them. He became so successful that he was able to purchase a house. He also determined to show God's favors to the poor. He particularly loved horses, especially race horses. He became an excellent horseman and one of the pictures used at his beatification shows him on a favorite mount, with his adopted niece riding behind him.

From the time he was about forty years old, Ceferino began to stay for longer periods of time in Barbastro, a small town close to the Pyrenees. Here, he stayed in the center of town in the district known as San Hipolito, sometimes called the Gypsy Quarter. With his Gypsy heritage, it was not important to Ceferino if he slept in a building or out in the open. In Barbastro, however, he made a home at 31 Via San Hipolito. The living quarters were above a small stable, and next to it was another stable large enough for ten or more animals.

Ceferino and his wife had no children, so they adopted his wife's niece, Pepita, and raised her as their own. Concerned that she not grow up illiterate as he was, Ceferino enrolled her in a school run by the Sisters of St. Vincent de Paul who taught her to read, write, embroider and play the piano.

Ceferino had many friends in Barbastro, Gypsy and Gajo (non-Gypsy) alike. Rich or poor, ordinary or important were all alike to him. He lived according to the Gypsy law with fortitude and justice. He developed a reputation for being extremely honest in his business dealings and for charity to those less fortunate. He became like a human bridge between the two worlds, that of the farmers and townsfolk and that of the gypsies. Respect for this man was so great that he often served as a peacemaker in disputes and more than once even his bishop sought his advice. With his special gift for getting people to reconcile their differences, the Kalderasha Romanies would have called him a "Krisitori," a "true

Ceferino with his adopted daughter (his niece)

judge." His niece Maruja said, "Everything that Uncle Pelé did, he did with love, and this love went out to everybody."

One of his particular friends was a wealthy professor, Don Nicolas Santos de Otto. He was a frequent visitor at the Otto home and the professor's children were very fond of him, and considered him one of the family. Once, Don Nicolas purchased a large new strongbox to store family documents and money. He asked his children what name of four letters to use as the combination for the lock. One of them immediately replied, "Pelé." Toward the end of Ceferino's life, he suffered a financial reverse and his final years were spent in straitened circumstances. At this time, he was forced to sell his house. He then began to work for Don Nicolas, taking care of his animals and his farmlands.

January 19, 1912, was a special day for Teresa and Ceferino. After thirty-two years of marriage according to Gypsy law, they were married according to the rite of the Catholic Church in the church of San Lorenzo in Lerida.

Ceferino had a particular love for all children. He would lead the children of the district to the little church of San Ramón on a hillside just outside the city and tell them many stories of the goodness of Jesus. Often, he sang and taught them to sing religious songs. He taught them to respect nature, even the birds and insects, and spoke to them as if they were adults, not talking down to them. He would kneel so as to be at their level as he taught them their prayers and their catechism. When they finished their lesson, he would reward each child with a piece of chocolate. When the children saw him in the street they would run to him, with the smallest ones pulling at his trousers to get his attention.

Ceferino's faith was a practical one. He was a member of the Society of St. Vincent de Paul and devoted much time and considerable resources to aid the less fortunate. He visited the sick and the elderly in the hospitals, and often fed beggars at his own table. Once, a young Gypsy mother was unable to breast feed her baby. Ceferino gave her the money to provide milk for the child. He was generous in loaning his animals to those who lacked transportation for their goods, allowing them to defer payment until the end of the working season.

At the age of sixty-five, Ceferino became a member of the Franciscan third order. He was chosen as a counselor of the men's group and proudly carried the banner of St. Francis in processions.

For about the last twenty years of his life, Ceferino was a daily communicant. He was a member of night adoration and joined the small processions when Holy Communion was taken to the seriously ill in their own homes.

In the fall of 1920, El Pelé was imprisoned, mistakenly, for two months. He was showing some animals at a fair when a man called the police, telling them that the animals Ceferino had been his and had been stolen from him at a previous fair. Fortunately, Ceferino was able to prove that he had legitimately bought the animals, not knowing they were stolen. When he was acquitted, he walked nearly a kilometer from his home to the chapel of Santocristo in the Cathedral in thanksgiving for his release. He walked on his knees, carrying two lighted candles.

One day Ceferino was walking down the street when he noticed the bishop, Monsignor Eliliano Jiménez, in the same street. He crossed over and greeted the bishop, whom he knew well. Just then, Father Jiménez, the rector of the Piarist school, came up. Father Jiménez joked loudly that someone should take their picture — the three most

The saint loved to catechize the little Rom children

Ceferino with his horse

prayerful Jiménez in Barbastro: the bishop, el Pelé and the Rector of the Escolapios!

Ceferino had a deep love for Our Lady. Often, he would take Pepita, riding pillion behind him, and ride his horse to the shrine of Pueyo, about five miles from Barbastro to venerate the Virgin there. In addition he joined the many pilgrims of the area each Easter Monday in an age-old traditional pilgrimage to the shrine.

The rosary was a favorite devotion of Ceferino's and he prayed it daily. He told his friends that he had made a vow to do so in gratitude to the Virgin of the Rosary for a favor she had done for him. He prayed at home, in the street, in the rooms of the elderly and bedridden or in the prisons. After the death of his beloved wife, he often prayed it before her photograph. He was so devoted to his rosary that he preferred to die rather than give it up and renounce his faith.

A priest who knew him said that "Ceferino had a true Christian and Catholic faith and he practiced it as many others do and even better, at the same time remaining a Gypsy like his parents and his neighbors in the district."

At the time of his beatification, Archbishop Giocanni Cheli, president of the Pontifical Council for the Pastoral Care of Migrants and Itinerant Peoples, said that "Ceferino had the wisdom and knowledge of things that God hides from the proud and the wise of this world and reveals instead to the small ones, to the humble. Ceferino was poor, but rich in charity which he used to help others . . . poor, but rich in virtue. Humble, but great in the faith." ✥

Notes

1. Bishop Asensio was beatified at the same time as El Pelé.

8

Charlene Marie Richard
United States, 1947-1959

A Cajun Saint?

The beatification in May 2000 of the two child seers from Fátima marked the first non-martyr children that young ever to be accorded this honor. The beatifications confirmed a belief that the church has had since the time of Christ — that children have received the love of God in a way befitting youngsters. As the Second Vatican Council pointed out, "Children also have their own apostolic work to do. In their own way, they can be true living witnesses to Christ among their companions."[1]

The United States may one day claim its own child saint: Charlene Richard, a little Cajun girl. She lived a simple life in her rural home at Richard, Louisiana, in the Diocese of Lafayette. The people of Charlene's small community live simply but are strong in faith. After her death, they began to ask Charlene's intercession for help over the rough spots in their lives. In return, she seemed to shower favors on those who asked in humble faith. In the past forty years, Charlene's name and story have spread far outside the boundaries of southwest Louisiana. Many are drawn to the great gift this young Cajun girl has to offer: the example of childlike faith shown by her acceptance of God's will in her life.

Charlene was born January 13, 1947, the second of ten children of Joseph Elvin and Mary Alice Richard. Joseph worked for the Louisiana State Highway Department and Mary Alice worked as a nurse's aide. The Richards were honest, hard-working, God-fearing people who lived in a small farming community in Acadia Parish. They cherished their Catholic faith and the traditions of their Cajun heritage.

As a baby, Charlene was tiny. She began to walk early, at the age of seven months. She liked to walk over to the kitchen windows and look outside. Even though the windows were low, Charlene had to stand on tiptoes to see outside.

When Charlene had just begun to talk well, about the age of two, her great aunt Ora came over. Her grandmother had made a new dress for her and she told Charlene to get it and show it to Aunt Ora. Charlene jumped down from the rocker and brought the dress. Aunt Ora asked, "Why, Charlene, who is that pretty dress for?" Charlene didn't answer and just began rocking again, so her aunt repeated her question, "Who is that pretty dress for?" Surprisingly, with a twinkle in her eye, Charlene looked up and mimiced her aunt perfectly, saying "Who is that pretty dress for?"

With the typical quiet humor of so many Cajuns, Charlene loved to "pick at" her friends and relatives. One summer evening when her Aunt Ora was spending the night, she got dressed for bed in a nylon gown that had developed a number of "wear and tear" holes in it. Charlene looked up and slyly said in French, "Oh honey, that's the gown!" Her older relatives would often speak in French to Charlene, but she didn't like to speak French so she would tell them, "*Je ne suis pas cajun!*" ("I'm not Cajun!")

The family always had pet cats and dogs and Charlene loved the animals. Many of the family photos show her with one of the pets. But she had no use for chickens and disliked being around them. When she was three or four, the family had gone to visit a cousin and his rooster attacked her sister Annie. Fortunately Annie covered her face with her hands because the rooster was making straight for her eyes. Cousin Boris took the rooster off and killed it, but Charlene never lost her fear of chickens.

In May of 1957, the family was living in Church Point, a town about seven miles from Richard where they later moved. Charlene made her First Communion when she was ten at Church Point. Her grandmother had made a special dress, trimmed with flowers and with a wreath of flowers crowning her veil. One Sunday

Charlene's First Communion
PHOTOS COURTESY OF MRS. MARIE RICHARD

that May, the family decided to drive over to Richard for Mass. Charlene was wearing her First Communion outfit. As they arrived, they noticed a large group of children outside the church. Without their knowledge, the priest had chosen that Sunday for the crowning of the Blessed Mother. To the family's surprise and Charlene's delight, the priest stood her at the front of the line and she was allowed to crown the statue of the Virgin.

The family moved to Richard when Charlene was in the fourth grade. Here, she was an avid sports enthusiast and played on the school softball and basketball teams. In sports as in her schoolwork, Charlene was competitive. She wanted to be "the best." In the summers, Charlene baked cookies, rode horses, and enjoyed playing with her friends who nick-named her "Charlie Brown." Her family nickname was "Sue-sue." At St. Edward's church, Charlene became an active member of the Junior Catholic Daughters.

Charlene with her kitten

During summer vacations, St. Edward's held a summer school program. Charlene and her brother John Dale especially enjoyed writing plays and acting them out with the other children. One summer they wrote a special play for their pastor in which John Dale played the priest and Charlene sang with a group of other children.

Charlene was close to all her brothers and sisters, especially her brother John Dale, who was her idol. Her baby brother Gene was her godchild. Gene was killed at the age of nineteen in an auto accident. Today, his remains lie next to Charlene's in the St. Edward cemetery.

Charlene's grandparents lived next door, and Charlene loved her grandmother very much. She always wanted to spend the night at her grandmother's house. The Richard children were supposed to take turns for the treat of a night over at their grandparents' house, but Charlene would always fool her sister and promise her all sorts of things in order to get to take her place. Charlene was close to her "Mom-Mom," and it was this grandmother who shaped and encouraged the spiritual development of the young girl. In the early part of 1959, she had two surgeries and was in a great deal of pain. "Many nights I can remember waking up and feeling Sue-sue's hand rubbing ointment on me," she remembered. "I guess she would hear me groan in my sleep and she would wake up and put the medicine on me to help my pain."

Charlene loved to be helpful. Her mother remembers that she would often get up after dinner and offer to clean the kitchen, telling her mother to rest on the couch. She would offer to wake her mother when she had finished the chore, and make a fresh pot of coffee for her.

She also stood up for the underdog. A certain little boy constantly picked on a little girl who lived near Charlene. One day, Charlene had had enough and she got all over the little boy. The school bus driver made her sit down and, telling her that he knew she wasn't normally mean, asked her why she had done that. "It isn't fair," Charlene said. "Why didn't you do something to him?"

Charlene had a strong love for Our Lady. When she was very young she had seen her grandmother praying the rosary and asked her to teach her the prayers. By the time she was seven, she made it a daily devotional. One year her religion teacher suggested that the children pray the rosary every day during May. Since Charlene already prayed the rosary each night, she decided to do something different. She got a small table and made a little altar for her room where she put a picture of Our Lady, a crucifix and an old Bible. Each morning she went and got fresh flowers from the rose bush in the yard to decorate the altar.

After reading a book about St. Thérèse of Lisieux, she took it home to read to her grandmother. Then she asked her if she, too, could become a saint. "Yes, if you pray in the right way," was the reply.

Charlene's family was not wealthy, and although clean and comfortable, their homes were modest, without a lot of modern conveniences. One day Charlene visited the new home of a friend and came home much impressed, telling her mother how beautiful it was. "It was so beautiful, I know I will never live in a house like that." After thinking a while, she continued, "Oh, well, when I die, heaven will be prettier than that."

One of Charlene's brothers says that the children never knew they were poor because they had so much fun. Charlene and her brothers or her friend Lucille would go down to the bayou to look for clams. Often the family would go out in the woods near their house to cook fish, or dig a pit to cook spicy barbecue.

Charlene Richard

In the late spring of 1959, Charlene was in the backyard of her home, standing near the clothesline, when she came running into the house, pale and shaken "Mama, you won't believe this. I know you'll laugh at me but it really did happen," she said. Obviously the young girl had been frightened by something and her mother encouraged her to tell her what had happened. "Mama, I saw a lady, a tall lady dressed in black. She stopped me. I looked up and saw something shaped like a woman but I couldn't see her face. I was scared. When I asked her 'In the name of God, what do you want?' she just sailed under the oak tree and disappeared." Her older brother John Dale remembers that Charlene was so frightened that she was shaking all over and their grandmother had to hold her to try to make it stop." The following day, Charlene and this brother were in the backyard emptying a tub of water when Charlene cried out, "Oh, I see her again." She never referred to the incidents again.

A few weeks later, Charlene became ill. Finally, she was diagnosed as suffering from acute lymphatic leukemia. She died just thirteen days after the diagnosis. During her last few days on earth, Charlene suffered terribly, although the doctors did what little they could to make her comfortable. Sister M. Theresita Crowley was the pediatric supervisor at the time Charlene entered Our Lady of Lourdes hospital in Lafayette. She remembers Charlene as a pious little girl. "Charlene suffered a great deal; it's the nature of the disease. The pain is awful and there is almost constant bleeding and hemorrhage. But, I remember her as a cheerful patient. She never complained." She continued, "Of all the beautiful, sick children I have tended to in my career as a nurse, Charlene stands out in a very special way. I learned a lot from Charlene, especially from her willingness to accept everything. Her life was full in a short span."

Nurses' reports show that at times the pain was so severe that Charlene asked for a shot to mitigate it. And her godmother says that for a short time she questioned, "Why me?" Father Frank Bussieres was the pastor of St. Edward's during the time of Charlene's illness and death. He was the one who had to go to her and tell her that her illness was incurable. He says there is nothing sharp in his memory of this other than a general feeling of a very quiet acceptance of God's will on her part.

Father Joseph Brennan, the hospital chaplain who attended her during her final illness saw Charlene as a witness for people of all ages to the power of resignation and acceptance of God's will. He says that Charlene wasn't different from other children her age in any way except that "when the crisis came in her life — and it came very early — she accepted it with faith and trust and love. "On his daily visits, he spoke with Charlene about offering her pain for others; Charlene asked him to suggest particular persons to offer her suffering for. She would say, "Okay Father, who am I suffering for today?"

One day Father Brennan was talking with her and told her, "Charlene, a Beautiful Lady is going to come to you one day soon and take you home." Charlene looked at him and said, "When she does, I'll say, 'Blessed Mother, Father Brennan was asking for you.' "

The day before her death, she kissed the chaplain goodbye and told him that she would be praying for him from heaven. Speaking at a commemorative Mass in 1989, the thirtieth anniversary of Charlene's death, Father Brennan said, "Charlene taught us lessons in humility, acceptance, simplicity and faith. We have many books teaching us how to live. Charlene wrote the book on how to die." ✝

Notes

1. *Apostolicam actuositatem*, Decree on the Apostolate of Lay People.

9

The Martyrs of Asturias and Almeria
(Turon and Tarragona)

The Martyrs of Asturias

Cyril Bertrand Tejedor and Companions
Eight Christian Brothers and a Passionist priest
martyred in Asturias, Spain, October 1934

Brother Cirilo Bertran (José Sanz Tejedor, 1888–1934)
Brother Marciano José (Filomeno Lopez y Lopez, 1900–1934)
Brother Julian Alfredo (Vilfrido Fernandez Zapico, 1902–1934)
Brother Victoriano Pio (Claudio Bernabe Cano 1905–1934)
Brother Benjamin Julian (Vicente Alonso Andrés 1908–1934)
Brother Augusto Andrés (Roman Martinez Fernandez 1910–1934)
Brother Benito de Jesús (Hector Valdivielso Saez 1910–1934)
Brother Aniceto Adolfo (Manuel Seco Gutierrez 1912-1934)
Father Inocencio de la Immaculada, C.P. (Manuel
Canoura Arnau 1887–1934)
Brother Jaime Hilario (Manuel Barbal Cosan 1898–1936)

Among the 2,365 religious men who gave their lives for the faith during the Spanish civil war, one hundred sixty five were members of the Institute of the Brothers of the Christian Schools. The martyrs of Asturias were beatified by Pope John Paul II on April 29, 1990 and canonized in October of 1999.

In beatifying the martyrs of Asturias, Pope John Paul II said, "In the eyes of their persecutors, they were guilty of having dedicated their lives to the human and Christian education of youth. The Passionist priest met occasionally with the de la Salle Brothers. In that way God in his inscrutable providence wished to unite in martyrdom members of two congregations who worked in solidarity for the Church's one mission. . . . Not being afraid of spilling their blood for

Christ, they conquered death and now participate in the glory of the Kingdom of God. That is why today I have the joy of inscribing them in the catalogue of saints, proposing them to the universal Church as models of Christian life and our intercessors before God. . . . They are not heroes of a human war in which they did not participate but were educators of youth. In their capacity as consecrated men and teachers, they faced their tragic end as a real testimony of faith, giving the last lesson of their life with their martyrdom."

Martyrs of Asturias/Turon
PHOTOS (EXCEPT PAGES 97 AND 105) COURTESY OF THE CHRISTIAN BROTHERS

The "Revolution of Asturias" was a Communist uprising that preceded Spain's bloody civil war. On the first Friday of October 1934, the local authorities of the Communist-led rebel forces in Asturias Province of the mining town called Turon, marched into the Christian Brothers' residence where they found the Passionist priest, Father Inocencio de la Immaculada (Manuel Arnau) preparing to say Mass. He and the members of the Turon Christian Brothers community were arrested and accused of "corrupting minds." They took the prisoners to the "People's House" Communist Party headquarters

Father Inocencio, C.P.
PHOTO COURTESY OF THE PASSIONISTS OF SPAIN

— where they were kept for four days without explanation. On October 9, before dawn, they were brought to Turon's cemetery and shot to death without even so much as a mock trial. The Spanish historian Vicente Carcel Orti has stated, "The martyrs of Turon were not victims of an act of war or of political repression. They were victims of plain religious hatred that would turn into a systematic policy of murders two years later with the beginning of the civil war."

In 1918, the owners of the coal mining company in Turon decided to found a school for the children of the workers and entrusted it to the Christian Brothers. The school opened in 1919 and became a well-loved institution in the town until the political ferment of the 1930s. In 1933 a law was promulgated forbidding members of religious congregations to engage in teaching. The brothers were withdrawn, but faced with exile or adaptation the superiors of the Brothers Institute in Spain chose adaptation. In the fall of 1933 a new group of professors arrived to take over the running of the Colegio Nuestra Señora de Covadonga. They wore secular clothing and were known by their secular names. No one was deceived, and one of the local anticlerical Masons remarked, "They are the same dogs but with different collars."

The superior of the little group was Brother Cirilo Bertran. Born at Lerma on March 20, 1888, he was the son of a road maintenance worker. Little is known of his early life. At seventeen, he went to the Brothers' juniorate at Bujedo and then to the novitiate where he received the habit in 1907. He began his teaching career in 1909 and made his perpetual profession in 1916. He had a reputation as an ex-

cellent teacher and attracted many to vocations to the priesthood and to the Brothers Institute. Although he was usually serious, he had an unassuming and affable manner and his students counted it a pleasure to be with him. He was good about repeating lessons for the slowest students, and administered punishment with understanding. One of his former students that he had encouraged in a Passionist vocation was one of the first to give his life at Mieres, only a few days before his former

Brother Cirilo Bertran, F.S.C.

teacher's own martyrdom. As superior in Turon, Brother Cirilo tried to keep on good terms with the local civil and religious authorities and to maintain a low profile. He encouraged the Brothers to show themselves as little as possible in public and to concentrate on their work at the school. The ultimate demand on this "serene captain" was to lead the Brothers of Turon with courage and serenity to the final confrontation with the forces of hatred and violence.

Brother Marciano José was born Filomeno Lopez y Lopez in 1900 in a small village in the province of Guadalajara, the son of staunch Catholic parents. His uncle had entered the Christian Brothers after the death of his wife, and Filomeno left home at the age of twelve to join him in the junior novitiate in Bujedo. At first he fit in very well and his career as a brilliant teacher was foretold. He was loved by his companions, especially the boys who were homesick and whom Filomeno made his special charges. Soon, however, he began to experience intense pain in his ears and despite the attentive care of his uncle and the infirmarian, the condition worsened. The superiors finally decided to send him home in hopes that the

Brother Marciano José, F.S.C.

change of climate would effect a cure. In time the pain did cease, but he was left almost totally deaf. At home, Filomeno worked as a field hand, but remained determined to rejoin the brothers. Even if he couldn't teach, he was ready to promote the cause of Christian education in any capacity where he might be useful. His appeal was heard and he was given the religious habit on November 4, 1916. Through the years, he worked in the laundry, the sacristy, and as a cook, happy to be of assistance in any way he could. He made his perpetual profession in 1925. He was so uncomplaining and ready to be of service that he was often moved with little notice to replace a brother where there was a need for his services. In the spring of 1934, the cook at Turon could endure the tense situation there no longer and asked for a transfer. Brother Marciano was sent to take his place. When the brothers were arrested on October 4, 1934, Brother Marciano was the doorkeeper and the cook. At first he was not recognized as a member of the community. He could have escaped by claiming to be only a servant, which in a sense he was. Instead, he replied, "I am the cook and a religious." So he was taken away with the rest.

Brother Julian Alfredo was born in the province of León in 1902. Known by his family by the nickname "Viyo" he was a happy and playful fellow to whom studies came easily. His mother died when he was quite young so he spent a large part of his time with his uncle who was a priest. He felt called to a religious vocation and entered the minor seminary of the Capuchins. At 17 he entered the novitiate but became ill and was sent home to restore his failing health. Unable to do any heavy work, he spent much time reading and became known for his learning

Brother Julian Alfredo, F.S.C.

and wisdom. In the afternoons, he gathered a group of friends and taught them catechism. At the age of 22 he became aware of the work of the brothers and joined the novitiate in 1926. He completed his novitiate and was admitted to final profession in the summer of 1932. Although he was always cheerful and amiable, he had a great love for silence. On holidays and in his free time he enjoyed helping the cook in the kitchen. He had a special devotion to Mary whom he called "our good Mother" and encouraged his students to wear the scapular, to say the rosary after school, and to join confraternities in her honor. He was zealous as a catechist and his students loved him for his complete explanations. He also was known for an exceptional ability to teach singing. A year after being transferred to Turon he was called upon to face the full force of hostility there as it erupted in revolutionary violence.

Brother Victoriano Pio was born near Burgos in 1905, and en-tered the junior novitiate of the Brothers when he was not quite fourteen. In the novitiate he took the motto "to do what the Rule requires, no matter what it costs." Brother Victoriano was a very intense and even an impatient sort of person, never wasting a moment. His intensity carried over to his professional studies and his work with the students. He was talented in music and art and had a contagious enthusiasm. Usually reserved in his manner and a stern disciplinarian, he was nonetheless loved as well as respected by his students. He

Brother Victoriano Pio, F.S.C.

willingly found time to provide extra classes to help those who were less gifted keep up the pace. Often congratulated profusely on the performance of his choir, Brother Victoriano would say that the glory belonged to God alone and that he was grateful that his choir motivated so many people to come to the religious ceremonies. In September 1934, the superiors had to replace a seriously disturbed brother in Turon who had been in charge of the senior class and sent Brother Victoriano. Twenty days after his arrival, the revolution broke out and he was taken prisoner with the others.

Brother Benjamin Julian was born in the province of Burgos on October 27, 1908. He and his cousin Federico became fast friends and inseparable companions and were often referred to as the "twins." Persistence and determination were the main elements of his character. After hearing a speech by the brother recruiter at the age of eleven, he declared his desire to enter with the brothers but was told that he was too young. He persisted and by a special exception of the Provincial was allowed to enter the juniorate in September of 1920. He wrote often to his cousin who joined him the following year. He was given the religious habit in January of 1925. Because he was, and looked, so young, he was given the name Benjamin. He was very short and this youthful appearance aggravated the difficulties experienced by so many teachers as they first enter the classroom. Fortunately he had a wise director who helped him and the diminutive Brother Benjamin, serenely and determinedly, gained ascendancy over his young charges. Later a visitor from the normal school asked the director how it was possible that such a small and youthful looking teacher was able to hold the respect and attention of the seventy pupils in his class. The director replied, "The reason is that the children regard neither the size of the teacher nor his age. All they see is a heart that loves them with an unselfish love." In 1933, Brother Benjamin and his cousin made a retreat together in preparation for their final profession. At the close of the retreat, Brother learned that he was assigned to Turon, so the two cousins, dressed in secular clothes, took leave of one another for the last time in this world. Brother Benjamin headed for Turon and the road that led to martyrdom.

Brother Benjamin Julian, F.S.C.

Brother Augusto Andrés was born May 6, 1910, in Santander. The oldest of three children, his father died while he was quite young and his mother relied greatly on him for help. He attended the Christian Brothers' schools where he was known for his fine native intelligence and his diligence at his studies. He attended Mass each morning at school until the day when he fainted. The superior suggested that due to the fast from midnight and his precarious health he should attend Mass at his home parish so he could return home and have a good breakfast before school. At the age of eleven he announced his desire to enter the Brothers, but his mother, barely adjusted to the loss of her husband, felt she needed his presence and support and his pleas were in vain. He fell seriously ill and his classmates began a novena to the Little Flower. The doctor advised his mother to send for a priest to give him the last rites. During the night

Brother Augusto Andrés, F.S.C.

which all believed to be his last on this earth, he fell into a deep sleep. Suddenly he awoke with the fever gone and his first words to his mother, said with a smile, were "Now will you let me go to Bujedo?" In gratitude for the remarkable recovery, his mother agreed. After his novitiate he was assigned to the school at Valladolid. He was successful in the classroom from the start. Daily his students entered class to find the blackboard decorated with the teacher's skillfully drawn designs that illustrated and enlivened his lessons. During most of his religious life, he had to endure continual pleas from his mother to return home. Often this reduced him to tears but he was determined to persevere. He sent her a picture of the Blessed Virgin on which he had written, "Why did I come to Bujedo? In order to become a saint, I have only one soul to save, and I will die only once." In 1931, universal military training was required and Brother Augusto entered the service where he was assigned to the motorcycle brigade. Because of his health his stay was short but his comrades were impressed with his spirit of valor and his forthrightness. In 1932 he fell seriously ill with pneumonia and complications from an intestinal infection and had to spend time in the infirmary at Bujedo where he was a model of patience in suffering and resignation. On his recovery he was sent to Turon in 1933. When concern for his safety was expressed by his family, he simply replied that he might be able to get to Heaven more quickly. At the time of his death a year later, he was still not old enough for his final profession.

Brother Benito de Jesús (Hector Valdivielso Saez) was born in 1910 in Buenos Aires, Argentina. His canonization in 1999 makes him

that country's first native-born saint. Shortly after his birth his family moved to Mexico where his merchant father had better opportunities. Because of the turbulent climate in revolutionary Mexico, his father sent his wife and children to the province of Burgos in Spain. As a child, Hector was fond of drawing and developed great skill at calligraphy. He was also an enthusiastic soccer player. His family saved many examples of his youthful work. He and his older brother José entered the junior novitiate at Bujedo in 1921. Later,

Brother Benito de Jesús, F.S.C.

Hector volunteered for a missionary apostolate and was transferred to the juniorate at the Brothers' international headquarters then in Belgium. He was happy there and wrote his mother frequent and joyful letters telling about his daily life. He received the religious habit in 1926 and made first vows a year later. He did not live long enough to be eligible for perpetual profession. He wrote to his father who was still in Mexico where the Church was still being vigorously persecuted, "I would consider myself happy indeed if, like you, I could be living in the midst of a persecution that would procure for me the palm of martyrdom. If God gives you the grace of martyrdom, know that I, your son, will be envious of you." After his novitiate, he returned to Spain to complete his studies. At Astorga in 1929 he was given a class with one humdred young boys. Equal to the challenge, it seemed that authority came to him easily and naturally. Outside of school hours, he was active with the St. Tarsicius Society and he encouraged the young members in devotion to the Eucharist and in working for the poor and disadvantaged. He also promoted the programs of Catholic Action. In spite of his youthful twenty-two years, he wrote a number of impassioned articles defending the Church which he signed simply "H" or using the pseudonym "Vezas." Aware of the dangers of his position, he wrote to his mother, "A religious is always likely to be persecuted, hated, insulted and rejected by society . . . nevertheless, I prefer my state in life a thousand times to all the other advantages that the world might have to offer." He was transferred to Turon in the fall of 1933. He had written his mother, "If God requires it of me, I am ready to suffer prison, exile and even death."

Brother Aniceto Adolfo was the youngest of the Turon martyrs. Manuel Seco Gutierrez was born in the province of Santander on October 4, 1912. His family was staunchly Catholic and recited the rosary each evening after the hard day's labor in the fields. The father taught his children catechism. When Manuel was only six, his mother died. A sacristan in the local parish, his father took his children to church for all the scheduled ceremonies. Three of his four sons entered the Christian Brothers Institute. Manuel was hot tempered and his violent and impulsive reactions when things did not go his way caused frequent rebukes from his saintly father. This was a life-long struggle for him. He worked off much of his excess energy by diligent application to his studies and domestic duties and in addition he was an enthusiastic competitor in sports. He joined the Brothers' junior novitiate at the age of twelve. When his aunt, a Dominican nun, heard of it she predicted, "He has a bad temper, that one; he won't last a month in religious life!" His brother Maximino says, however, that from the moment he entered the juniorate Manuel rarely showed any display of his horrid temper and seemed to be well beloved and per-

fectly at ease. Manuel developed a special devotion to the Blessed Virgin and managed to recite all fifteen decades of the rosary daily. At fifteen he consecrated himself to her according to the practice of St. Louis Grignon de Montfort. He entered the novitiate in 1929. His tenacity and will power came into full play to control his lively temperament and to make up for what he lacked in native intelligence. This was not made any easier by the onset of persistent migraine headaches. He was assigned to his first school in 1932 and his first class numbered 87 students. His enthusiasm

Brother Aniceto Adolfo, F.S.C.

for his subjects, especially catechism, rapidly gave him the ascendancy over the class. In the community he was rather shy. In 1933 he made his first and last visit home, by which time both of his parents had died. When his younger brother made his first vows, Brother Aniceto wrote him, telling him "Never cease to thank God for having deigned to choose three members of our family for the privilege of cooperating with him in the salvation of souls." Aniceto was transferred to Turon in September of 1934. As the Brothers were led out to be executed, Brother Aniceto handed his rosary to the parish priest with the request that he give it as a souvenir to his brothers, but the precious relic was lost in the confusion that followed.

Father Inocencio de la Immaculada, C.P., was born in the province of Lugo in 1887. From his early years, he was impressed by the Passionist priests who came yearly to conduct a parish mission. At fifteen, with the consent of his pious parents, he was sent to the Passionist house of studies at Penafiel. In 1904 he entered the novitiate at Duesto and made his first vows in 1903. He was ordained in 1913. For most of his religious career he was a professor of literature and philosophy in the various Passionist houses of study, although from time to time he was assigned pastoral work in the parishes. In September 1934 he was assigned to the Passionist monastery at Mieres, not far from Turon. He taught philosophy to the seminarians while occasionally assisting with the priestly ministry for the nearby parishes. In October, he was called to go to Turon to assist in hearing confessions in the parish and the school in preparation for the First Friday devotions. This assignment proved to be his death sentence. Confessions that day were so numerous that he was persuaded to spend the night with the Brothers and to say Mass the next morning for them after which he was to preach to the students. He was arrested with the Brothers the following morning and shared their fate. Although the revolutionaries eventually freed the par-

Father Inocencio, C.P.
PHOTO COURTESY OF THE PASSIONISTS OF SPAIN

ish priests, the fact that Father Inocencio was a religious priest and associated however briefly with the Brothers in the religious education of the young was enough to present him the crown of martyrdom.

On Friday morning, October 5, the Brothers arose as usual at 4:30 a.m. and assembled in the chapel. At about 6 o'clock, Brother Aniceto answered a persistent knocking at the door. It was Juana Gonzales, the housekeeper of the parish priests who had just come from the Communist headquarters and who announced that the revolution had begun and that her husband, her son, and the three local priests had been arrested. She begged the Brothers to flee. After some hesitation, the Brothers decided that flight was unrealistic and decided to proceed at once with the Mass. Father Inocencio had just begun the offertory when there were sounds of fanatics in the street outside. To save the Blessed Sacrament, he distributed all the consecrated hosts and the brothers retired to their rooms to quietly await the outcome. Brother Marciano went to the door to confront the invaders who demanded the weapons hidden within. Once he realized what they were asking he told them there were no arms of any sort. The angry group entered and made a thorough search. Finding no weapons, and disappointed in the fruitless search, they informed the priest and the brothers that they were under arrest and they were led, under arms, to the Casa del Pueblo which would serve as their jail. The school was commandeered as a central headquarters for the Committee of the Revolution.

Father Inocencio's religious habit was particularly annoying to the captors so they ordered him to take it off. One of the guards went to bring a cloak from the brothers' house, as the priest had no other clothes to wear. The garment was made of wool and was so ill fitting that it was very uncomfortable; the best they could do was give him a scarf to put around his neck in place of a shirt. Other prisoners in the building were allowed to have their families bring them food but there was no one to bring meals to the brothers. When Don Rafael del Riego, director of the mining company, detained in an adjoining room, heard of this, he gave orders that food for them be supplied from the company kitchen but nothing was done about that until the following day, so their first day was spent in a complete fast.

On the second day more detainees were brought in, so the parish priests and the young members of Catholic Action were put in the room with the Brothers and the Passionist priest. One of the village doctors was called to give an injection to calm Brother Marciano who had become increasingly restless on account of suffering from a spinal ailment. The brothers asked if they could get a mattress for him from the school, but they were refused and the ailing brother, like the others, slept on the tables or on the floor. The brothers began to pray together and recite the rosary and their resigned and prayerful attitude was a source of comfort to the others. The parish priest, a fellow prisoner, said that the brothers asked if their deaths would constitute a true martyrdom in the theological sense of the word and on his assurance that it would, they seemed filled with great joy and devoted themselves to preparing worthily to make the supreme sacrifice. At about five o'clock on Sunday evening, two members of the Committee of the Revolution came, ostensibly to show some concern for the prisoners. One purpose of the visit seemed to be to verify the function of Brother Marciano. Because of his deafness and his nervousness he was unable to answer their questions so the officer asked the Brother Director if he was a member of the community. On receiving an affirmative answer they seemed satisfied and left. Because of the tone of their questions, the prisoners decided to receive the sacrament of penance. Afterwards, all seemed filled with a great calm. On Monday, many friends of the brothers came before the Committee to plead their cause, but their intervention was in vain.

It took all day long for the rebel leader to round up enough riflemen to serve as a firing squad. Lacking enough volunteers from Turon he recruited a motley crew from Mieres and Santullano. The committee met in their new headquarters, the former school, and spent the day in drinking the liquor from the well-stocked cellars of the mining company. Any hesitation was effectively masked by the alcohol and towards midnight the order was given, "*Adelante, en marcha!*" ("Hurry up, let's go.") The most touching account was written by the pastor, Father Jose Fernandez, shortly after he witnessed the event. A little after one in the morning, four armed vigilantes entered and demanded that the brothers and the priests surrender everything they had in their pockets. For some reason, the coadjutor was allowed to keep his watch and the pastor was allowed to keep his rosary. Father Inocencio was sleeping with his head covered by a blanket. Awakened, he revealed a peaceful smile as if he had been dreaming of paradise. Even when he stood, he kept the same serene expression. The prisoners were lined up in groups of three and told they were going to the front lines. The captors then told them that there were two too many and the two local priests were pulled aside. When the order to march was given, the parish priests raised their hands and silently pronounced the words of absolution. Two former policemen were taken along with the religious. The details of the execution have been well documented by some of those who took part in the murders.

As soon as the prisoners were taken outside they were informed that instead of being taken to the front lines they would be marched to the cemetery to be executed. One of the leaders of the death squad testified that the religious listened to the sentence calmly and then with a firm step marched along. He said, "Although they knew perfectly well where they were going, they conducted themselves like lambs being led to the slaughter, without complaint, to the point where I myself, hardhearted as I am, had to admire their self-control. . . . Arrived at the place where the trench had been prepared, we lined them up in front of it and then we dispatched them with two rounds of fire. . . It seemed at the last that I heard them praying in a low voice." Castanon's account leaves out some of the more ghastly details. When the bodies were exhumed some days later there was evidence that some of the victims did not die at once but were given the coup de grace by blows on the head with a heavy club. Also, the executioners despoiled the bodies of their outer clothing and anything else of value.

By October 19, civil guards and government troops were back in control at Ruton and the Christian Brothers first learned of the fate of the little community. A high priority was put on the exhumation of the mortal remains of the martyrs and this was accomplished on the afternoon of October 21 by a group of soldiers appointed by judicial order. The remains were identified by the laundry markings on their undergarments and a Passionist priest identified the body of Father Inocencio. The bodies were placed in individual caskets and reburied in another part of the cemetery. Later the bodies were transferred to the provincial center at Bujedo, and Father Inocencio's remains were interred in the Passionist cemetery at Mieres.

Although criminal investigations were undertaken to bring to justice those responsible for the atrocities committed during the October reign of terror and sentences of death and imprisonment were handed out to the leaders, not one of the sentences was ever carried out. The outbreak of a full-scale civil war was not far away.

While the cause of the Turon martyrs was being examined by the Congregation for the Causes of the Saints, the case of Brother Jaime Hilario (Manuel Barbal Cosan) was moving forward in a parallel investigation. After consultation with committees of cardinals and theologians, the Congregation joined Brother Jaime's cause to that of the martyrs of Turon and they were beatified together on April 29, 1990 as the Martyrs of Asturias.

Manuel Barbal Cosan was born January 2, 1898, in the province of Lerida. Under the influence of his hardworking and devout parents, he became distinguished by a serious nature that had, at the same time, a touch of poetry and romance. After elementary school, he sensed a vocation to the priesthood and at the age of 12, he entered the minor seminary of the Vincentian Fathers at La Seu d'Urgell. Although he was successful in his studies, he began to have hearing problems and returned home. Still convinced that he was called to the Lord's service, he began to look for an alternative to the priesthood. He was delighted when he learned that the Christian Brothers would accept him. After spending some months learning French, he went to Irun, France, to make his novitiate where he was given the habit and the name Jaime Hilario. After his novitiate, he was assigned to Colegio San José at Mollerussa where he taught successfully for five years. In 1923 he was sent to Manressa to teach Latin, but his hearing problems returned and he was forced to abandon the classroom and work for a time in the garden. In 1926 he began teaching religion to the novices at Pibrac, France, and in 1927 he made his perpetual profession. By 1934 his deafness had made it impossible for him to continue teaching and he was sent to the house of formation in Tarragona to work in the garden. In the silence of his labors, he found the opportunity to speak with God and to accept the action of Grace which was steadily preparing him for his ultimate witnessing. Among his personal notes the brothers later found this statement, "If God had revealed to me the difficulties I would have to face as a brother, I would have been afraid and would never have entered. But now I would not give up my robe for all the gold in the world, nor my way of life for all the land in Enviny." In spite of his handicap, his authentic faith triumphed to the end.

On July 17, 1936, he was on his way to visit his family when the civil war broke out. In Molleussa he was immediately identified as a Brother and put under house arrest with a local family. In August he was taken to a cell in the jail at Lleida. On December 5 he was transferred with four other Brothers to Tarragona and confined in a prison ship where still others of their confreres were being detained.

Brother Jaime Hilario, F.S.C.

January 13, 1937, Brother Jaime was brought before the People's Tribunal at Tarragona. His lawyer advised him to simply state his occupation as a gardener so he would be perceived as a worker rather than a member of the clergy, but he refused to do this, saying that he couldn't deny that he was a religious. During his interrogation, he had difficulty in hearing the questions and they had to be repeated in a loud voice. When asked about the apparent contradiction between his work in the garden and his status as a religious, he replied that there was no contradiction. He explained that since he was deaf, his gardening was his contribution to his religious Institute. His honest testimony sealed his doom. Two days later a formal trial was held before the same tribunal in a makeshift courtroom which had previously been the diocesan seminary. The prosecutor demanded his death in these words, "Either we kill these people, or they will kill us. If we condemn to death those who fight against our comrades in the front lines, how much more should we condemn those who dedicate themselves to educating fascists." Brother Jaime received the verdict tranquilly and quoted St. Jean-Baptiste de la Salle, the founder of the Brothers, saying, "God be blessed."

He wrote to his brother who worked for the Trappists near Toulouse, "I have just been condemned to death by the People's Tribunal. Don't cry, dear brother. When you hear my name mentioned, don't give way to sadness but raise your eyes to Heaven and be assured that I shall not forget you there. I am going to shed my blood for God, for my country, and for my Institute." To the rest of his family he wrote, "I accept the sentence joyfully. They could not accuse me of anything. I was condemned simply because I am a religious. Do not weep. I do not deserve to be wept over, because I am not a criminal. . . . Farewell. I will be waiting for you in paradise."

When he was led out to execution, he told those around him, "God be blessed! In heaven I shall pray a great deal for all of you. What more could I ask for than to die, when my only crime is that I am a religious and that I have worked for the Christian education of youth?"

On the afternoon of January 18, Brother Jaime was taken to the cemetery and positioned a short distance from the firing squad. He stood with his arms crossed on his chest and his eyes raised to heaven. He exclaimed, "To die for Christ is to live, my friends!" Shots rang out. A bit shaken and pale but smiling, Brother Jaime had not even been touched. Again the commander ordered the volley. Again the victim remained standing slightly wounded in the arm but staring courageously at his assassins. The soldiers threw aside their weapons and ran away crying "a miracle!" Enraged, the commander walked up to Brother Jaime, shouted a gross insult and fired five shots at close range. The valiant brother fell dead at his feet.

The Martyrs of Almeria

Diego Ventaja Milan and Companions
Two Spanish Bishops and Seven Christian Brothers
martyred in Almeria, Spain, August and September 1936

Monsignor Diego Ventaja Milan, Bishop of Almeria
Monsignor Manuel Medina Olmost, Bishop of Gaudiz
Brother Aurelio Maria (Bienvenido Villalon Acebron 1890–1936)
Brother José Cecilio (Bonifacio Rodriguez Gonzalez 1885–1936)
Brother Edmigio (Isidoro Primo Rodriguez 1881–1936)
Brother Amalio (Justo Zariquiegui Mendoza 1886–1936)
Brother Valerio Bernardo (Marciano Herrero Martínez 1909–1936)
Brother Teodomiro Joaquin (Adrian Sáinz Sáinz 1907–1936)
Brother Evencio Ricardo (Eusebio Alonso Uyarra 1907–1936)

When Pope John Paul II beatified the Martyrs of Almeria on October 10, 1993, he said, "All of them, faithful servants of the Lord, were like those messengers of the king who according to what we heard in the Gospel were also mistreated and killed. [Mt. 22:6] The Church hears these words of the martyrs. She looks with veneration at their witness."

One of these martyrs, Brother Aurelio Maria, after learning of the deaths of the Brothers in Turon wrote, "It would be a great honor for us to shed our blood for Christian education. If we redouble our efforts for education, we also may perhaps have that honor." Little did he realize that he would, indeed, be accorded the "great honor." The great honor was a double celebration for Brother Teodomiro Joaquin. The day of his birth into Heaven was the same as the day of his birth into this world twenty-nine years previously.

In July of 1936 the Popular Front, the party in power, recommended that each locality set up a committee and hold trials for all the enemies of the revolution. In Almeria, the first decision was to arrest all who were not supporting the revolution, especially priests and religious.

On the twenty-second, Father Martin Salinas, chaplain of the Brothers school, went to the school and, fearing the worst, decided to

The Martyrs of Almeria/Tarragona
PHOTOS COURTESY OF THE CHRISTIAN BROTHERS

Brother Teodomiro Joaquin, F.S.C.

Brother Evencio Ricardo, F.S.C.

consume the Hosts reserved in the tabernacle. Within hours a noisy crowd was outside the school, demanding entrance to search for arms. They took the five brothers they found there and moved them to a number of temporary holding places. Brothers Teodomiro Joaquin and Evencio Ricardo were arrested in the street the same day as they were going to mail some letters to their families

Brothers Edmigio, Amalio and Valerio Bernardo were kept in prison until August 12 in very primitive conditions. They remained calm and gave a fine example to the other prisoners, keeping up their spirits. On the twelfth they were taken to a coal ship called Astoy Mendi, which had been converted into a prison ship. Here they were kept until the night of the thirtieth when they were taken by van to the outskirts of Tabernas where there were several dried up wells. They were shot, one by one, and thrown down the well. Months later when the bodies were recovered, doctors stated that they believed that Brother Valerio Bernardo was thrown in while still alive, breaking both legs in the fall. Brothers Evencio Ricardo and Teodomiro Joaquin were taken to the barracks and kept in a cell for forty-four days. One

Brother Elmigio, F.S.C.; Brother Amalio, F.S.C.; and Brother Valerio Bernardo, F.S.C.

Brother Aurelio Maria,
F.S.C.

Brother José Cecilio,
F.S.C.

of their wardens constantly harassed them. As he brought their food he would call out, "I am going to feed the dogs." Allowed out of their cell for only a few minutes each day, their health began to fail. On September 4, they were taken to the prison ship and joined the other brothers, some priests and a crowd of Catholic laymen. On September eighth they were taken out on the road and shot at an isolated spot. Their bodies were left where they lay and some pious people from nearby respectfully buried them. Brothers Aurelio Maria and José Cecilio had been arrested in the school on the twenty-second and on the twenty-seventh they were released to see to some arrangements for the new school building. They were arrested again on the twenty-ninth. They were held in various temporary prisons until September 12 when they were driven to some abandoned wells on the boundary of Tabernas. They were shot and their bodies were thrown down the wells. Monsignor Diego Ventaja Milan, Bishop of

Two Martyr Bishops of Almeria —
Monsignor Diego Ventaja Milan, Bishop of Almeria, and
Monsignor Manuel Medina Olmost, Bishop of Gaudiz

Almeria and Monsignor Manuel Medina Olmost, Bishop of Gaudiz, were arrested on August twenty-fourth and imprisoned with some of the brothers. Like the others, they were moved to a number of temporary holding places before being taken out for execution on August 29 along with fifteen other detainees. Along the road to Motril they were taken off the van and lined up to be shot. Bishop Manuel asked to speak and according to later testimony of one of the executioners he said, "We have done nothing to deserve death, but I forgive you so that Our Lord will forgive us. May our blood be the last to be shed in Almeria." The leader interrupted him with the order to fire. Gasoline was then poured on the bodies and lit. Some pious people from nearby buried the charred bodies. After the Civil War, the remains were translated to the Cathedral of Almeria. ✢

Notes

1. Catholic Action was defined by Pope Pius XI as "the participation of Catholic laity in the apostolate of the hierarchy." Its influence was great in Western Europe and the United States in the early twentieth century. Though the title is not used any more, the spirit of this original organization lives on in Pope John Paul II's apostolic exhortation of January 1989, *Christifideles laici* (the Christian faithful laity).

10

Dina Belanger
Marie St. Cecile de Rome, R.J.M.
Canada, 1897-1929

Musician and Mystic

"I'm sorry, Dina, I can't find a single saint with your name," the elderly sister sighed and closed the book where she had been trying to find a patron saint for the little Belanger girl.

"Well," the child replied, "Then I'll be a saint and give a protectress to those who take my name."

Who would suspect that this interchange between the eight-year-old girl and her teacher would be prophetic? It was, and today Dina Belanger is called Blessed by the Catholic Church.

At the age of five, Dina had a beautiful dream where she saw the little Jesus who appeared about her own age. He was standing with open arms above the foot of her bed, and he said with a smile, "What would you like?" With childish naïveté, the little girl replied, "Would you please give me your picture?" At Christmas when she was presented a little crib with the Infant Jesus smiling with open arms, Dina exclaimed, "I knew he would send me his picture!" She believed her childish wish had come true in the gift. Instead, Our Lord implanted the picture of his love on Dina through the gift of mystical lights throughout her life. It was not, however, until after her death from tuberculosis in 1929 that the religious of her congregation as well as the public discovered the secret of her intense and mystical interior life. From her first glimpses of reason, she experienced a

Dina as a young nun

great nostalgia for Heaven. She recalls that when she was just eleven years old, "Our Lord manifested himself to my soul through a new light. It was the first time that I understood so well His voice, interiorly of course, a soft and melodious voice which flooded me with joy."

Dina kept on receiving Our Lord's communications and, feeling as if she were plunged into a sea of graces, she heard Jesus speaking to her of suffering and of the total gift of oneself. Her Divine Master made her feel his presence. At first Jesus stayed beside her, then within her. With her willing consent, he replaced Dina's will with his own. Boldly, the talented musician questioned him, "What can be the purpose of my work in music?" Jesus replied, "Your musical knowledge will protect your vocation; but you will do good especially through your writings." Dina was surprised and wondered if she had heard correctly. Jesus continued, "Yes, in the convent you will devote yourself to a literary work."

Discreet by nature, Dina lived her entire life in a manner that exteriorly appeared quite ordinary. Her superior in the Religious of Jesus and Mary suspected unplumbed depths in this favored soul, and in 1924 requested that she write her autobiography. For Dina, this was her greatest sacrifice. Writing about her life was the greatest act of obedience she ever made. She would have preferred to be forgotten, to pass unnoticed. After her death, it was this autobiography that Dina called her Canticle of Love, which showed her mysterious relationship with the world beyond. It shows her gradually abasing herself while in her place rises Christ, dazzling and divine.

A mere two years after Dina's death, Cardinal Rouleau, O.P., Archbishop of Quebec, wrote of the Autobiography, "I have read this with deep interest and edification. The perusal of these writings is of a nature to do good, particularly to consecrated souls." In 1934 his successor Cardinal Villeneuve wrote, "It is not yet time to pass a formal judgment

Age 2, holding her rosary

on the virtues and mystical states of Mother Marie St. Cecile de Rome, but it is opportune to seek edification from her writings."

Dina Belanger was born April 30, 1897, in Quebec City, Canada. She was baptized the same day at St. Roch parish, receiving the name Maria Marguerite Dina Adelaide. She was the only surviving child of Octave and Seraphia Belanger, a pious couple who doted on Dina, but who strove to raise her in such a manner as to avoid spoiling her.

As a very young child she was somewhat stubborn and self-willed. Later, she credited her father with preventing her strong will from developing into a bad temper by a gentle lesson he taught her at the

Dina as a young girl

age of three. "I went into a tantrum one day. I was not yet four years old. First, I refused to obey my mother. When she insisted, I flew into a rage. I began to stamp around, to scream and to dance. Then Papa got up, took my hand and calmly said to me: 'Come, I'll help you dance and scream so we can get this over with sooner.' When I heard my father imitating my spiteful screams and sobs, I stopped on the spot; my pride was hurt. I no longer wanted to dance; nevertheless, I had to keep on hopping with my part-

ner. That was my punishment, and since it hurt me in my innermost wicked ego, I never forgot that most gentle and yet so beneficial lesson; I was cured forever of any wish to dance to the rhythm of my discontent."

The habits of devotion developed in Dina were nurtured by her parents, and from her youngest days she felt a love for God in her young soul. Charity for the poor and sharing were also virtues Dina learned early from her family. Dina wrote, "I accompanied my mother on the visits she made for purposes of charity. Throughout all my life, I saw my parents helping the poor generously, giving large amounts right and left, consoling with their religious and encouraging words, making many prolonged visits, eagerly giving nursing care, very often of the most vile and repulsive kind, comforting and helping the afflicted, the sick and the suffering. Their joy always was to give silently and discreetly."

Dina the young student

From six to twelve years of age, Dina completed her elementary schooling in the Saint-Roch school in Quebec. Her secondary schooling was in the Jacques-Cartier convent in her parish and from the age of fourteen to sixteen she studied at the Bellevue College. These schools were under the direction of the Sisters of the Congregation of Notre-Dame, and that was the first order Dina considered in later years when she was seeking her vocation. At the age of eight, she began to study the piano, which she admits she had a natural liking for.

Dina made her first Communion at the age of ten in 1907. She tells us, "My happiness was immense. Jesus belonged to me and I belonged to him." Her attraction for the Eucharist and her devotion to Mary constantly grew stronger through the succeeding years. After finishing boarding school, at the age of sixteen, she asked her parents, her pastor, and her spiritual director for permission to enter the convent. The two priests counseled her that she should wait until she was twenty-three or twenty-four.

Dina had a natural aptitude for music and she excelled in this subject as she did in most of her academic subjects. In 1915, Dina and two friends traveled to New York where they studied music at the conservatory for two years. In order that her parents would not miss her so much, Dina wrote to

Dina's First Communion

them every other day, affectionate letters, overflowing with vitality, enthusiasm, good cheer and optimism. Of her courses she says, "I was right in the midst of artistic delights. We had to speak in English, listen, understand, study in English! It was fun, especially at the beginning. Fortunately, pianos produce the same sounds in all the different countries." The boarding house where the three Canadians stayed was run by the Sisters of Jesus and Mary of whom Dina wrote, "Their kindness, their charity, their thoughtful attentions, of which I was the object, edified me; their examples of patience, self-denial inclined me to do good."

For the three years after Dina finished her studies in New York, she gave a number of concerts in Quebec. Her works were acclaimed and most of the time the profits would be directed to charitable works.

Dina, dressed for a concert

Before her concerts, however, she played for her true master. "I would invite him with the Blessed Virgin, the angels, the saints to listen to them."

In 1920 Dina again began to think of entering a convent but was undecided which order to enter. Jesus told her, "I want you in the Congregation of Jesus and Mary," Dina responded to him that she was willing to enter whichever order he wished, and then reminded him that she didn't have any inclination for teaching. (The Sisters of Jesus and Mary were primarily dedicated to education.) "You will not teach long," he replied. Dina entered with the sisters as a postulant in August of 1921 at their novitiate in Sillary.

At first, Dina found life in the novitiate difficult, and she was beset by terrible homesickness. She struggled to overcome the temptation to leave, feeling that Our Lord wished her to make this her home. Then, on the final evening of the retreat made in preparation to her entrance in the novitiate, "I felt I was surrounded with pure delight, it was peace, love. Then, the good Master took my poor heart, picked it up as one removes any object and placed, in its stead, a gift of infinite loving tenderness, his Sacred Heart and the Immaculate Heart of Mary! Again, that was a tableau; but there certainly occurred a divine operation in me that no pen could describe." On February 15, 1922, Dina took the habit under the name of Mary St. Cecile of Rome. She made her religious profession on August 15, 1923.

After her profession, Dina was sent to teach music at the Convent of St. Michel de Bellechasse in Quebec. She was to have three short stays there, each one interrupted by illness. Eventually she was diagnosed with tuberculosis. In March of 1924, in obedience to her superior, Dina began writing her autobiography. On her deathbed she confided that this was the act which had cost her the most in all her life. One by one the superior collected Dina's notebooks, putting them in the drawer of her desk without reading them. Jesus had told Dina, "You will do good through your writings," but Dina never suspected that his words would apply to the account of her life.

Dina made her perpetual vows in August of 1928 and by the following April she entered the isolation section of the infirmary where she remained until her death. From July on, Dina no longer had the strength to write. On September 4, 1929, without any death struggle, she breathed out her last, fully conscious, her eyes fixed on the picture

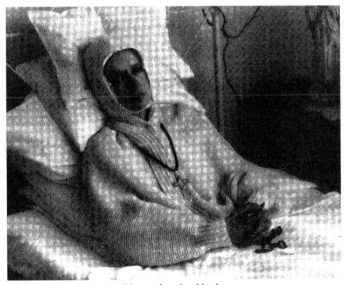

Dina on her deathbed

of the Eucharistic Heart of Jesus hanging in front of her bed. A few hours before her death as she was being exhorted to have courage, she replied in a tone of voice full of conviction, "Jesus is praying."

One of the sisters who had known Dina well tells us, "When those in the convent heard about the kind of graces the Lord had showered upon her and, through her, on her congregation, there was first a current of restrained emotion, then one of enthusiastic gratitude toward God, as the sisters exchanged memories."

What can we, as ordinary Christians, learn from the life and example of a mystic such as Dina Belanger? Dina received many extraordinary mystical gifts, but the essence of her life remained union with Christ and surrender to divine love. Her writings are inspiring. Her example shows us a journey through stages that are progressive, slow, sometimes painful but one in which, in fidelity, the soul can reach for the summit. We can struggle to make Dina's motto our own: "Love, and let Jesus and Mary have their way." In attempting to live out this motto, we can hope for the day when we may say with St. Paul "It is no longer I that live, it is Christ who lives in me." [Galatians 2:20] ✢

11

Eileen Rosaline O'Connor
Australia, 1893-1921

Little Mother of the Sick Poor

In front of the horrified eyes of their mother, the two little girls tumbled out of the family pram and landed with a hard "thunk" on the ground. Scooping them up, she soothed them; soon she calmed their loud, frightened cries. It did not appear as if either three-year-old Eileen O'Connor or her younger sister, Mary, was seriously hurt. In Mary's case, this was true. She was not injured. But by the time Eileen was five years old, doctors had told her heartbroken parents that her spine was broken and that she would have to have one operation after another.

Although the best of surgical attention was obtained for her, her case seemed hopeless from the beginning. From the time of her first operation until the day of her death of tubercle osteomyelitis at the age of twenty-eight, Eileen was never to be free of pain. A curvature of her spine retarded her normal growth. She never grew taller than three feet, ten inches. Her disability and constant illness kept her from normal attendance at school. She was bedridden much of her life and spent many hours in a wheelchair. Sometimes the pain was so severe that she became unconscious.

In spite of her disability, the young cripple began a work with Father Edward McGrath, M.S.C., to serve God through his sick poor. After founding a pious association to nurse the sick poor in their own

Eileen O'Connor

homes, Eileen endured misunderstandings, calumny, and the opposition of eccelesial authorities, defending herself, Father McGrath, and their ideas, and taking over the practical direction of the work. Her suffering and prayers at home were on behalf of the nurses who went out, working for God's poor.

Eileen Rosaline O'Connor was born February 19, 1892, in Richmond, Melbourne, Australia, the oldest of four children of Charles O'Connor and his wife, Anne. An Irish immigrant, Charles worked as a bookkeeper and accountant. The family was loving, affectionate and devout.

When Eileen was ten years old, the family moved to Sydney where her father became one of the chief accountants with a large firm. Eileen attended the local school run by the Sisters of Mercy but since she had to be carried much of the time, she went for a while as a boarder at the Sisters' school in Pymble. She had missed a great deal of school because of her constant medical problems and she never really caught up on her primary education. Eileen's condition varied from fully bedridden to some mobility, but she was determined to overcome her limitations. This determination remained with her throughout her brief life.

Although Eileen's constant medical needs must have been a drain on the family's finances, Charles earned a good income and the family was moderately well off. Eileen learned at an early age the value of home nursing care and saw at first hand the financial strain of illness.

Eileen as a youngster

Australia at this time was suffering a depression, unemployment was high and there were few government benefits available to the less fortunate.

Charles O'Connor became ill and died suddenly in 1911. This was a crushing blow for Eileen who had been very close to her father. Her condition worsened and she became completely immobile except for the use of her left hand. For the entire family, the death of the bread winner was a disaster. They moved to Coogee in search of cheaper housing. Here, Mrs. O'Connor went for aid to the Missionaries of the Sacred Heart and the superior arranged for his curate, Father Timothy Edward McGrath, to call on the family and see what he could do to help them. Through his aid they eventually located a home known as "Restwell" where Mrs. O'Connor was able to keep the family together by taking in paying boarders.

In spite of her physical disability, Eileen was intellectually bright and had a cheerful and winning disposition. The young and enthusiastic curate brought Holy Communion to the teenage invalid regularly. Eileen wanted to become a nun, but when she mentioned her hope at school she was told she would not be able to because of her limitations. In a letter to Father McGrath, she admitted that on having these hopes dashed "I had a cry. But I soon got over it by going to Our Lord and telling Him I would and did love Him best and that He must have me; and if I could not have beads and live like his other nuns and like them tell everyone that He is the best to love, it would not matter; I'd be a nun just the same. . . ."

Which of the two first thought of nursing the sick poor in their homes is not known. Eileen certainly realized what a worthwhile work this would be and Father McGrath had wanted to do something special for Our Lady from his seminary days. Their thinking came together and Eileen began to plan for a group to carry out such a work. They began to interview young women who were attracted to the idea.

Eileen with a young friend

With one of these young women, Cissie McLaughlin, Eileen established an instant rapport. She later wrote her a note in which she asked, "Don't you think it is a most holy and needed work and wherever you are you will pray for it won't you? I wonder if Our Lady will give you a religious vocation for this work. Do you think she will and do you want it? Anyway, we are friends for always are we not?" Eileen signed the letter "from your little friend, Eileen, the Pest." Cissie later recalled that she never forgot the interview and that at the tram stop on the way home an overwhelming conviction came over her that she was meant for this work. She said she felt that Eileen had sent an angel after her to persuade her. Eileen's ideas had revealed a new way of following the Gospel, a work she could and did enter wholeheartedly.

Eileen with one of Our Lady's Nurses

Father McGrath and Eileen obtained the promise of twenty girls to join the work and rented a house and set Founding Day for April 15, 1913. Later, this home was purchased through the generosity of Father Edward Gell and his sister Frances, two great benefactors. That morning, Eileen was taken from her home to the new house in a horse-drawn ambulance with Father McGrath walking alongside. The jolting of the ambulance caused Eileen so much pain that by the time it arrived at its destination, she was unconscious. Four of the M.S.C. priests came and the house was blessed. A Mrs. Derrick and her daughter Mary moved in to be the housekeepers. But the rest of the day was a fiasco! Only seven of the twenty who had promised to come turned up. By the end of the day, all of these had left, leaving only Eileen and the housekeepers.

After the debacle of opening day, twenty-one-year-old Eileen settled in and revealed a flair for practical management. Over the next eighteen months, seven recruits came to form the nucleus of what came to be called Our Lady's Nurses for the Poor. Of these, Cissie McLaughlin was the first. A nursing sister was hired to instruct the girls in their nursing skills and by 1914 their territory covered most of the near-city suburbs and the lower North Shore. Their first distinctive uniform was adopted: a white dress with a brown pillbox hat and cloak. It was a nurse's uniform, suggesting their professional status, and later became a religious garb once they had obtained the necessary approvals.

For some years, Eileen had been paralyzed in both legs and on one side and had to be carried everywhere. In 1914, she began to walk again without assistance. She walked from her bedroom to the kitchen and continued to be able to walk, apart from some periods of illness, until her death.

Eileen at the beach

Eileen's cheerful nature and beautiful smile drew others to her. She had a simple and effective spirituality. Although because of her lack of education her writings are sometimes ungrammatical, her spirituality shines through the letters and little works she wrote, almost poetically. The simple rules she wrote for Our Lady's Nurses are not canonical in form but they clearly express the spirit she had and which she passed to others in her words and her example. In writing of charity she said, "True charity is never idle, for if we wish to be really charitable there is always someone we can make happy or happier, someone we can help a little — make things a little easier for them with our love."

Eileen especially enjoyed visiting and playing with the children who came to visit. She also enjoyed her dog, Rags. She made a number of scrapbooks to amuse the children. These contained cutouts of the latest dress styles, of pets, of children and of theatrical scenes. She showed by example her belief about idleness. For the nurses she had written, "Be not idle. We must try to be sweet and busy and happy, our minds must be willing and our hands outstretched, we must do much . . . we must never be idle, there is so much to do."

A busy invalid, Eileen used the phone regularly to conduct business or to show concern for others. She continually instructed and encouraged Our Lady's Nurses in prayer and spirituality. Many of her writings survive. She was granted a number of spiritual favors, some of which she confided to Father McGrath. When it was possible to be taken out, she enjoyed visits to the beach or Centennial Park, joined by friends and children. A short drive by car was a welcome break away from her indoor existence.

Toward the end of her life, people flocked to meet her and receive help from her. She told the nurses that no one was to be turned away and in spite of her constant pain the visitors never realized how much she was suffering and they came away consoled, helped and counseled. Peace and cheerfulness seemed to radiate from Eileen, and Our Lady's Home at Dudley Street became a haven for worried and unhappy people.

At the beginning of the work, people of the community rapidly became interested in these "brown nurses." With youthful enthusiasm and naïveté, Eileen and Father McGrath made a number of errors of discretion such as failing to ask the bishop for permission for fundraising efforts. In addition, a Father Hubert Linckens arrived in Sydney as a visitor for the MSC's in 1914. A rigid, by-the-letter-of-the-law type of man, he and Father McGrath had a disagreement that led to problems for Father McGrath within his order, and at one point he was actually dismissed from the Missionaries. Although he appealed his dismissal and won, he was assigned far away and was not able to return to Australia on a permanent basis until he was elderly. Eileen remained to guide the fledgling group alone. At one point, when some of the nurses

"Little Mother" with flowers

left, Eileen's calm reaction was merely to say, with all assurance, "The best ones will stay."

Father Gell and his sister thought a vacation would be good for Father McGrath, so they organized and funded a tour by ship of the Pacific Islands for Father, Eileen, a nurse, and a few other friends. On their return they found that a hurricane of calumny had erupted. Father Linckens had dismissed Father McGrath from the M.S.C. on the grounds that he had "fled from the Monastery with a woman." The words, which implied a sordid affair, were ones that Father Linkens had found in a decree originally written about a priest who had left the order to live with a woman.

Keeping her head in this crisis, Eileen intended to see that justice was done. She urged her nurses to continue to trust in Jesus and Mary and to see the gossip as a share in the suffering of Christ. With financing provided by Father Gell and his sister, she, her nurse and Father McGrath left for Rome to appeal the order. She hired a Roman solicitor, obtained the help of a Pallotine priest who became an enthusiastic supporter and did all the translation work, and did much to prepare the case for Father McGrath. She remained calm, although with her sensitive nature she felt things very deeply. She wrote to Frances Gell and told her that she "felt sick and frightened." At the trial, her presence made it very clear to everyone, just as she had hoped, that "people believe their own eyes and can see that it is impossible for me to be more to Father McGrath than I should be." The sight of the brave young woman with her physical disability and deformity led to the Tribunal's lifting of his suspension in June of 1915 and he was received back into the General House in July. He was not, however, to return permanently to Australia until 1941 and eventually in 1969 he was allowed to return to Coogee as a resident chaplain where he remained until his death in 1977.

Back in Australia, Eileen continued to organize the work. She drew up a Rule of Life for the nurses. They lived the life

"Little Mother"

of religious and she adopted the Ignatian exercises of morning and evening prayer, and particular examination of conscience. She gave the nurses a daily meditation, and prayed with them. Each morning before they went on their rounds, they came to her room and reported back to her in the evening. Monthly, they brought their case books and discussed their cases with her. Eileen taught them how to deal with the poor. Daily, they renewed their promise to work and live for the poor. Before they were allowed to have the Blessed Sacrament reserved, they attended the parish church for Mass and Benediction.

Eileen's teachings on how to deal with the poor were practical and inspired the nurses in their work. Some of their patients, unused to kindness, tended to be rough and hostile even to those who were trying to help them. Eileen's advice was always sensible: "Never leave people poor and hungry while you investigate a case. The cause of poverty is nothing to do with you; you don't ask questions; you help the poor. Who are poorer than those who have lost the faith? You will never have hospitals or home; you will nurse the sick poor in their own homes. The really poor are the friends of Christ."

In the short space of the six years of her remaining life, the dreams of Eileen O'Connor and Father McGrath were put into living, vibrant practice. Archbishop Kelly, originally opposed to the group, became an enthusiastic supporter after seeing the good the nurses were doing for the poor. During the influenza epidemic of 1918-19 and the recurrence of the bubonic plague in 1921, Our Lady's Nurses worked tirelessly, ceaselessly visiting the poor and sick. The rector of St.

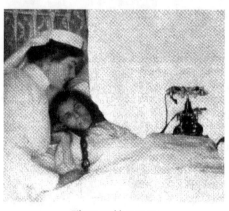

Eileen and her nurse

Patrick's College in Manly, Dr. Hayden, was brought to visit Eileen by his sister. As he said, "I came to criticize but left to pray." Eileen's deeply spiritual magnetism completely captivated him.

After the initial problems at the beginning of the work, Eileen rapidly learned to use her great patience, prudence, and discretion to accomplish her aims. She was careful not to appear to be dressing as a nun. During her life she did not represent her companions or herself as nuns but simply as pious women. Her long-term aim, of course, and the way she trained and shaped the Brown Nurses in their dedicated lifestyle, was that they should be religious.

As a patient

In 1920, Eileen's sufferings intensified. In September an operation for bladder stones resulted in prolonged agony. She confided, "I must not ask for any alleviation of the pain; souls are in need of my pain." She considered her physical suffering a special gift from God, and offered it for the souls of the sick, the poor, and for those who worked for them. She died January 10, 1921, surrounded by seven of her nurses, her mother, and several close relatives. Her final thoughts included the words: "I am always with you, I will bless you."

Eileen's body was originally buried in Randwick Cemetery. In 1936, Archbishop Kelly gave permission for it to be taken to Our Lady's Home. The body was exhumed and found to be in a wonderful state of preservation. Today, her mortal remains lie in the Chapel of Our Lady's Home.

Before she died, Eileen O'Connor had said, "If it were ever possible for me to be unhappy in Heaven, the only thing I feel would make me unhappy would be if the nurses ever turned away from the poor." They have not. Eileen's vision lives on today in the work of Our Lady's Nurses for the Poor, who were recognized as a religious congregation of Diocesan Right in 1953. The poor are still the special focus of this dedicated band of professional women, now serving in six cities, who rely solely on donations and do not charge for the services they provide. ✝

12

Felipe de Jesús Munarriz and Companions

The Claretian Martyrs of Barbastro
Fifty-one priests, religious brothers, and seminarians, members of the
Congregation of the Missionary Sons of the Immaculate Heart of Mary
(the Claretians) martyred in Barbastro, Spain, August 1936

On July 20, 1936, rebel militia forces entered the Claretian seminary in Barbastro, northern Aragon, and arrested the entire seminary
community. Within two weeks of their arrest, Father Felipe and two
other priest professors were taken to the local cemetery and shot on
August 2. The rest were imprisoned for over a month. Six more of the
group were called out on August 12 and as they went to their deaths,
they called out, *Viva Cristo Rey!* ("Long live Christ the King"). At midnight, a group of twenty died with the same religious fervor, and later
in the day of the thirteenth, another twenty died, a number of whom
were celebrating the anniversary of their religious profession. Two
seminarians who had been hospitalized were shot on the 18th along
the road from Barbastro to Berbegal. Of the entire group of Claretians
of Barbastro, seven were spared because of their advanced age and
two foreigners, from Argentina, were exiled. The two Argentinians
were later able to give testimony about the others.

When the anarchists broke into the gatehouse of the missionaries, they used as their excuse a search for hidden weapons. The superior told them, "There are no arms and no politics here. We are
religious and we are forbidden by our Constitutions to belong to any
party." In spite of failing to discover any weapons, the anarchists took
the three superiors to jail, and gave orders that the others should be
imprisoned in the lecture hall of the Piarist fathers on the square near
the jail. Father Masferrer was able to save the Eucharist from the community chapel, which he hid in a small valise which was later brought
to the auditorium-prison by the two priests who were allowed to remain behind to help take two sick seminarians and one feeble old
brother to the hospital. The rest left in lines of three under the watch
of armed guards. At the request of Father Cunill, Brother Simon

Sanchez and the five oldest brothers were allowed to be taken to the asylum of the Little Sisters of the Poor, across the square. The Piarists extended whatever fraternal care they could to the Claretians who were being detained in their house. The Piarist rector encouraged them and provided them some food, drink, and a few mattresses, pillows and sheets. He took the valise with the Eucharist and hid it in the physics lab, inside a film projector. At the time of the arrests, the community cook, Brother Vall, had been dressed in secular clothes. With his callused hands and smelling of food and cooking oil, the captors believed he was an "unenlightened proletarian" and an "exploited victim of the religious." Although he assured them he was a religious and a missionary, they did not pay attention to him and he was not detained. The three superiors were imprisoned in a cell of the municipal jail along with several canons of the cathedral and some Catholic laymen. Surviving witnesses testify that the three missionaries were exemplary. They were interrogated individually, and when Father Leoncio Perez returned he was in good humor. Questioned as to what he had been asked, he replied, "I was asked where we had hidden our weapons. I took out my rosary and told them: I don't have or want any other weapon but this." On July 25, the three missionary superiors were taken along with 350 other prisoners to the old convent of the Capuchin Nuns. From there, they were taken out with 17 other detainees and shot in the local cemetery. They had been given no sort of trial. They were priests and that was enough to find them guilty. At the same time, another group of priests and laity also marched into the cemetery. Among the laymen was a likable Gypsy, Ceferino Jiménez Malla, who had been arrested a few days earlier for trying to defend a priest and for carrying his rosary. Against the cold wall of the cemetery all the condemned men fell, riddled with bullets. All, that is, except one. Camilo Sabater Toll, a civil guard, was only wounded in the hand and was able to make his escape. Later, he was one who was able to testify to the great blood bath of Barbastro.

By a special providence from God, the religious articles of the prisoners were not taken away, so they were able to retain their rosaries, medals and crucifixes and to be led to the firing squad carrying them. Also, for the first twenty-five days of their imprisonment they were able to receive Communion on most days. Some of them had the joy of keeping the Eucharist on their person, becoming living tabernacles. Others received the host slipped inside the sliced roll they were given for breakfast.

In those hottest months of summer, the prisoners were provided with only a meager ration of water. They had to do without even the most basic hygiene and the oven-like heat aggravated the buildup of sweat and dirt. Forty-eight bodies shoved in a furnace-like room led to a stifling stench and true human misery with even their underwear chafing and cutting wounds into their skin. They were afflicted with head lice which added to their physical misery. Although they were given a little water to drink, they were not given any to wash with. One of the militiamen, seeing how dehydrated and dirty they were, had pity and sneaked them a little extra water on the sly.

Often the guards amused themselves at the prisoners' expense, standing them against the wall and pretending to be ready to shoot them. Prostitutes and specially trained female soldiers came into the auditorium during siestas and often at night to tempt the basic passions of the group of pious young men, most of them between the ages of twenty-one and twenty-five. Witnesses are unanimous in stating that not one of them fell for this. Throughout their ordeal, the Claretian seminarians waited with faith and calm, leaving written testimonies of their courage and hope in Christ and forgiving their tormentors publicly. All of them were offered their liberty on innumerable occasions, if they would throw away their cassock and become good revolutionaries. In a precious letter written to his family, Ramón Illa said, "I am writing to you with deep joy of soul, and the Lord knows I'm not lying. . . . The Lord has seen fit to place the palm of martyrdom in my hands. By these lines, too, I'm sending you my only will and testament, namely, that when you receive them you will sing to the Lord for the great and single gift of martyrdom that He has deigned to give me. . . . I wouldn't exchange my jail for the gift of working miracles, nor my martyrdom for the apostolate, which has been my life's dream. I'm going to be shot for being a religious and a member of the clergy, or, if you will, for following the teachings of the Roman Catholic Church. Thanks be to the Father through Our Lord Jesus Christ, Amen."

At three thirty in the morning of Wednesday, August 12, fifteen armed revolutionaries arrived carrying thick manacles of twisted, bloodstained cord. The leader called for the seven oldest who stepped down. Brother Gregorio Chirivas had been sick for several days, and he left all his things on the bench where he had been sleeping, including his broken dentures. The guards tied the prisoners' hands behind their backs and then bound them together, two by two, at the elbow. Father Pavon discreetly lifted his hand and pronounced absolution before he serenely bade them farewell. The little group was joined by a diocesan priest who was tied to Father Calvo and they were marched through the town square to a waiting truck. A few minutes later the

The Claretian Martyrs of Barbastro
PHOTO COURTESY OF THE CLARETIANS

remaining prisoners heard the volley of rifle shots. The truck had not completed the journey to the cemetery; rather, it stopped about three kilometers along the road in a wide bend. Before the firing started, they were offered one last chance to apostatize. Afterward, some were given the coup de grace in the head and they were left there alongside the road so as not to soil the truck with blood as they bled to death. Their executioners went off to a nearby farmstead to drink some wine, and returned to load the stiffening corpses and transport them to a big ditch in the cemetery. Quicklime, dirt and buckets of water were thrown over the bodies.

The remaining seminarians intensified their preparations for death. Faustino Perez wrote, "We have spent the day in religious silence, preparing for our death on the morrow. Only the holy murmur of prayers can be heard in this room, a witness to our deep anguish. When we talk, it is to encourage one another to die as martyrs. When we pray, it is for the forgiveness of our enemies. Save them, Lord, because they don't know what they are doing."

Pablo Hall, one of the Argentenians who had already been informed that he would not be killed, asked the others for a memento that he could take to the Father General as a souvenir for the Congregation. They took out a handkerchief that had belonged to Father Sierra who had been shot a few hours earlier. One by one they kissed it and touched it to their forehead, saying, "Let this be my farewell kiss to the Congregation which I love so much, for having the joy of dying in its arms. That same evening, José Amoros and Esteban Casadevall made their perpetual profession to Father Ortega who made a record of it, which was signed by several witnesses.

Lacking stationery, they wrote in and on whatever they could find: breviaries, prayer books, stair steps, the walls, and even on a chocolate wrapper. These messages of love and pardon were hidden with the hopes that they would be found one day. Although many of them were lost, a few have survived to bear mute testimony of the courageous martyrs' spirituality. Almost all testified to their love of Christ and their country, their forgiveness of their executioners, and their happiness of the grace they felt their martyrdom to be. Some dedicated their martyrdom to particular groups such as the workers or the Chinese missions. One precious relic that has endured is a piano bench whose underside is covered with the testimony and last words of six of the youthful martyrs. The front and back of a plain chocolate wrapper contains their official farewell. "August 12, 1936, in Barbastro. Six of our companions are already martyrs. Soon we hope to be so ourselves. But before this happens, we want to make it clear that we die forgiving those who are going to take our life, which we offer for the Christian order of the workers' world, for the final reign of the Catholic Church, for our beloved Congregation and for our dear families. Our last offering to the Congregation from its martyred sons." Then each wrote a single line and signed their name. The humble testament was given to the Argentine students in case the revolutionaries made good on their promise not to execute them.

About midnight, twenty executioners arrived. The leader called out for all those over the age of twenty-six to step forward, but none did. Then he called those over twenty-five years of age. Again, there was no response. At last, he turned on the lights and commanded another of the revolutionaries to begin reading off the names on a list he carried. As each person's name was called, he jumped down from the stage and took his place in line against the wall. Twenty were lined up and tied. Astilio Parussini, the other Argentine seminarian, testified that their faces seemed supernatural; Hall added that not one flinched or showed any sign of cowardice. As they were leaving, Juan Echarri turned towards those who remained and called "Farewell brothers, until heaven!"

The twenty condemned were led to a van and joined by an old-time civil guard who took the initiative and began the cry "Long live Christ the King." The others joined in and then began to sing canticles. Infuriated, the guards began beating them with the butts of their rifles to silence them. Again the van stopped about three kilometers from the city. A witness saw the missionaries kneeling on the heaped up earth of the embankment, trying their best to stretch their bound arms in the form of a cross. A final challenge, "Come with us and fight against the fascists," was answered with "Long Live Christ the King."

A number of farm workers in the area heard the executions as well as the boasts of the executioners. Again, the bodies were left to bleed before transporting them to the cemetery and a common pit which some Gypsies had been forced to dig. The following day, the workers who went to look at the site of the execution found some holy cards, some books, and a shoe belonging to the missionaries. Some years later the bodies of the missionaries were identified thanks to the numbered tags on their clothing which corresponded with the brother tailor's well-kept list.

At five thirty in the evening, the two Argentinean seminarians were taken from the prison and put on a train for Barcelona. They were able to leave the country and lived to testify as to the last days of the martyrs.

Early in the morning of the fifteenth, the glorious feast of the Assumption, the final twenty were called for. Tightly bound and accompanied by three priests of the town, they were loaded onto the van. Although they had been warned not to, they began shouting "Long Live Christ the King." The angry driver stopped the van and went to the back, striking the missionaries with his rifle butt. To the last, they prayed ejaculatory prayers, clutching their crucifixes and rosaries.

Later on the morning of the fifteenth, the last two seminarians were released from the hospital along with the elderly Brother Joaquin Munoz and were immediately taken to the municipal jail. On the 18th the militiamen judged Brother Munoz too old and sick, so they left him alone. They took the two seminarians and shot them in the same place as their brothers.

Most of the 51 martyrs were young seminarians in their early twenties. For a month they knew what their destiny could be and they prepared for it with joy and determination. They were killed in the first weeks of the Spanish civil war, when political confusion and human passions were high and crimes and atrocities were committed on both sides. Their martyrdom is a not a political or moral judgment for either side. They were killed quite simply because they were religious, and they would not betray the vocation they received from God.

The martyrs of August 2, 1936

Father Felipe de Jesús Munarris Azcona, priest, age 61; Father Juan Diaz Nosti, priest, age 56; Father Leoncio Perez Ramos, priest, age 61.

The martyrs of August 12, 1936

Father Sebastian Calvo Martinez, priest, age 33; Wenceslaro Claris Vilaregut, student, age 29; Father Pedro Cunill Padros, priest, age 33; Brother Gregorio Chirivas Lacambra, religious brother, age 56; Father José Pavon Bueno, priest, age 35; Father Nicasio Sierra Ucar, priest, age 46.

The martyrs of August 13, 1936
Javier Luis Bandres Jiménez, student, age 23; José Brengaret Pujol, student, age 23; Brother Manuel Buil Lalueza, religious brother, age 21; Antolin Clavo y Calvo, student, age 24; Tomás Capdevila Miro, student, age 22; Esteban Casadevall Puig, student, age 23; Eusebio Corina Milla, student, age 21; Juan Codinachs Tuneu, student, age 22; Antonio Dalmau Rosich, student, age 23; Juan Echarri Vique, student, age 23; Pedro Garcia Bernal, student, age 25; Hilario Llorente Martín, student, age 25; Brother Alfonso Miguel Garriga, religious brother, age 22; Ramón Novich Rabionet, student, age 23; José Ormo Sero, student, age 22; Father Secundino Ortega Garcia, priest, age 24; Salvador Pigem Sera, student, age 23; Teodoro Ruiz de Larrinaga Garcia, student, age 23; Juan Sanchez Munarris, student, age 23; Manuel Torras Sais, student, age 21.

The Martyrs of August 15, 1936
José Amoros Hernandez, student, age 23; José Maria Badia Mateu, student, age 23; Juan Baixeras Berenguer, student, age 22; José Blaso Juan, student, age 24; Rafael Briega Morales, student, age 23; Brother Francisco Castan Messeguer, religious brother, age 25; Luis Binefa Escale, student, age 23; José Figuero Beltran, student, age 25; Ramon Illa Salvia, student, age 22; Luis Llado Teixidor, student, age 24; Brother Manuel Martínez Jarauta, religious brother, age 23; Father Luis Masferrer Vila, priest, age 24; Miguel Massip Gonzalez, student, age 23; Faustino Perez Garcia, student, age 25; Sebastian Riera Coromina, student, age 22; Eduardo Ripoll Diego, student, age 24; Francisco Roura Farro, student, age 23; Jose Rios Florensa, student, age 21Alfonso Sorribes Teixido, student age 23; Agustin Viela Ezcurdia, student, age 22;

The Martyrs of August 18, 1936
Jaime Falgarona Vilanova, student, age 24; Atanasio Vidaurreta Labra, student, age 25.

13

Georges and Pauline Vanier
Canada, 1888-1967 and 1898-1991

A Couple United in the Values of the Heart

Georges Vanier once said, "Let us never be afraid to remind the world that standing above purely economic, material, or psychological values, there are human values, values of the heart, moral and spiritual values, values that find their source and their strength in the intimacy of a united family where peace and love reign supreme."

In spite of the highly public life that Georges and Pauline Vanier were called on to live because of his work as one of Canada's most able diplomats, the couple maintained an intimate and united family in a home where Christ the King was given the key. The temperaments of the loving couple complemented each other. He was quiet and gentle; she was outgoing and effervescent. Their married life shines with the beauty of the sacrament. One day they may be held together in veneration as holy models of the sacrament of marriage, and how, lived faithfully, it can serve as a highway to heaven.

Georges Phileas Vanier was born April 23, 1888, in Montreal. He was the oldest of five children of Phileas Vanier, a real estate man, and Irish-born Margaret Maloney. Growing up, Georges spoke both French and English. As a boy, Georges was gentle, intelligent and a serious student. He was devout, committed to saying the rosary daily and to frequent communion. These practices became lifetime habits for him. He studied at Loyola College and Laval University, graduating in law and being called to the Bar in 1911. While at Loyola, he was Prefect of the Sodality of Our Lady and for a time thought of becoming a priest. Georges's law career was brief. At the outbreak of war in 1914 he joined the newly formed 22nd (French Canadian) Battalion known as the Van Doos, and within a year he was in the trenches in France. In 1916, for his part in a daring maneuver, he was promoted to Captain and received the Military Cross. In 1918 in a bloody battle near Arras, the young regiment leader was wounded in the chest and both legs; his right leg was amputated the following day. On the way to the dressing station, the chaplain asked Georges if there was anything he wanted. "Yes," he replied with a smile, "absolution for my sins, a drop of rum and a cigarette." He was awarded a bar to the Military Cross for "conspicuous gallantry and devotion to duty" and the Companion of the Distinguished Service Order for inspiring the Van Doos to take Cherisy. After the Armistice, he was walking on crutches by the time he was sent home in 1919. Immediately he asked to rejoin his regiment and the Inspector General of the Armed Forces laughed at him, telling him "But you've lost a leg!" Georges retorted, "I know that. Don't you want officers with brains as well as legs?" He was promoted to major and posted to Quebec City as second-in-command of the battalion. Shortly thereafter he met twenty-two-year-old Pauline Archer. Pauline told the dashing young major that she was to sail to France for a vacation and he replied, "I'll send you roses en route." The roses never arrived but once back in Canada Pauline discovered to her delight that they had indeed been sent, just to the wrong ship.

Pauline Archer was born March 28, 1898. She was the only child of a Montreal attorney, Charles Archer, and Therese de Salaberry. When Pauline was six years old, her mother took her to visit with Père Almire Pichon. The priest had been the spiritual director of both Thérèse de Salaberry and also Thérèse Martin, the little flower of Lisieux. He took a lifelong interest in the Archer family, and his wise advice continually repeated the same theme: be confident in God's love, even in the midst of problems. He also inspired them all to trust in the loving Heart of Jesus. Until the war, the Archer family made summer visits to France and Mrs. Archer always made time for a visit with Pere Pichon. After the war, when traveling across the Atlantic had begun again, the family set out for a six-month vacation in France. Pauline was a tall and lovely girl of twenty-one. Although her parents had kept her at home to be educated, she was lively and full of high spirits. One day she accompanied her mother on a visit to the priest; it was the first time she had seen him since she made her first confession, sitting on his lap. Definitely older, and in poor health, Père Pichon still spoke with the same gentleness. When he asked Pauline about her plans for the future, she had no reply. She had a strong inclination to prayer and the spiritual life but although she had briefly considered a vocation to the religious life, she did not really want to become a nun. She had joined wholeheartedly in many social activities and had met a number of attractive young men. In particular, the young Georges Vanier had captured her interest, but she did not know if he felt the same way about her. She could not spill out her conflicting emotions to the kindly priest and asked him simply to pray for her. He replied that he would begin a novena for her intention. Mother and daughter took a sad leave of the frail priest; he died on the last day of his novena for Pauline's intentions.

Pauline Archer and Georges Vanier were married in Montreal September 29, 1921. Georges became an aide-de-camp to the Governor-General of Canada and they left for Ottawa immediately. Two years later a diplomatic move took them to England. For the rest of their married life, army and diplomatic appointments moved the Vaniers back and forth across the Atlantic. Some of his appointments included being Canadian minister to France, becoming Brigadier General in command of the Quebec Military District, Canadian minister to the Allied governments in exile, Canada's representative to the United Nations and Canadian ambassador to France. He retired from diplomatic service in 1954, but in 1959 he was asked to become Governor-General. By this

Governor-General Georges Vanier and Pauline Vanier
PHOTO COURTESY OF THE CANADIAN NATIONAL FILM BOARD

time, he was in his seventies and had suffered a heart attack, but he told Pauline, "If God wants me to do this job, he will give me the strength." When a friend declared "Good heavens, Vanier, you've already got one foot in the grave," Georges replied, "I know, but it's been there 41 years."

In his public life, Georges gained the reputation of a peacemaker who sought justice. He felt a particular personal concern for the refugees of World War II, especially the Jews and the orphaned children. During his years as Governor-General of Canada, he displayed an interest in the humble and the poor, in the problems of youth, and in the condition of modern family life, which won the hearts of all Canadians. Realizing the imprint of happy marriages on society as a whole, he wrote, "A close look at the family in Canada could help more people to find the warmth and delight we have found ourselves." He established the Vanier Institute of the Family to ensure aid to families in need of counsel and to deepen the understanding of the importance of good family life.

During his viceregal years as the nineteenth (and first French-Canadian) Governor-General, times were turbulent. Georges charged people of all ethnic origins to go forward hand in hand, saying, "The road to unity is the road of love; love of one's country and faith in its future will give new purpose in our lives, lift us above our domestic quarrels, and unite us in dedication to the common good. . . . I pray God that we may all go forward hand in hand. We can't run the risk of this great country falling into pieces."

Five children eventually blessed the Vanier's union: Thérèse, Georges (nicknamed Byngsie after his godfather, Lord Byng), Bernard, Jean, all born in quick succession, and Michel, a lovely surprise born when Pauline was forty-three. . .They were a happy young family who enjoyed seaside holidays. The boys took boxing lessons. Georges rolled on the floor and played with his children, and read them Shakespeare. There was always time for laughter and companionship. They entertained prime ministers and dined with royalty but were equally at home in an intimate family setting.

Although there was little outward piety or sentimental devotion in the religious practices of the family, both Pauline and Georges devoted time each day to prayer, meditation, and spiritual reading. Each evening, Pauline knelt with the children for prayers while Georges, unable to kneel because of his prosthetic leg, sat in a nearby chair.

Every year they also observed a novena in November in honor of Père Pichon, the spiritual director of Pauline's mother, asking for his beatification. Georges' daughter inherited his Bible after his death. In it, she found a slip of paper on which he had penciled a record of moments given to meditation. He had told her, "We can all find time to do what we want." The couple gained deep strength from their Catholic faith. Pauline's mother, guided by Père Pichon, had taught her to trust God's love and goodness. She passed this confidence on to her children. Georges, however, had been brought up in a home that emphasized a Jansenistic form of Catholicism and although he admired his wife's joyous faith, his own had a somber tinge. In 1938, Georges heard a sermon on the love of God that brought a change in his spiritual attitude. Suddenly he felt free of the fear and guilt that had characterized his earlier religious outlook and his spiritual life progressively deepened and a new sense of communion arose between him and his wife. From this time, Georges resolved to accompany Pauline to daily Mass, with few exceptions, until his last days. The couple developed together in harmony and understanding until their friends declared, "We always think of them together." When his job required Georges to be away from his family, he wrote Pauline every day.

The experience of the war years affected Georges all his life, strengthening his sense of duty and his compassion. Some of his war wounds caused him to be in almost constant pain for the rest of his life. He always made light of his disability, the loss of his leg. Jokingly, he would let the children drive a hatpin into his artificial leg. When out walking, he'd show them how oddly hollow the limb sounded when he tapped it with his cane.

During the 1930s, Georges Vanier's family wealth vanished and the family lived through a number of lean years. In addition, Pauline, always high strung, suffered from depression and had an operation to remove an ovarian cyst that fortunately proved to be benign. Because they were in diplomatic service, they had to keep up appearances while making do with less. Later, Pauline was to say that the hardship of these years was the best thing that had ever happened to her children. At the beginning of World War II, the Vaniers had to flee their home in France and for the rest of the war years, family life was somewhat disrupted. After the war they returned to Paris, along with the latest addition to the family, Michel, who had been born in 1941.

By the early 1950's most of the Vanier children had grown and dispersed. Thérèse studied and became a medical doctor. Byngsie became a Cistercian monk in Quebec. Bernard became a painter. Jean studied philosophy in Paris and Michel remained at home with his parents until he finished school. In 1954, Georges retired as ambassador to France and he and Pauline returned to Montreal.

Georges Vanier became Governor-General of Canada on September 15, 1959. He set up a chapel in the family home at Rideau Hall where daily Mass could be said. He wrote, "We will have an altar where Christ the King will reign. To Him will I give the keys of my house."

In the summer of 1964, Jean had gone to help a Dominican priest at an institution for persons with mental handicaps in the town of Trosly-Breuil, near Paris. Here, he found his own vocation. He bought a house and took two of the men with handicaps to live with him. Within a few years, others joined him and Jean called the young community L'Arche (the ark). Here he began to live out his vision based on the teaching of Christ that the poor and rejected should be at the center of the Christian community. A doctor of philosophy with a brilliant academic career ahead of him, he chose to spend his life with people whose brains had been damaged and whose hearts had been wounded by society's rejection and by the indifference of institutional life. His grandmother who, in her youth had known abandonment and loneliness knew the importance of living where one is loved and wanted to join him in his work but died in 1968 before she could do so.

Georges Vanier died on March 6, 1967. Although he had been ill for a few weeks, he had continued with his normal activities. An avid hockey fan and supporter of the Montreal Canadians, the day before his death he had watched a hockey game. That Sunday morning, he felt too weak to attend Mass, so he received Holy Communion in bed and was anointed. He breathed his last in peace.

Pauline was appointed a member of the Privy Council in 1967 because Georges had died before the end of his term, which is when a Governor-General is normally appointed a Privy Councilor. She was among the first recipients of the Order of Canada, Chancellor of the University of Ottawa, and was named Canadian Woman of the Year for 1965. After Georges's death, she moved to Montreal and settled into a comfortable townhouse not far from her childhood home. She began to visit her children, and to become active in a number of social works including visiting prisoners.

In 1974, at the age of seventy-three, Pauline returned to France and began to live and work with her son Jean in the midst of the L'Arche community. Although someone had suggested she do so shortly after Georges' death, she had rejected the idea because of her age, her fear of people with handicaps, and the fact that she was settled in Montreal. But a seed was sown. During a retreat at the Montreal Carmelite monastery the Gospel reading about the rich young man came across as a personal message to her. When she left Canada, she told the press, "There is no great dramatic story. All I'm doing is getting rid of some luxuries that I don't need with the permission of my children, and using the money to help the poor in general and my son's work." Although it was not an easy transition, she remained there as a rock of support until her death. In particular, she was appreciated by those young people who joined L'Arche in a burst of enthusiasm and then felt overcome by the challenge.

Pauline died in 1991 at the age of ninety-two, and was buried next to General Vanier at the commemorative chapel at La Citadelle in Quebec City. "Let's be together in our weaknesses and strengths," the couple had pledged. Together in life and in death, they may one day together share the honors of the altar. A cause for their beatification is being considered with the permission of Ottawa's Archbishop Marcel Gervais. ✢

14

Jacques Fesch
France, 1930-1957

Murderer, Convert, Contemplative, Mystic

Jacques Fesch, a young Frenchman, was a convicted murderer who was guillotined for his crime in 1957 at the age of twenty-seven. He has left us a testimony in his letters that can bring hope to even the most hardened of sinners. His letters show that he was successfully able to resist the terrible temptation of despair, and present a clear witness to the unconquerable strength of a God who is Love and whose love no crime can overpower. The letters display a glowing testimony to the fact that Love is stronger than even the most horrible of deaths. On the last night of his life, Jacques Fesch wrote, "I wait in the night and in peace . . . I wait for Love."

September 30, 1957, knowing he was to be executed in the morning, Jacques went to bed, to sleep, and awoke at three o'clock in the morning. He asked his prison guard for a light, saying that he had to "get ready at once." He made his bed and took up his missal. He was reading it peacefully when the prison chaplain arrived at 5:30. The chaplain testified that the young man made his final confession and a moving Communion. As they bound Jacques's hands, the chaplain faced him in order to comfort him, but Jacques remained peaceful and serene.

Jacques refused the traditional glass of rum and the cigarette offered to the condemned at the moment of execution, but as he mounted the scaffold he said to the chaplain, "The crucifix, Father, the crucifix," and kissed it fervently. Those were his last words; he said nothing further. The blade of the guillotine fell. The chaplain tells us that Jacques had offered his life for his father, for those whom he loved, and for the man he had killed. He says that there was not the slightest note of rancor or bitterness, and that Jacques "died a great Christian."

Jacques Fesch entered prison an atheist. The first time the prison chaplain visited him, he courteously sent the priest away telling him that he had no faith. In the nearly four years he spent in prison, he returned to the Catholic faith and became a true contemplative.

In addition he was given a number of mystical lights and went to his execution in a spirit of faith and joy. During his time in prison, his greatest preoccupation was how he could share this faith with his family, whom he loved.

Some people may think that Jacques's conversion was a normal reaction. Imprisoned, stripped of everything, who else can you turn to but God? But that is a simplistic view. It is no

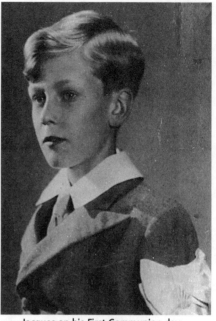

Jacques on his First Communion day
PHOTOS COURTESY OF SOEUR VERONIQUE, CARMEL
OF SAN REMY, ITALY

easier to allow yourself to be drawn from darkness to the point of emptying yourself of your own ego in prison than in the world.

Over a period of time, a great interior transformation took place in the soul of Jacques Fesch. "Little by little I was led to change my ideas. I was no longer certain that God did not exist. I began to be open to Him, though I did not yet have faith. I tried to believe with my reason, without praying, or praying ever so little! And then, at the end of my first year in prison, a powerful wave of emotion swept over me, causing deep and brutal suffering. Within the space of a few hours, I came into possession of faith, with absolute certainty. I believed, and could no longer understand how I had ever not believed. Grace had come to me. A great joy flooded my soul and above all a deep peace. In a few instants everything had become clear. It was a very strong, sensible joy that I felt. I tend now to try, perhaps excessively, to recapture it; actually, the essential thing is not emotion, but faith."

In his journey to faith and joy, Jacques was helped by the prison chaplain, Father Devoyod, O.P., who visited him and who loaned him books, by a childhood friend of his wife's, a religious named Brother Thomas who prayed for him, and maintained a close friendship with him through their correspondence, and by his lawyer, Paul Baudet, a sincere Christian. In addition, Jacques maintained a close friendship and correspondence with his mother-in-law.

Some of Jacques's letters have been translated into English in the books *Light Over the Scaffold: Prison Letters of Jacques Fesch from Cell 18: unedited letters of Jacques Fesch.* In reading them, one receives not only the picture of the psychology of this extraordinary prisoner, but also a map to holy joy and peace and the introduction to a stairway to Heaven. In his own words, he tells the story of the ascent of a soul. Along the way, the reader tastes some of the spiritual fruits Jacques gathered along his journey.

Jacques Fesch was born in Saint-Germain-en-Laye on April 6, 1930. The son of Belgian parents, his father was a bank president, an autocratic man and an atheist who made family life unbearable. His mother was loving but ineffectual.

Jacques attended a religious school for the first nine years of his education but the problems of his family had damaged his sense of security and his enthusiasm and he did poorly in school He attended a boys' high school but after a single year he quit. Jacques worked for his father at the bank until he left for military service. Toward the end of his enlistment, his parents separated.

Tall and slender with nice features, Jacques's silence and timidity came across to many as apathy. He appeared absent-minded and non-chalant. Even after his conversion, some took his natural reservation, his withdrawn nature as one of cynicism.

While he was in military service, he married Pierette Polack, a young girl from his hometown. He fathered a daughter, Veronica. Later, he wrote with brutal honesty: "I was a disturbed, unbalanced, and deeply unhappy person. I married because, in the first place, my wife was pregnant, and then too because I had found a semblance of warmth in my new family. . . . I did not love my wife, but we got along well and peaceably. My child I did love. But what is a child when one is twenty and has no moral stability?" Later, in prison, he apparently grew to love Pierette. In his letters he apologizes to her and even gets his mother-in-law to purchase a bracelet as a gift for her. He maintained a continued love and concern for his daughter. He often drew little pictures and made cut outs for her, and his letters show his deep love for her. In a letter written shortly before his execution, he says "be sure that from heaven I will protect her and watch over her with all the love Jesus will give me."

After his military service, his father-in-law gave Jacques a job in his factory, a thermal coal company in Strasbourg. The young couple, both immature, separated in October of 1953 with Pierette taking Veronica and moving home with her family and Jacques going to stay with his mother.

Jacques had the idea to found a branch of his father-in-law's business and obtained a thousand francs from his mother. Unwisely, he spent half of the money on a car and realizing the impossibility of his plan and the foolishness of spending the money on a car, he became discouraged and longed for an easy solution. His very existence seemed dismal, his life was in a shambles and he realized he was a total failure. He returned to Pierette, but dreamed of an impossible escape; he would set sail for the distant lands of Polynesia in a small boat!

Jacques went to LaRochelle where he had plans for a small, but seaworthy boat drawn up. Short two thousand francs for the cost, he appealed to his father who refused.

The thought of his escape from his miserable life became an obsession and he made plans, with two other young men as accomplices, to rob a moneychanger named Alexander Silberstein who kept a shop in the Paris stock exchange. Before the planned attack, Jacques went to his father's home and, unbeknownst to his father, stole a loaded gun and a hammer. During his trial, this evidence was used to prove premeditation.

One day in late February of 1954, Jacques went to Silberstein's place to

Jacques and his wife, Pierette

order some money and returned in the evening, presumably for the remainder of the cash. He struck the old man with the butt of the revolver. Although the man's head was bloodied, he managed to cry out for help and the gun discharged a bullet which wounded Fesch's own hand.

Streaming blood, he ran, but the blood caused him to be noticed and after hiding briefly in a building, he attempted to leave when he was recognized. A policeman shouted for him to put his hands up. Instead, seized

Jacques Fesch on the day of his capture

with panic, he drew the revolver and fired a single shot that hit the policeman in the heart, killing him. Frantic to escape, he wounded a second man who attempted to capture him. He fired twice at two other pursuers, missing both, but was finally caught at a nearby subway station.

On his arrest, Fesch was subjected to the usual police interrogation and taken afterwards to the Prison de la Sant in Paris. That evening, Pierrette was waiting to meet Jacques at a café. There, the police found her and ordered her to follow them. She saw her husband, handcuffed, with his face bleeding.

The police gave her the third degree, questioning her until the wee hours of the morning without ever telling her why she was being detained. The following afternoon she was allowed a newspaper whose headlines carried the story of her husband, the assassin. To her credit, Pierrette stood by Jacques until his death. She forgave him and even told her young daughter that he was away on a trip. She married him in a religious marriage only a few days before his execution.

After some time in prison and at the request of the prison chaplain, Jacques wrote a report of his crime. In it, he says, in part, "it is impossible for me to look at my own actions as a simple spectator, taking into account only the brutal facts, overwhelming though they may be. Each time I go back over what happened, not only my own actions but all the things that preceded them — my thoughts, intentions, states of mind — I find it absolutely impossible to describe because the whole is too complex. These events hold me in their grip and create a certain impression in which nothing can be understood clearly. It is very difficult for me to record my thoughts because although they run deep, I don't know how to express them."

Jacques continues by recording the fact that the disturbances in his family life where his parents often fought and where there was "no respect, no love," left him as a disturbed, unbalanced and deeply unhappy person. Jacques does not make excuses and never claims that he is not culpable of the crime with which he has been charged. He does make the point that he was acting on reflex and that he does not feel that he was making a free, balanced choice. He explains, though, that he is guilty of sins other than the robbery and murder. He feels he will also have to answer for the pain he has caused his wife, his child, and more. Once he had been converted, he prayed constantly for the gift of faith for those he loved.

In speaking of his father's atheism, Jacques wrote: "I beg the Blessed Virgin to hear my prayers, she who is at the source of infinite mercy." And again, "At home, we had about as much religion as you would find in a stable, and since I've been here the members of my family have each begun to examine their consciences. Little by little they are growing united again, and renewed. My mother and one of my sisters have already formed a little nucleus. All that remains is for them to bring back my father and my other sister. This will come about, perhaps, if God wills it." In other letters and in his journal he mentions his concern for his wife and his daughter, and his mother-in-law.

Jacques's mother died of cancer on June 7, 1956. She had offered her life that her son might die well.

Jacques' faith was purified as he suffered through a period of spiritual desolation common to the mystics. He wrote to Brother Thomas, "Then, morally, an upset which is actually over now but which left me disoriented for some time. Instead of referring everything to God so as to be strengthened by faith, I made the great mistake of examining my situation from a human angle, looking to the future and wishing vehemently for a kinder fate from a worldly point of view. Of course, easy solutions came to mind, acceptable at first so to speak, and then ones that were more and more evil, drawing me once more into the quagmire of sin. In the end, little brother, I swept all these villainous thoughts aside and climbed back up the slope with determination."

Jacques was not by nature either a poet or a mystic. He never studied theology; his theology came from the inner workings of God in his soul. He realized that his conversion was a gradual, progressive thing, but he moved from atheism to a marked, sincere faith. "Before that, the true God was an indifferent tradition as far as I was concerned. Now, He is all that matters. . . . Then comes the struggle — silent, tragic — between what I was and what I have become. For the new creature who has been planted within me calls for a response which I am free to refuse. . . . I am amazed and surprised at the change which grace has effected in me. . . . In this radical experience which is overturning my life and marking it indelibly, I perceive an ongoing need for spiritual renewal. . . . But God is here. In Him I have the strength to see and do whatever I must, so as to be conformed to His image. He unites my prayer to His will. The vocation He gives me arouses a prayer within me, which I address to Him."

Although there were appeals made in his case, Jacques seems to have received an interior light of knowledge that he would not be pardoned. He accepted his death and offered it for those "whom the Lord wants to save."

He begged his family to prepare themselves in prayer, offering their grief to God, so he may go in peace. Above all, he cautioned them not to see divine injustice in his execution, and tells them, "God is not an automatic distributor of temporal benefits to sinners who have come upon hard times. He loves men, and has only one object: to give Himself to them for all eternity, not to give them a pleasant life on earth which will generate sins, and then bring souls who have injured Him to Paradise!"

He wrote what is perhaps his greatest message, the joy of the cross. "I hope that my recent letters have helped you a bit to see things from a different point of view than the strictly human one. Above all I have wanted to make you understand the cross. Crucified love! Was there ever a greater crime? It is this sacrifice which saves us, and it is through it that Jesus continues to live here below."

"This execution which frightens you is nothing in comparison with what awaits sinners in the next world! It is not for me that you should weep, but for sins which offend God. As for me, I am happy. Jesus is calling me to Himself, and great graces have been given me. If you could only taste for a single instant the sweetness of the transports of divine love!"

Realizing that love continues to exist, Jacques promised "If God permits it, I will pray for all of you from heaven. There is a communion of souls, but for that we must be in the necessary state."

In his final letter to his mother-in-law he urged her to reconcile with the Church and told her: "Now, my life is finished. 'Like a little spring flower which the divine Gardener plucks for His pleasure,'[1] so my head will fall — glorious ignominy — with heaven for its prize! I am happy. . . ."

On death row, Jacques had made friends with another prisoner and he sent him a final message, a poem. These words highlight his faith and his holy joy:

"To my friend Robert, with the hope that he too will rejoice in the dawn!

He said, it is good to part in the night
Toward the end of exile, toward the shining dawn
He whose soul here below was covered in veils.
Then forth he went to the sound of sobs
Forth to the black scaffold and the bloody block
Eyes open, eager, upon the stars.
Until we meet in God.
Your brother Jacques." ✝

Notes

[1] Here Jacques is quoting St. Thérèse of Lisieux. He often quoted Scripture and other spiritual writers in his letters.

15

Jerzy Popieluszko
Poland, 1947-1984

Priest of Solidarity

With tears in his eyes, his voice breaking, the priest directed the
congregation, "Repeat after me," as for the third time he spoke the
line from the Lord's prayer, "as we forgive those who trespass against
us." At last, the line was repeated with enormous force by the voices of
the congregation at the packed vigil at St. Stanislaw's church in Warsaw. It was October 30,1984, and the death of their beloved Father
Jerzy Popieluszko had ·just been announced. The congregation was
holding a prayer vigil in hopes that the priest had not been killed and
that he would be returned safely. He had been missing since his abduction on the night of October 19.

Panic, grief, and shock followed the finding of the battered corpse of
the priest. The body was pulled from a reservoir on the river Vistula,
about eighty miles northwest of Warsaw. The priest had been tortured,
and the body was beyond recognition. A sack of rocks had been hung
from the legs, and the body had been tied with a nylon rope so that if he
had resisted Father Jerzy would have strangled himself. The corpse had
been gagged, and the body was covered head to foot with deep, bloody
wounds and marks of torture. The face was deformed, the hands were
broken and cut, the eyes and forehead had been beaten and the jaw, nose,
mouth and skull were smashed. Part of the scalp and large strips of skin
on the legs had been torn off. When Father Jerzy's mouth was opened,
all of the teeth were found to be completely smashed.

One of the doctors who performed the post-mortem reported that
be had never seen anyone so mutilated internally. Identification from a
birthmark on the side of his chest was finally made by the priest's brother.

Of what crime was this fragile, defenseless priest accused? Officially, none. Why was he kidnapped, horribly tortured, and murdered?
Father Jerzy Popieluszko preached and lived a defense of human rights,
a song of freedom. In speaking of the steelworkers he said, "These

people knew their strength lay in their unity with God." Marshall law had silenced millions of Poles, but Father Jerzy refused to be silenced. He preached a non-violent, Christian solidarity, and a moral victory over the forces of evil and Communist oppression. In his priesthood, he took seriously the gospel command to free the oppressed.

"One must suffer for the truth. That is why I am ready for anything," Father Jerzy had written to Pope John Paul II. At his last Mass, a special Mass for the Working People in the provincial town of Bydgoszcz, Father Jerzy preached a final sermon that exemplified all he stood for, "Overcome Evil with Good." His last words to the congregation were, "Most of all, may we be free from the desire for violence and vengeance." In the spirit of these final words of the valiant priest, the congregation at his vigil prayed, "as we forgive those who trespass against us." On the day of his funeral, ten thousand steelworkers in hard hats marched past secret-police headquarters. One of the slogans they chanted over and over was "We forgive."

Jerzy Popieluszko was born in 1947 in Okopy, a small hamlet in eastern Poland about twenty miles from the Soviet border. His parents were poor farmers. The family of six lived in a small two-room house with only a stove for heat. As a child, Jerzy was in chronic ill health. He was

Jerzy Popieluszko, the Solidarity priest
PHOTOS COURTESY OF PAULINE FATHERS, NATIONAL SHRINE OF OUR LADY OF CZESTOCHOWA

born covered with yellowish ulcers all over his tiny body. Friends recall him as self-effacing, always doing things for others. Before school, he would rise early and walk three miles to serve as an altar boy at the nearest church. He was a loner, nicknamed "the philosopher" for his habit of being caught up in his own thoughts. He loved Polish history and, even in the state-run schools he attended, he spoke his mind. St. Maximilian Kolbe was one of Jerzy's heroes, and after high school Jerzy attended a seminary in Warsaw in order to be close to the monastery that Kolbe had created. He did not mention his desire to become a priest until after his high school graduation for fear that his examination results might be altered or that his parents might be pressured by the authorities not to allow him to enter the seminary.

After a happy first year at the seminary, Jerzy was drafted into a special army-indoctrination unit in 1966. Here he became the spiritual leader of his unit. For leading prayer services, Jerzy was assigned extra-hard labor. He was forced to crawl around the camp like a dog because he recited the rosary to brain-washing specialists. When an officer found him with a rosary, he demanded that Jerzy renounce his faith. The young seminarian refused, so he was beaten severely and put in isolation for a month. In a letter to his father describing the ordeal, Jerzy wrote, "I have turned out to be very tough. I can't be broken by threats or torture." The stay at the indoctrination unit ruined his health, although Jerzy told one of his seminary masters, "One doesn't suffer when one suffers for Christ."

After his ordination in 1972, Jerzy was appointed chaplain to Warsaw's medical students and nurses. Everyone admired his readiness to be with people in all circumstances, his easygoing nature, and his courage.

During the Pope's first visit to his homeland people were lined up to present him with presents and remembrances of the trip. The secret police were checking each gift. Three young girls carrying only a letter were standing in the long line when the police seized their letter. Father Jerzy witnessed their dismay and in a flash he jumped the barrier ropes, tore the letter out of the policeman's hands and returned it to the girls just as they were about to step up to greet the Pope.

Though he tried to hide it, his illness was taking its toll, and his fainting spells became more frequent. One day while saying Mass, Father Jerzy fell unconscious. He was suffering from a serious blood disorder that would require transfusions with each recurrence. A quiet life and a special diet would help prevent further deterioration from the disease, so in June of 1980 he was assigned to the parish of St. Stanislaw Kostka near the huge Warsaw steelworks. This post was normally reserved for retired priests, being considered an easy job. Here, Father Jerzy would be able to rest more and to have the special diet and medications he needed.

Despite threats from the Kremlin, the Polish workers stood united and Solidarity was born. By the end of August 1980, the Polish people had won the unprecedented right to free trade unions and some other key reforms. The steelworkers wanted to celebrate Mass, and although other clergymen had refused their request to come to the plant, Father Jerzy heard their call and came. The first priest ever to enter the factory, the frail young Father Popieluszko said Mass at a makeshift altar for a group of tired men in grimy overalls, who knelt on the concrete to receive communion. As he entered to thunderous applause, he passed a sea of faces smiling and crying at the same time.

A peasant's son, Jerzy Popieluszko knew work and workers. His straight talk and his cheerful dedication impressed the workers, who listened as he spoke about overcoming evil with good. He reminded them, "We are created to be free, free as God's children." He calmed the hotheads and blessed the long line of men. Soon the men realized that this young priest would stay by them, and affectionately began to call him Jurek. At last, when the thousands of workers ended their historic strike, Father made a vow, "to stay among my workers as long as I can." In honoring this vow, he became the most popular priest in Poland, and the spiritual patron of the Solidarity movement — he vowed to stay and stay he did. After his death, pressure was brought by the authorities to bury the martyr priest in his home village, far away from Warsaw and the workers. This was done in hopes that the priest, as a symbol of freedom, would be forgotten sooner. Father Jerzy's own mother, along with a delegation of workers, went to the Polish primate, Cardinal Glemp, and on her knees she pleaded, "The shepherd should be where his lambs are." In the face of this heartfelt plea, burial at St. Stanislaw's was allowed.

Father Jerzy loved the steel mill and its workers. "My whole strategy is the dignity of human labor and the struggle with hatred," he said. He wanted the workers to recover the spirit of pride, honor, and dignity that the state had denied them. During the fifteen months of Solidarity's partial freedom, the secret police constantly shadowed the dangerous little priest. In October of 1981, Father Jerzy went to America for the funeral of a relative. American friends asked him to stay and declare political asylum. He replied, "My people will be in danger if I abandon them. They need me and I need them."

When the Solidarity movement was forced underground, Father Jerzy accepted it as a challenge to be with his people "in their days of trial." After martial law was imposed, he became busier than ever, attending to the temporal as well as the spiritual needs of his parishioners. From the rectory, he ran the center that distributed medical aid to all of Warsaw, and people came from far away to give him aid for the victims of repression. One woman asked him, "How can I take help from the church? My husband and I aren't even believers." "That doesn't matter now. We are divided only into people who need and people who can give," the courageous priest answered. Commenting on Father Jerzy's constant concern for others, Solidarity leader Lech Walesa said, "He really didn't care about himself." In spite of his poor health, Father Jerzy visited the sick and brought aid and cheer, at all hours, to his parishioners. Mounting stress and pressure began to take its toll on him. After one service he surprised the congregation by asking for their help: "Now I need your prayers."

Martial law silenced millions of Poles, but Father Jerzy would not remain silent. The political trials of the workers inspired him to begin a monthly Mass for the Homeland, dedicated to all of the victims of the regime's harsh policies.

This Mass grew into a national event, and Poles came from all parts of the country to attend. He said, "[You] will rise again after any humiliation, for you have knelt only before God." Constantly he repeated, "Overcome evil with good." When he preached against fear, it enraged the government for it threatened the state's most effective weapon.

Father Jerzy received threatening letters and death warnings. After one particularly vicious threat, he told a friend, "The most they can do is kill me." In December of 1982, a first attempt on his life was made. He had just gone to bed when his doorbell rang. He was too tired to get up, and in a few moments, a bomb crashed into the next room, exploding where he would have been standing had he gone to answer the door. The

Father Jerzy at Mass

state media began propaganda attacks against Father Jerzy. In December of l983, he was arrested on trumped-up charges and taken to jail briefly. He was released after Church-State negotiations. The incident did seem to create a problem, with Cardinal Glemp, and there were rumors that he was preparing to transfer Father Jerzy. At this time, two messages arrived from Rome. The pope sent Father Jerzy a rosary with his blessing. Father kept this rosary until the end. He was buried with the rosary wrapped around his battered hands. The pope also sent a message to the cardinal: "Defend Father Popieluszko — or they'll start finding weapons in the desk of every second bishop."

Some students had given Father Jerzy a little black puppy. With his customary quiet sense of humor, he named the little dog "Tajniak," Polish for "secret agent," because he said the puppy followed him everywhere.

Death threats by phone and letter began to increase and grow more alarming. In the first half of 1984, Father Jerzy was called to thirteen interrogations, staged to terrorize him. A group of supporters always accompanied him to secret-police headquarters, waiting outside, chanting hymns and prayers until the end of the ordeal. Inside, with his hands behind his back, Father Jerzy would finger the rosary the pope had sent him. His interrogators' ruthless questions were answered by his reciting the rosary, again and again. At last the furious authorities would release him.

He kept a map of Poland on the wall of his apartment marked with the prison camps where Solidarity activists were interred. When a visitor asked if he weren't afraid to have the map, Father Jerzy replied that because they had jailed the activists, it was the government that was afraid. At a large Mass in August of 1984, Father Jerzy said, "We must fear only the betrayal of Christ for a few silver coins of empty peace." He predicted that Solidarity would endure because of "the hunger in the heart of man, the hunger for love, justice and truth."

Father Jerzy remained determined to preach. He told an Italian journalist, "If I shut up, it means they have won. To speak out is precisely my job."

Shortly before his death, Father Jerzy made a trip home to his native village. He told the parish priest there that he was expecting the worst, but that a man "should fear only betrayal." His mother watched him as he walked the farm and fields and lingered in each room of the small house. She felt as if he were saying good-bye.

On October 13,1984, another attempt was made on Father Jerzy's life. Thanks to the quick reflexes of his driver-bodyguard, Waldemar Chrostowski, the car in which they were riding was able to elude the secret-police ambush. On Friday, October 19, Father Jerzy spoke at a special Mass for the Working People. Secret agents waited outside. Father Jerzy was very ill and barely able to speak. Parishioners begged him to spend the night but he decided to return because he was supposed to say the first Mass at St. Stanislaw's in the morning. He and Chrostowski left Bydgoszcz to return to Warsaw. About a half hour from Bydgoszcz, the secret police overtook the priest and his driver. The driver was held at gunpoint, while the kidnappers beat the priest with fists and clubs. Unconscious, the frail priest was bound, gagged, and thrown into the trunk. An ex-commando, Chrostowski was able to hurl himself out of the car in a desperate escape. He made it to a nearby workers' hostel and quickly raised an alarm. With his escape, news of the abduction quickly spread across Poland. The nation's churches were filled with people for twenty-four-hour vigils, and the nation's workers prayed and hoped for the life of their priest.

The last Sunday of October, a record fifty-thousand people engulfed St. Stanislaw's for an outdoor Mass for the Homeland. While listening to a tape of his last sermon, they hoped against hope to see Father Jerzy again.

At last, the fateful word came. The state held an unusual trial, and, as the assassins had feared, they were thrown to the lions to protect their higher-ups. In 1987, Grzegorz Piotrowski was convicted for the killing of Popieluszko and sentenced to a twenty-five-year term. Also sentenced was Colonel Adam Pietruszka, Piotrowski's superior, convicted of instigating the murder, and Lieutenants Leszek Pekala and Waldemar Chmielewski. Within three years, however, the Polish Supreme Court, citing "humanitarian reasons" greatly reduced the sentences of all four. Piotrowski's sentence was lowered to fifteen years; the sentence of one of the lieutenants was reduced to four and a half years. Piotrowski was released from prison intending to work for an anti-clerical newspaper. He said he did not regret killing Father Jerzy.

On the day of Father Jerzy's funeral, half a million people filled the streets leading up to the parish church of St. Stanislaw. The country stood united again around its heroic martyr priest. Overnight the church became a mighty national shrine. Since his death, new converts have flooded into Polish churches. Many who had lapsed have returned. His murder has given courage to many priests, and his example is inspiring vocations to the priesthood. Although there were hopes that the trial of Father Jerzy's killers might mark a change in policy, the persecution, torture and unexplained deaths of priests continued throughout the 1980s. In August of 1984, the stonemason who built Father Jerzy's tomb was kidnapped and pushed out of a moving truck when he refused to give details of the vault to his unknown assailants.

In 1987, then Vice President George Bush, on a trip to Poland, laid a wreath on Father Jerzy's grave, saying, "His soul is in the hands of God, but his spirit lives on in the people of Poland and the world."

In the summer of 1999, 700,000 people flocked to Bydgoszcz to attend one of the most emotional Masses of the pope's trip to Poland: a Mass in honor of the martyrs of all times. Special mention was made of Father Jerzy Popieluszko. "The world needs people who have the courage to love and do not retreat before any sacrifice, in the hope that one day it will bear abundant fruit." His voice breaking with emotion, the aging pontiff said, "Indeed, rejoice and be glad, all you who are ready to suffer for righteousness' sake, for your reward is great in heaven!"

Father Jerzy's cause has been opened in Rome. ✞

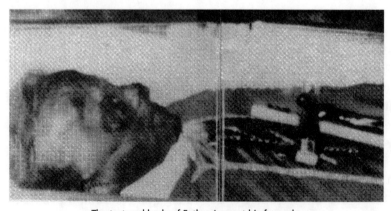

The tortured body of Father Jerzy at his funeral

16

John Ziang-bai Nien
China, 1922-1959

The Fragrant Cypress

The elderly Chinese farmer trudged slowly and wearily along the mountainous path of Chun Ta Ping. The warmth of his breath made white puffs in the frigid air. The peaceful blanket of snow covering the ground was beautiful, but the beauty could not stem the rumbles of hunger inside the farmer's stomach. This winter of 1960 was a winter of hunger; for two years a terrible famine had ravaged all of China. Hunan was hard hit and many were starving to death. The government, the so-called People's Commune, had not helped.

Ahead of him, the farmer noticed what he first took for a bundle of rags alongside the road. Perhaps he would find something of value there. On approaching, however, he realized it was the dead body of the prisoner who had been sent there by the police in Yuanling the year before. When the police left him in the custody of the village, they told the people he was a reactionary, an American spy, an enemy of the Communist party and a great danger to the rule of the Chinese government. There was no food to feed the prisoners, so the villagers were to guard against his escape and were told they should have no pity for him. The prisoner's life in Chun Ta Ping had been difficult. He had no home nor any land to grow food. He found a natural shelter in a cave to shield himself from the cold of winter and the heat of summer, and he was reduced to begging, here and there, for food. Some kind-hearted local people gave him their leftover food during his first year, but when the famine got worse, everyone in the area was suffering from hunger and nobody had any extra to give him. At last he had died of starvation, here along this mountain road, cold and alone.

Looking about to make certain there was no one to notice him, the kind old farmer rolled the body in a light quilt and dug a shallow hole to bury it. As he worked, the farmer began to notice a sweet odor as of fragrant flowers. Deep in the dead of winter, no blossoms were to be found on this frozen mountain countryside. And yet the odor was powerful. At last the elderly Chinese realized that the smell was coming from the body of the reactionary who, by all the signs, had been dead for several days. Confused, the old man kept silent about the strange sweet smell. In fact, he told no one he had buried the revolutionary there by the side of the road.

A few years later, Joseph Chu came to the little village as a cadre, part of a group sent to propagate socialism in the area, and to re-arrest the prisoner. Joseph had been working as a clerk in the department store of Chenki and the government, believing him to be from a very poor family, thought he would naturally be in favor of the Communist regime. On his trips through the countryside to propagate the tenants of Mao Zedong, Joseph was especially kind to the poor peasants he met and easily earned their trust. The old Chinese farmer showed his trust in the young cadre by telling him of the burial of the reactionary and of the strange odor he had noticed. Instinctively the farmer felt that his secret was safe with this kind young man. He had no way of knowing that the cadre was a Catholic. He would have been shocked to find that Joseph knew this dead reactionary who, in life, was the Catholic priest, Father John Nien. The young cadre pondered the farmer's strange tale about the fragrant odor of the body. How strange, he thought, that the priest's Chinese name, Ziang-bai, means "fragrant cypress."

Nien Ziang-bai was born May 2, 1922 in Kiaokiang, Supu Hsien in western Hunan province. His pagan father died when he was just a child and his mother entered a Buddhist convent and became a nun. Young Ziang-bai, her only child, stayed with her as a little Buddhist monk.

One day a great storm arose and Mr. Hu, a catechist of the Shupu Mission who was traveling in the area, stopped at the convent for refuge. Mrs. Nien offered him hospitality and shelter. The two began to discuss their different religious beliefs. Mrs. Nien became so interested in Catholicism that she asked Mr. Hu for some books that would tell more about it, and invited him to come back for further discussions. With his help, the Buddhist nun became a convert to the Catholic faith. She and her young son were baptized June 30, 1934. She took the Christian name of Monica, and the boy was named John after the beloved Apostle. At confirmation on May 30, 1937, John added the name Felix.

As a child, John showed extraordinary piety and devotion. He played around the mission compound of Paotsing and became friendly with the Passionist priests there. By the time he was thirteen, his mother had become a catechist herself. She had dedicated her son to the Church in 1935 and with the recommendation of Father Raphael Vance, one of the sturdy Passionist missionaries of the area, he entered St. Joseph's minor seminary in Yuanling.

John is remembered by his classmates as being prayerful, cheerful and outstanding in sports. Of all the seminarians, he was the best in swimming and basketball. In the summer of 1940, John and his friend Bernard Chu accompanied their rector, Father Reginald Arliss, for a vacation at Wusu, a small mountain village close to a river. After daily Mass, the boys studied for several hours and then devoted the remainder of the day to recreation. Each afternoon they went swimming or fishing. John loved to dive into the river from a high cliff and enjoyed the dangerous rapids in the river without any fear.

A former roommate, tells that John knelt by his bed each evening, saying three Hail Marys in addition to the regular prayers. He had learned this practice from his devout mother. The same man relates that John was very diligent in his study of Latin and that he often used to find him in a corner of the schoolyard reading aloud from a book called *Thesaurus*, a collection of Aesop's Fables in Latin.

The seminary was a well-built old Chinese house set in a yard about as large as a tennis court, surrounded by high walls and protected by a large barred gate. The seminarians slept on the second floor of the house; the ground floor housed the classrooms, a small chapel and the rooms and offices of Fathers Leo Berard and Michael Campbell. These two Passionists along with two Chinese gentlemen constituted the faculty of the seminary. In the interior of the house the young seminarians studied peacefully, oblivious to the bustling street outside filled with soldiers, merchants, coolies, peddlers, beggars and rich men going to and fro bent on the things of this life. The seminary was just a few doors from the mission, and on Sunday evenings the bishop, the missionaries and the semi-

The young seminarian

PHOTOS (EXCEPT PAGES 171 AND 177)
COURTESY OF PASSIONIST ARCHIVES

narians would enter the little chapel, and kneel in the stalls on either side to receive Benediction accompanied by the sweet sound of the seminarians chanting in faultless Gregorian, their youthful voices rising in the beautiful strains of "Tantum Ergo." The missionaries were filled with great pride. One of the main jobs of a missionary is to teach the faith so effectively that a native priesthood evolves. The little seminary of Yuanling held great promise of providing Chinese priests for their people.

One night in the spring of 1938, the seminarians were rudely awaked by the cries of "Ch'i Hoa! Ch'i Hoa!" A fire had broken out and a fire in the heart of a city in China with nothing at hand but the most primitive equipment to fight the peril, the water supply remote and made available only by an organized link of water-porters is a dreaded terror. If it were not controlled, much of the city could be burned, as the houses were linked together by flimsy wooden walls. By the grace of God and the loyalty of the Christians who rushed to help, the fire was contained and only a single classroom was destroyed.

When the war with Japan broke out, the seminarians left their little haven to make room for the poor, homeless refugees and the wounded soldiers. They moved into the mission proper, occupying rooms once reserved for visiting priests. They heard Mass in the Bishop's tiny chapel and held their classes in an old wooden storehouse, a rice bin.

In 1941, John began higher seminary studies in Hankow, but transferred to the major seminary in Kunming when the situation in Hunan became more disturbed. The seminary was run by the French Sulpician Fathers. Here he began his studies in philosophy. Kunming was an important military base for the Guomingdang government and as such was the frequent target for bombing by the Japanese Air Force. Bishop Cuthbert O'Gara, C.P., took John and another seminarian with him to India, intending to have them continue their studies there, but no suitable solution could be found so they continued on with him to America.

John Nien Tao Teh, arrived in San Francisco aboard the U.S.S. West Point on September 14, 1943, to begin his seminary studies at St. Mary's Seminary in Baltimore, Maryland. The Sulpicians who run the seminary provided him with a scholarship for tuition, and the Passionists met his other expenses. John's seminary records show two dates of birth for him: July 9, 1921, and May 2, 1922. The confusion stems from the Chinese practice of counting the probable date of conception as the date of birth. The seminarians wore cassocks and a minor mistake was made on John's. A letter from the seminary to the uniform company apologized for omitting his height on the order form. He was five feet, five inches and his cassock was made for a man five feet, four-and-one-half inches. His wearing of a "floodwater" cassock apparently didn't matter, however, as he seems to have gotten along very well with his seminary peers in spite of this. A later alumni newsletter points out his cheerful disposition, his quiet smile, and his pleasant cordiality, which had gained for him the deserved admiration of all his fellow seminarians. Yes, he got along well with his peers — almost too well, in fact.

Although he had done well in all of his class work and studies, a somewhat scolding letter from his bishop in August of 1945 informs him that the Sulpician faculty members had withheld their recommendation for his advancement to orders because of his deportment (conduct) in chapel and at spiritual exercises. The bishop continues, "had this condition been reversed and you were being held up by reason of studies, I would have considered the matter much less seriously than your present status. The most important factor in your seminary course is the progress you make in spiritual development — everything else is secondary. That you might receive the best possible training is the reason why I took you to America. If you fail in this regard, your seminary course will be a complete failure." Bishop Cuthbert continues his lecture-by-letter, and closes with the recommendation that John cultivate a tender and constant devotion to our Blessed Lady. "She will help you to form the image of Our Divine Lord in your soul."

In a fatherly letter written from China in February 1947, Bishop Cuthbert wishes John a blessed Easter and tells him, "Above all, personal holiness is necessary if you are to be a successful teacher. You must first show in your own life that you are the convinced follower of the Divine Master. Hence you must be humble, docile, mortified and possessed with a burning zeal for souls. Pagans will ask, not whether you are a learned man, but whether you are a virtuous one. Our Catholic people will want to know whether you are a good priest — one who is ready at all times to sacrifice himself for them."

Apparently the young man took both the lecture and the advice to heart, as later events were to prove. In a letter of April 1947, Bishop

Cuthbert congratulates him on his completion of the courses in theology and tells him of the arrangements made for his return to China. In the same letter, he also informs the young seminarian that he himself will soon be installed as the first Bishop of Yuanling and reminds John to thank the Sulpician fathers for the gift of his scholarship.

A letter to Bishop Cuthbert from Very Reverend James A. Laubacher, the rector of St. Mary's Seminary in June of 1947 reads, in part, "I thought it would be safer to have Mr. John Nien carry with him to you his various canonical documents. You will find enclosed a certificate of the last orders received by John, a testimonial letter from the Archdioceses of Baltimore and Washington covering the period of his stay here at the Seminary and a Rector's letter certifying that he has completed his course, taken the canonical examination for priesthood and has given satisfaction in piety and character. I might mention also that John successfully passed his examination for the Licentiate of Theology and was given his S.T.L. degree cum laude. . . . John received tonsure on June 26, 1946, porter and lector on June 27, and exorcist and acolyte on June 27." Without doubt Bishop Cuthbert would have been happy at hearing of John's cum laude scholastic achievement, but even more delighted at the "piety and character" references.

John with a young friend

In July, John wrote to Bishop Cuthbert telling him, "This profound teaching, which though I have heard or read [it] myself, did not attract my attention before, or if it did it certainly did not remain long in my mind, now sounds like a thunderclap, rushing in my brain, and deep down to the bottom of my heart. "The Priest is the Alter Christus" is still sounding within my mind. I am listening to it and I will continue to listen forever."

On John's return to China, following missionary custom, he

lived for a full year in the bishop's house before ordination. Sister Carita Pendergast, S.C., says that she remembers him as being tall for a Chinese, slender and quick in movement. "He was a delight to us sisters for he had become Americanized enough to remind us of our brothers and nephews at home. But the bishop was heard to exclaim, 'I sent Johnny Nien to the States for a good clerical education. I expected to get in return a polished Chinese gentleman. Instead, I now have an American college boy!'" Sister Carita laughs as she recalls a tall, thin Chinese rushing about Yuanling, clad in the customary Chinese gown, topped by a brown leather jacket adorned with a white silk scarf and with a paperback book poking out of a side pocket.

In a letter he wrote to an American friend, the sister of one of the Passionists, John tells her, "I am doing very well at present. I am staying in Yuanling since I came back to China. I don't have much to do, except a little studying, playing with the children, and visiting sick in the hospital nearby." In another letter to a priest friend he writes, "The conditions in China are very bad. The high cost of living, the difficulties in communication and the poverty of the people make everything uncomfortable. Christmas in China is also very dull. On the feast day the Christians come to church to attend the solemn high Mass and receive holy Communion. That's all for Christmas. There is no Christmas shopping, no cards and no presents. The Christmas decorations and celebrations are unknown to the people here. Yet they enjoy their Christmas as much as any one in the United States. For this reason I can have more chances to write letters to my friend instead of cards."

John was ordained to the priesthood on the Feast of Christ the King, October 31, 1948, in the Cathedral of St. Augustine, Tuanling. The Passionist Provincial, Gabriel Gorman was making a visitation of the China Missions and assisted at the ordination ceremony. Thus, John became the first native priest of the Yuanling Diocese.

On October 10, John sent out invitations to his ordination. Not the fancy printed ones as are sometimes made, but a touching letter to his American friends. He wrote, "Properly speaking, this is not an invitation card at all; it is a home-made card, the one I have made myself, to invite you all, my friends, to come to my Ordination to the Priesthood on Oct. 31, 1948. It seems funny to send invitations abroad to the friends who are not able to come, but in reality, it isn't so. Though your bodies can not come, your hearts can. I invite you to be present at my Ordination in spirit and heart, praising God, Jesus Christ Our Lord, with me, for the great Thing He is about to bestow on me. Therefore, I ask of you all, my dear friends, to remember me in your prayers that I may be worthy of the Holy Priesthood I am going to receive."

A week before the big day, John received notice that Father Lardner, the Sulpician provincial had died. He wrote a tender note of sympathy, saying, "I feel very sad when I heard it, for before my leaving for China he had told me, as I can remember, that he was going to wait for my first priestly blessing. But now, he has left before the time comes. Not only I feel sad on account of my personal friendship with him, but also, I am very sympathetic with all the Sulpicians to have lost a great, kind, and a very capable Father. I assure you, Father, though my body can not be present at the last rites for him, my heart is always there, and I will remember him in my Masses, if by the Providence of God, I shall get up to the Altar."

One of the Passionists wrote home about the preparations for the big event. "About one half of the missionary personnel will be present. Our neighboring and parental diocese of Changteh will have several priests in the sanctuary for the event. The ceremony will be carried out as solemnly as we can manage here in the interior. It is bound to make a very deep impression on our converts and likewise upon any pagan guests who may attend. The following day, All Saints, the newly ordained will be the celebrant at a Solemn Mass . . . with all the priests attending. The girls choir of the Sisters High School will furnish the music. And there will be the customary festivities in the refectory." A group of the sisters came from their outlying mission areas and John and his mother were breakfast guests in the convent. Afterwards, the visiting sisters left in a weapons carrier stacked with mission supplies.

The local Christians were deeply impressed by the solemn ordination ceremony.

John wrote to a friend, "As for my ordination, the day was grand. People here have never seen an ordination before, in fact, there wasn't any, since I am the first one ordained here. They have made a great noise about. Firecrackers were all over. Personally I prefer spiritual things to all these. I have celebrated my first Solemn Mass the day after All Saints Day, during which I have remembered all my friends all over the world. One week later, I had my appointment as an assistant here in Yuanling." He concludes this letter by saying: "Here, we are all right. Anxiety of course is always there in the time and conditions like this. We are under fear of being run over by Communists, which are not far off at present. If they take Naking and if the government falls, the Church will suffer a great loss."

A number of John's first priestly blessings were sent to friends in

Father at a wedding in China; he is at back, middle
PHOTO COURTESY OF JOHANNES ZHENG

America. One, to the rector and the Sulpicians at St. Mary's seminary, was sent by cablegram. The vibrance and enthusiasm of the young priest shines in his letters which all conclude with the request for prayers.

As the first native priest of the Yuanling diocese, John did missionary work, visiting poor families and comforting the sick and dying at the mission hospital. He was a strong helper for his bishop and a valuable co-worker with the Passionist Fathers. His friend Father Marcellus White, C.P., remembers that Father Nien was particularly well informed of the problems. Father White says, "he was a tremendous assistance to us American Fathers because of the disturbed conditions."

A beautiful statue of Our Lady of Fátima was donated for the shrine planned for her in the humble Yuanling cathedral, but Bishop Cuthbert had to write and ask that it be held in America because of the unrest in the diocese and the possibility that they would have to move. He says, "she alone can protect us against this tide of Communism; we surely cannot put much confidence in the present tottering regime."

In October of 1949, the Chinese Communists took over the government and the National Government of China moved to Taiwan.

Immediately, the Communists began to persecute the Christian churches.

Foreign missionaries were placed under house arrest, forbidden to contact their flocks. The only exceptions were the two native priests, Fathers John Nien and Bede Zhang (who was awaiting ordination). They were still allowed to move about the area, ministering as they could to their little flock. Father White says that Father Nien was constantly questioned about the activities of the Catholic community of Yuanling. Matters became more critical as the Korean War developed with the invasion of South Korea in which the American government was involved. Though it was distant from the war front, Yuanling was a center of activities. Father Nien was questioned again and again.

In December of 1949, Father Nien wrote to the St. Mary's alumni newsletter The Voice, telling them that he would never forget them and his "old home" especially now that "I am faced with the new 'Red' ungodly faces. Do not be surprised, fellows, since we have been 'liberated" (a special term!) two months ago and are under the 'Red Rule.' All priests are at their posts. The church functions are still unhindered; several mission houses have been 'borrowed' (a polite word). There were plenty troubles in the beginning; since then, things became better. As for the future, God will take care of it. May I ask of you all, Fellows, prayers. We need lots of prayers in a crisis like this. So would you be kind to us 'Reds' and convert us 'Reds' to Christ through your prayers? So long!"

In April of 1950, Father Nien went on a missionary journey to Luki, Soli and Fengwang. On a sick call, he was arrested briefly, but by September he was back in Yuanling where he served as deacon at the ordination of Bede Zhang, the second native priest of the diocese.

In a letter of July 4, 1950, Father Nien wrote to the Sulpician provincial in Maryland, "The Godless faces are everywhere, but under God's protection we struggle and continue our works. Things here in general are fine except a fair part of most of the missions of this diocese are taken by the Communists. They are living with us right in the same compound! The people fare worse than the mission. In general the iron rule in the larger cities is more lenient than in the small towns; Yuanling is much worse than the bigger cities of Hunan down river but at the same time it is much better than the [other] part of Western Hunan. I have been sent out to the various missions. . . . I have traveled some parts of Western Hunan and saw several towns. The people in these towns suffered a lot. In fact, they are much worse than Yuanling. The rich become poor and the poor starve, although the new party says and propagates that they are the people's party, especially for the working class and for the poor. Just a few instances will show what I mean. Formerly the water carriers for instance made their living by carrying water for the better ones, now the better ones are doing it themselves and the water carriers have to starve. The mission has her trouble, too. Although the Communists have taken part of all the missions, they still want more of it. Sometimes they threat [sic] to take all. A month ago I came to Feng Wong, a far away mission. On my arrival I found a few soldiers living in the priest's quarters. A few days later the local authority came to me to order me to evacuate the whole mission for them. We have carried the arguing for three days. They have put up a great threat, and we on our part were very stubborn. Finally they gave up and use the part they already have. Do not think that this is of our merit, for at that time, we have been praying very hard and have offered a novena to the Little Flower for protection." He continues, "we don't care what will happen to our lives; when we have one free day we will stick to that day. Of course, prayers can never be omitted. So far we are still somewhat unhindered in the mission work. The foreign fathers have difficulties with the new party to go round the mission. They are more or less confined to the cities or towns proper. The Christians on the contrary are much better disposed than before; they become more fervent and go to the Sacrament more often." He also mentions that the pagans even have a better attitude towards them and although there are no signs of conversion they do not have any enemies among the people.

In October of 1950, Father Nien paid a visit to the mission area of Father Reginald Arliss. Father Arliss said, "It was the first time our people had seen a Chinese priest. They were delighted. On the ninth he went to Paotsing to spend a week with Father Harold who had not seen a fellow priest since February."

John Nien with his Passionist friends

Some time in November or December of 1950, Father Nien was arrested at Ankiang and held in parts unknown. At his disappearance, his mother Monica went to the bishop. She said she would get a peddler's pack and hawk her wares wherever it was rumored that there were prisoners until she found her son. Monica was an old-fashioned Chinese woman whose feet had been bound as a child. This practice, which was later forbidden by the government, resulted in the women having deformed feet and made it very painful to walk. Just like St. Monica, this humble Chinese Monica suffered terribly for her son. Posing as a fruit peddler, she hobbled from town to town for nearly seven months. She was outside Ta-Kiang-K'ou prison, near Supu, when the prisoners were led out for roadwork. She looked up to find herself staring into her son's eyes. He was ill clad and tied hand and foot to other prisoners. Neither mother nor son gave any sign of recognition, but Monica hastened back to Yuanling to inform the Bishop.

Bishop Cuthbert and his Vicar General were arrested on June 30, 1951, and thrown into jail without any trial or determinate sentence. Throughout that year and early in 1952, the Communist government arrested four other missionaries. By March, six of them were detained in the same prison and Father Nien was transferred to a cell adjacent to Father White. For nearly a year, Father White was never given a chance to speak to Father Nien in any way. After the armistice was signed in July of 1953, some of the Passionists were released, but Father White and Father Justin Garvey were held until November 1955.

For six years Father Nien was forbidden to have any visitors and, in spite of threats, he consistently refused to speak against the bishop or the mission priests.

Conditions in the jail were miserable. The Passionists dubbed it "Little Alcatraz." It was filthy. Prisoners were not allowed to bathe or wash their clothes and infestations of lice and fleas added to the discomfort.

For some years, Father Anthony Maloney, C.P., edited a newsletter called Hunan News, made up of letters he had received in Hong Kong from the Passionists in Hunan. The original letters were written in a sort of code that Father Maloney decoded. The newsletter was then sent out to Passionists and friends of the Passionists in the United States. There are a number of mentions of Father Nien in the newsletter.

In September of 1951 it was rumored that Father John was being held in the Chinkiang jail. Later that month he was in the local jail with the bishop. At the end of the year he was thinner but undaunted. In April, the Passionists were happy to receive a note from Father Nien which asked for some clothing and confirmed that he was back in Yuanling. In October, Father Bede Chang met a man who was in jail with Father Nien for almost a year and who helped him sweep the jail floors. He said Father Nien was doing janitor work but not in the part of the jail where the bishop and the other fathers were imprisoned. In spite of all the Communists tried, he remained firm in his refusal to give in. In December, Father Lombard wrote, "Last night during Benediction a cop walks right up to the altar and yells at Father Raphael, 'Here's a note.' The few in church and myself, the organist, thought it was a summons to go to Changsha. Instead it was good news! A handwritten Chinese note from Father Nien asking for a cotton padded suit and that his food bill since August 12th be paid. You know, you have to pay your board bill in the jails here. We found a suit of Father Bede's and Father Raphael will take the cash up tonight. Does it mean that Father Nien will be freed or is he being sent elsewhere? It is the usual custom to pay food bills when one is leaving jail. We are hoping this is the case for Father Nien."

By February of 1953, only ten Passionists remained in Hunan, the bishop and four priests held incommunicado in the Yuanling jail. The other five were at their missions. Father John by this time had been jailed since October 1950. In April the bishop and his two confreres were released from jail and expelled from the country. There was only speculation, no solid knowledge, about Father Nien. Father Lombard wrote, "Only those who have lived under 'liberation' can appreciate how 'cordial, pleasant and cooperative' the Comrades are! The Sphinx is a gossip compared to them. Even the super-efficient bamboo wireless has developed a short circuit. All we can do is pray for those in custody and hope for the best."

In September, Father Mullin got good news — a note from father Nien from the Yuanling jail, asking for some clothes. "We sent them down pronto, with Father Bede doing the honors. The greatest surprise was that Father Nien was brought to the jail entry-way where Father Bede could see him and speak a few words in the presence of the guard. We sent him a clean 'pu-kai' (cotton quilt). You should have seen the ragged thing brought back in exchange! It is still out in the sun drying before we burn it. It was full of fleas, too, so much so that Father Bede stripped immediately after carrying it home and gave his own clothes a few days sun bath." The turnkey (guard) told Father Bede that Father Nien was "very, very stubborn."

On September 15, 1953, Father Lombard wrote, "A note from Father Nien to Father Bede has just been delivered: 'my pu-kai (quilt) is almost rotting and falling apart and I have only a few clothes to cover my bony body; please send to the address given as soon as possible. If you can find a piece of soap, send it.' Father Bede cried as he read the note to us and perhaps we will too, as to just think of what he is in is enough for a hundred nightmares. This is the first note from him in a year." The following day, he wrote again. "Last evening Father Bede carried up to the jail a pu-kai, clothes, towels and a bar of soap. Asked by the guard at the gate what he wanted Father Bede showed Father Nien's note and was told, 'wait a while.' Then, in the distance he spied Father Nien heading towards him and instead of passing by, as Father Bede expected, came right up to him, the guard saying 'Since you two are from the same county you may talk to him about his mother and his home, but nothing else.' So, with twenty others crowded around listening, he gave him some news of home with no chance to say anything else. After a few minutes the guard ordered Father Nien, 'Look at the clothes and take what you need.' The exchange of pu-kais was made but the guard said, pointing to the towels and underclothes, 'You can't have all those fine and fancy things as your mind is still unwashed.' Turning to Father Bede the guard added 'If this Nien would only change his thoughts he could go out into the free air of this paradise.' So Father Bede had to bring back much of the stuff but at least Father Nien received some clean clothing; all he had on was a dirty, ragged pair of shorts. He told Father Bede that he had been in the Yuanling jail all of the time except the first few weeks when he was in the Chinkiang jail. Father Bede says he looks about the same though his head is shaven and his eyes look strained as he has no glasses; he is very brown but no thinner than before. He talked in the same direct, incisive manner so Father Bede concluded that his mind is still O.K. As the two of them stooped over during the exchange of pukais Father Bede whispered 'We are praying for you' and he whispered back, 'Thank everyone.' Father Bede was then politely ushered out as 'the government now has the new doctrine of moderation' — so said the guard. You may imagine how Father Bede rushed home to tell all."

Father John Nien
PHOTO COURTESY OF JOHANNES ZHENG

The son of one of the Catholics was allowed out of jail for a "vacation" and he brought the news that Father Nien had to attend indoctrination for a full year but when the course ended in July he did not receive a passing mark so is now in the work gang. Father Raphael paid his board bill for the year of jail and indoctrination. Now, though still in jail, he is working, so his board will be free. In November they took him another bar of soap and a cotton-padded coat. When the guard asked Father Bede why he was so solicitous of the prisoner, Father Bede was clever enough to say it was because they were from the same county and had been schoolmates, rather than saying it was because he was a priest. The jailer remarked that Father Nien was a good worker but that his mind remained as unwashed as ever.

In December when Father Bede took the customary bar of soap, he saw Father Nien washing the vegetables near the gate and was allowed to speak with him a few moments. He was also allowed to take a pair of leather shoes to Father Nien to wear when it rains.

In March of 1954 Father Lombard wrote ". . . we do have another chapter in the mystery of Father Nien. When Father Bede went up with his monthly bar of soap the prisoners had been moved."

By September 1954 there were only two Passionists left in Red China, and both were in jail. There was no one left to send letters to be translated and printed in the Hunan News.

A final edition of Hunan News was printed in January 1956. At that time the two jailed Passionists had finally been released and sent home. Father Nien was still in jail but was apparently released some time during the year. We do not know full details of this. During his brief period of freedom, he worked for a time with Fathers Bede Chang and Gabriel Chang, a young Augustinian, before he was rearrested.

In 1957, all Hunan clergymen were forced to take a course in "correct political thinking," and told that future Chinese bishops would be elected, instead of being promoted by the Holy See. In 1958, they were again gathered and told to sign a written declaration making a complete break with the Holy See. Father John, forced to attend, refused to sign the betrayal. On his return to Yuanling, the local government launched a "popular movement" against him, and one of the instigators slapped him in the face publicly. Father John responded mildly, "You can treat me as you please." He was then immediately re-arrested and "disappeared"; none of his friends knew where he was jailed. At his sentencing, he was referred to as a "stubborn running dog of the American imperialists," and a "diehard counter-revolutionary."

Eventually, friends discovered that he had been exiled to a lonely mountain village, placed in the custody of the villagers as a criminal. Although assured of freedom if he denied the Holy See, Father John preferred the difficult exile, which led to his death of hunger and cold in the bitter winter of 1960.

In a 1984 letter written by a Chinese Catholic to one of the Sisters of Charity, the girl who has signed herself only as "your little sister" wrote, "Father Nien stopped living in about 1959. He is the pride and glory of Father William and his brethren and of the whole diocese. If we are not mistaken, we even think that you may start working at his beatification right away."

A 1985 letter from one of the Chinese Augustinians to Father Marcellus White reads, "Father Nien is for sure your pride and glory. Because of his stubborn defending [of] the relation with the Holy See in summer of 1958 he was condemned for a second time to hard labor far away from Yuanling. And the next year (1959) we stopped hearing anything of him."

The final chapter of Father Nien's life, his death, was not made known until it was secretly carried out of China in the mid 1980s. It was written by his former classmate, Bernard Chu, the brother of the young cadre who heard the story from the old farmer who had buried the young priest who so obviously died in the odor of sanctity.[1] ✢

Notes

1. The Passionist, Augustinian, and Franciscan Fathers and five religious communities of Sisters worked in the mission territory of Hunan from 1922-1956. Their

area embraced fifteen thousand square miles and had a population of five million. Hunan was one of the most backward provinces of China and the missionaries faced famine and pestilence as well as war. Smallpox, typhoid and cholera added to the toll of misery. Three of the Passionists were murdered by bandits, and other priests and sisters died of disease. At no time was there a sustained period of peace and prosperity. When the last of the missionaries were expelled from China because of the vengeful fury of the Red hatred of the church, they must have felt a sense of failure as well as sadness. By the mid 1980s, the government began to loosen their restriction against contact with foreigners and mail from former students and friends reached the United States. Some of the religious were allowed to visit China in the late 1980s and early 1990s. A small but dedicated group of Catholics in the area have weathered the storms of persecution and remain strong in their faith, proving that the missionaries' blood, sweat and tears have not been in vain. The seed has been well planted. Today, Christians in China still face persecution, living daily in uncertainty. For that reason, some of the Chinese names in the story of Father Nien have been changed.

17

Luis Espinal Camp, S.J.
Bolivia, 1932-1980

Bolivian Voice of Those Who Have No Voice

Oh Lord of Silence, we offer you our loneliness,
Our absolute loneliness,
For even now you are not absent.
We don't have anything more intimate,
And more ours.
We offer you our finiteness, the roots of our being;
We offer you the anxiety of being human.

Father Luis Espinal, S.J., offered God his finiteness in the above poem, and gave Him his life in reality.

Luis Espinal Camp was born in Sant Fruitos de Bages, Barcelona, Spain, February 4, 1932, the son of a simple working family. His mother died when he was only a small child, so his older sister became a mother to him until she entered the Carmelites. Two of his other older siblings also left to follow their religious vocations when Luis was still a teenager.

From the time Luis was four until he was seven, Spain was in the midst of a bitter civil war, where he learned first-hand the sadness of war, hunger and tragedy. One of his older brothers was killed in the conflict, which bloodied his native land. Luis grew up with a great love of liberty and life, and a passion for Jesus Christ. In the profoundly religious context of the traditional Catholic families of the region near Manresa, Luis was strong in his solitude and his sadness but he was also a youth in robust health who loved sports. He played soccer, loved all sports, and in his primary studies at the pre-seminary "Aspotolica" he worked hard and was an excellent student. He finished his secondary studies at the Colegio y Seminario Menor San José de Roquetas. He made excellent grades, especially in language and literature.

August 14, 1949, Luis entered the novitiate of Our Lady of Veruela in Zaragoza. Here he experienced a profound interior maturity and consecrated himself to Christ, who became the light of his life, and who accompanied him as a friend until his death. His companions saw in him one who had a deep spiritual life, interiorly rich, with a great wish to serve and to help the dispossessed. He was idealistic with a passion for justice. He was serious, reserved and a little timid, but happy and amiable. He was also intelligent and blessed with a wonderful sense of humor. His writing skills enabled him to communicate his experiences and convictions brilliantly. He completed his novitiate and made his perpetual vows as a Jesuit on August 15, 1951.

That same day, he was supposed to leave for India, but due to problems with his passport, he never went there. He felt, however, that his vocation was to work in the Third World. In the following years, he continued the traditional formation of a Jesuit, studying many disciplines including Latin, Greek, and literature. Until his death, he preferred to read and meditate on the New Testament in its original language, and he always kept a small copy of it in his shirt pocket.

During the 1950s he obtained his licentiate of philosophy at the University Eclesiastica de San Cugat del Valles. Immediately thereafter, he entered the Universidad del Estado in Barcelona and obtained a second licentiate. At this same time, he began to write scripts for Radio Barcelona and for Vatican Radio as well as publish some of his writings, translations, and poetry. In 1959, he returned to the Univer-

Playing soccer at age 15
PHOTOS COURTESY OF ALFONSO PEDRAJAS, S.J.

The young chemistry student

sity in Sant Cugat del Valles to finish his theology studies. He completed his licentiate in theology in 1963.

Luis was ordained on July 29, 1962 at San Cugat, Barcelona. He said his first Mass on July 31, the feast day of St. Ignatius Loyola, the founder of the Jesuits.

In 1964, Luis went to Bergamo, Italy for two years to study audiovisual journalism with a specialty in films for television. His studies here indelibly marked his future ministry. Videography, a method of communication so divine and yet so mundane, was a primary channel for his vision of life and his response to the grand problems of humanity. He understood that his priesthood was a service to modern man. He wrote the book *Oraciones a Quemarropa* during this time. It shows clearly that for him, Christ was the Son of God and that we are not only *called* sons of God — we *are* sons of God. The poetry in this book was written in the youthful enthusiasm of his thirty-three years. Years later, when the poems were broadcast by Radio Fides in Bolivia, they had an impact that Luis Espinal could never have envisioned when he wrote them.

In 1966 at the conclusion of his studies, Luis began working in the film industry in various positions including that of a film critic for the magazine Reseña in Madrid. He worked for Television Española and produced a program called "Cuestion Urgente" (Urgent Question.) The program examined social questions each week: immigration, illegitimate children, single mothers, alcoholism, prostitution, suicide, juvenile delinquency, etc. The programs were wildly popular and were bought by the B.B.C., but in 1967 a segment showing the miseries of the marginal barrios of Barcelona was prohibited by Franco's government censors. Espinal refused to work further under the control of the dictator's censors.

Fortunately, at this time Monsignor Genaro Prata, the head of the communications media for the Episcopal Conference of Bolivia was visiting Barcelona. Luis made the biggest decision of his life. He went to Bolivia on August 6, 1968. Bolivia became his second homeland and Luis Espinal became "Lucho" (the fighter).

Here, little by little, he began to investigate and understand the problems of his adopted country. He studied the history and geography of Bolivia. He familiarized himself with its different zones. He admired the richness of its cultural diversities. Soon he realized that with all of its rich resources, the country made no progress and was among the poorest of Latin America. He asked himself why. He soon discovered the historical and structural conditions that caused unstable politics, favoritism of a minority and of foreigners which had impoverished the majority of the country and had converted it into the scene of continuous warfare. In the twelve years Espinal lived and worked in Bolivia, there were no less than thirteen major coups and changes in the hierarchy of the government of Bolivia! He was killed during the time of a government of narcotic traffickers and of brutal repression. The Bolivia of Espinal's time was an epoch of terrible dictatorships, repression, jails, shootings, disappearances, exiles, and violence against human rights.

With his journalistic tools and members of the press at the inauguration of "Aquí"

Luis Espinal identified with the Bolivian people, and he began a campaign to denounce social injustice and defend the poor and

The young Jesuit

marginalized, working with a number of causes. He actively collaborated in the creation of the Permanent Assembly of Human Rights. In particular, he denounced the leaders of the Mafia and the narcotics trade in the country. In his work, Lucho changed an esthetic instrument into a prophetic one. He spoke out fearlessly. For him to tell the truth was a sacred task. During Ovando's regime, he suffered his first political detention. His criticism of the narcotics traffickers was one of the reasons for his death. Against the imminence of the narco-trafficking government of Garcia Meza stood the annoying presence of Luis Espinal.

He was named by his colleagues as the director of the seminary. Although this was an obligation, which he did not want to take on, he accepted the charge with his characteristic humility. For him, the charge was a charge and only another service.

At one time, he joined a hunger strike with a number of the wives of miners who had been detained without justice This became one of the most intense times of his life. Although he had felt hunger as a child in Spain, this was the first time he voluntarily felt the way that so many of the people suffered involuntarily every day. He began to realize the efficacy of the non-violent activism of Mahatma Gandhi and Martin Luther King.

Lucho was naturalized as a citizen of Bolivia on June 11, 1970. His work in Bolivia was primarily dedicated to Christ as a journalist. He collaborated with Radio Fides in their magazines "Presencia" and "Ultima Hora"; he produced various programs for Bolivian television and worked in the film industry. He was a professor of communication at two universities and from 1979 worked on the weekly "Aquí." He wrote twelve books on cinematography, which were published by the Salesians and collaborated with other authors in a number of publications. Lucho, however, did not love his art for art's sake; he saw the cinema as an instrument in the service of the people of Bolivia. He produced a series of programs to define the Bolivian social situation. One segment was cut by the government censors, and Lucho wrote to his sister, Maria Soledad, a religious contemplative, explaining that there were some things he couldn't talk about at home because it would alarm the others without any reason. He explained about the programs he had made which had caused him to be expelled from television and said that the daily papers were full of the news and of protests against his expulsion, but that he hadn't joined in his own defense. He considered the expulsion providential in that it would allow him more time to work with the poor and the workers.

He closed with a sad comment, "Here, life is of little value; the miners die young of silicosis; there is a large infant mortality. To live long is a luxury here. Because of this, it is logical that the people want revolution and social change."

Although as a youth he had been in robust health, in Bolivia Luis's health left him. His external aspect remained healthy, but he went through three sicknesses of a grave nature. In 1974 he had a medical problem with his brain that caused him to have strong convulsions similar to those of an epileptic. In 1975 he had a back problem that kept him in bed for a week.

Finally, he came down with hepatitis that caused him several weeks of inactivity.

The last editorial that he wrote for Radio Fides was aired March 21, 1980, the eve of his detention and assassination. In it, he said: "Those who believe that they, and only they, have the political truth are in a neo-nazi scheme. . . . Those that believe in the logic of the gun, and who sponsor terrorism are neo-nazis. The following day, Lucho was the victim of those same proponents of terrorism.

Father Espinal disappeared during the night of March 21, 1980. His fellow priests and the father provincial became worried and began to search. The following day his body was found abandoned near a small village. The corpse showed signs of terrible torture and was riddled with bullets.

His body was taken to the chapel of the Colegio San Calizto in the city of La Paz where large numbers of people paid their respects

Luis "Lucha" Espinal

to his remains, praying and crying. Seventy thousand people accompanied his body to the cemetery, where on his tomb you may read this inscription: "Assassinated for helping the people."

Four months later with their boots mired in blood, Garcia Meza and Arce Gomez were overthrown in a bloody military coup. Both were then detained in maximum-security prisons. Meza in La Pas for his responsibility in innumerable tortures and assassinations and Gomez in the United States as a drug trafficker.

In Bolivia, Father Espinal is remembered as one who kept his Christian social principles until the end, giving his life for the most poor and marginalized. Four pillars were the base of his interior life: Jesus Christ, true Man; the people; the truth; and peace. The wide distribution of his writings and his poetry and the many conversions among the youth and the poor all over Bolivia are seen as a clear sign that God did not want his life forgotten. Hidden in the heart of the South American continent, the fire of Luis Espinal's imitation of Christ and of his evangelism and concern for the poor still burns brightly in the work of those who have so generously continued to work for the reign of God in Bolivia.

Luis Espinal is the synthesis of the voice he wrote of in an editorial:

"To be the voice of those that have no voice.
To be the voice to cry out those things that others keep silent about.
To be the strong, brave voice of the people."

His message can be summed up in his own political-spiritual testament:

Life is for this, to spend it for others. ✢

18

Margaret Sinclair

Sister Mary Frances of the Five Wounds
Scotland, 1900-1925

Scottish Factory Worker

"Father, is it wrong to break an engagement?" the lovely young woman asked her Jesuit confessor. Then she poured out her dilemma to him. While on holiday at the seaside in Bo'ness, she had met a young man, a lapsed Catholic named Patrick Lynch who had recently demobilized from the Army. By gentle persuasion, she had induced him to accompany her and her sister to Mass and Benediction and obtained his promise to go to Confession. He returned to the practice of his Faith and saw her regularly that year. On her birthday he had presented her with a ring and asked her to be his wife.

"Maggie" Sinclair was a pretty girl. With her big gray eyes, her infectious gaity and witty tongue, it is no wonder that the young man fell in love with her. She was distressed at the way the relationship had developed, although her parents liked the young man and were delighted at the prospect of a wedding. She had prayed, "If it is necessary that I should make the sacrifice, I will, dear Jesus, but you will have to make me love him, for I do not." Initially she had refused his request, telling him "No, my love for you is not the love a wife should have. I do not feel called to marriage." Her parents were grieved; so, to

Margaret Sinclair
PHOTOS COURTESY OF REV. STEPHEN MCGRATH, O.F.M.

please them, she accepted the engagement reluctantly. Her attitude of indifference at last angered her father who forcibly told her to make up her mind. "Margaret, it makes me ashamed of myself to see you sitting beside the boy, so sad and miserable. If you don't love him, tell him so plainly and let an end be made."

Margaret and her sister Bella prayed together, thought together, and cried together. It was an awful time.

Father Thomas Agius told her that what she had done for the young man was an act of charity, and carried no obligation to marry him against her will. Greatly relieved, Margaret wrote to the young man, ending the affair as gently as she could. "I had done what God inspired me to do, to help you, the little I could, to regain the Light. From that moment God and his Blessed Mother must have showered down their blessing on you, because you have remained steadfast since. And I trust in God that you will continue doing so, because you know He is the only real happiness. . . . You will recollect a year ago I wrote a similar letter to this, but when you came, you implored me not to. I must be rather chicken-hearted because I agreed, but I feel I cannot let it go on any longer. Perhaps you will be hurt at my saying this, but if you take a broad view of it, you will see that it is better now than after."

The ending of the engagement helped the popular young factory worker realize that the call of God was clear and unmistakable for her. She told her confessor that she wanted to become a Poor Clare nun. "I am longing to suffer with Our Lord Jesus Christ." When Father Agius pointed out the rigorous lifestyle the Poor Clares live, Margaret simply replied, "He will give me the grace to bear it. With the help of Our Lord, I don't think it would be too hard." She confessed that she had already been "practicing" penance. She had made a small wooden cross with the points of nails sticking out of it which she wore between her shoulders. In addition she fasted, sometimes severely. The priest immediately forbade all excessive penance and just as immediately, Margaret obeyed. He told her she must "leave the crosses" till Our Lord would send His own — "in His own way and in His own time. She must save up her strength for His sake." Margaret's replies convinced her confessor that her vocation was truly from God, and he advised her to seek admittance at the Poor Clare convent in Liberton Edinburgh. She applied, asking to be admitted as an extern sister, but there was no vacancy and she was directed to apply to the Poor Clare Colletines in Notting Hill, London, who accepted her.

Margaret Sinclair was born March 29, 1900, in the basement flat of a run-down Edinburgh tenement. She was the third child of a dustman who was employed by the Edinburgh Corporation. Later, three other children were born to this devout laborer and his wife. Shortly after Margaret's birth, the family moved to another tenement in Blackfriars Street, an area scarcely more cheerful than the grimy, dilapidated one where she was born. The new home, however, was close to the parish church of St. Patrick where, every morning, even in winter, Margaret went to Mass and Communion usually barefooted and thinly clad, a sign of the family's poverty. In spite of their poor financial situation, the home was normally a happy one. Andrew Sinclair was proud of his family and spent a great deal of time with them. He had never been to school himself, so he was determined that his children would receive an education. Elizabeth Sinclair brought up her large brood with great devotion under circumstances that were far from ideal.

Margaret attended St. Anne's Catholic School where she is remembered as a quiet, well-behaved pupil who worked hard. She gained prizes in running and swimming. Her natural cheerfulness and habitual smile gained her friends at school and made her the sunshine of her family. She was the family peacemaker when little arguments erupted between her more volatile sisters. When her mother was depressed, Margaret would urge her, "Dinna give in." Margaret stroked her mother's hair and said, "Try again mother, I'll say a wee prayer for you." Her irrepressible and cheerful faith seemed to move the mountains of her family's problems.

Margaret knew the power of a smile. She told her sister, "Sometimes a girl may just be waiting for you to give her a smile first, and

Just "Maggie" Sinclair

others may be in a little difficulty or out of sorts, as you never know one's troubles. A little smile like that given in passing brightens up the way for them, and you give them a little courage and you help them to support their little trouble."

From an early age, prayer was a large part of Margaret's life. Each evening after family rosary, Margaret would climb the stairs to her sparsely furnished, spotlessly clean room. She kept a colorful display of holy pictures on the wall and had made herself a little shrine on a narrow ledge by her bed where she knelt to pray. As a teenager she loved parties, dancing, and dressing in the latest fashion, but even when she arrived home late she would say her prayers. She told her sister, "Well, I enjoyed myself very well, now I must give God his share. Look at us dancing and enjoying ourselves and yet how many religious Orders were up praying for us, and how many souls God has called home during that time." As Margaret grew older, her prayer life deepened, but this did not make her dour and cheerless. Instead, she continued to enjoy the parish dances and retained her cheerful nature. She persuaded her sister Bella to attend daily Mass and Communion and when Bella protested that she wasn't good enough, Margaret replied, "You are not going to Holy Communion because you are good, but because you want to try and be good." She also told her sister, "You will see when you begin to go every day, you will find out you cannot live without going."

Margaret modeled her life on the Little Way of St. Thérèse of Lisieux. She read the Gospels, the Imitation of Christ, and the lives of the saints over and over again.

Even as a child, Margaret was known for her patience and gentleness, but the patience was won by her mastery of a tendency to be proud-spirited and to speak her mind. She learned to hold her tongue when necessary and to check any hasty word. She would leave the room when anyone was annoyed, returning only when they had sufficiently calmed down. Faced with a temptation, she would repeat the name of Jesus very slowly until the temptation receded.

Margaret was a "little mother" to her younger brothers and sisters. Andrew was her shadow and when the others objected to the baby tagging along, Margaret would reply, "Poor wee soul, he has no one to play with. Let him come with us." The neighborhood children called her "the kind girl" because she would stop and give them pushes on the swings. She told her sister, "Let's give them twenty each and make them happy."

Margaret attended the Atholl Crescent High School of Domestic Economy where she was awarded certificates in sewing, cooking and dressmaking. She sewed her own clothes and made them fashionable although not immodest. During her last year of school, she took a part-time job as a messenger for a local business firm, a dress shop, to help provide for the family. What little money she didn't pour into the family coffers she often gave to the missions or to the beggars in the streets.

At the age of fourteen, Margaret left school and took a full-time job in the Waverley Cabinet Works as an apprentice French polisher, putting a professional sheen on wooden furniture. Here she became an active trade union member. She was a committed member of the union. The work was arduous and the hours were long — from eight in the morning to six in the evening. She attended daily Mass before work. This was in the days before the relaxation of the fast rules and Margaret often worked all day without eating as she spent most of her lunch hour before the Blessed Sacrament at a nearby church. Margaret was a quiet and competent worker and she won the admiration of her employers. Often, co-workers engaged in telling ribald jokes or indecent stories, but Margaret simply kept her head down toward her work and ignored these. One man, seeing her rosary and prayer book lying beside her work area, advised his colleagues to leave her alone "for she is a holy girl."

The young factory worker

Margaret's mother, who had gone to work at the age of ten, worried when her girls had to go out to work for she knew the dangers of the modern workshop with its monotony and its dangers to morals. Margaret reassured her, "Don't worry, mother, I'll be in the factory what I have been at school and at home." At first, Margaret's efficient work and her withdrawal from unkind or objectionable conversations roused the ire of some of her workmates. Spitefully, they took Margaret's coat and hat from the pegs in the cloakroom and threw them on the floor. She simply paid no notice and continued to give her sweet smile to all her fellow workers who soon grew to respect her moral courage.

During the First World War, Margaret's brother John was called up and her father volunteered. Since her mother could not write, Margaret became the family scribe to write to her father and brother on her mother's behalf. One letter became a family joke. She closed it with "God keep you from your loving wife." She had absentmindedly left out the comma.

To do their bit for the war effort, Margaret and her sisters took an allotment (a plot of ground loaned to citizens to grow food) and Margaret won prizes for the cabbages she grew there.

After the war, work was precarious and Margaret felt the frustration of being unemployed when the factory closed down in 1918. She was lucky, however, and soon found work in McVitie's biscuit factory.

Much of her spare time was spent in works of charity. At the convent of the Helpers of the Holy Souls, she sewed for the church and polished the altar furniture. Margaret often visited the slums, seeking out the elderly and bringing them presents of flowers or coal.

On July 21, 1923, Margaret and her brother Andrew left for London, she to begin her life in the convent and he to immigrate to Canada. After seeing her brother off, she went to Notting Hill where she became a postulant of the Poor Clare Colletines. A loyal Scot, Margaret was not always understood. She did not lose her gifts of wit and gaiety, though, and in her letters home there is no mention of the discouragement and homesickness she must naturally have felt. Margaret had entered as an extern sister. In the Poor Clare convent, it is these sisters who perform the necessary domestic duties and do the work outside the enclosure that allows for the choir sisters to spend their time in prayer. Margaret was given the name Sister Mary Frances of the Five Wounds, and her tasks included taking charge of part of the garden, begging for funds, and the duty of portress, or doorkeeper, to welcome visitors to the convent. Like her favorite saint, Francis of Assisi, Margaret loved nature. She wrote of her delight in growing "flowers for sweet Jesus" and was able to tend a barren apple tree so well that it eventually bore fruit. The begging, however, was against her nature. "The Sinclairs were always proud, and I must and shall fight to acquire humility," she wrote.

Margaret received the habit on February 11, 1924.

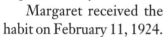
Margaret as Sister Mary Frances of the Five Wounds

Her family was present, including her closest sister, Bella, who was now a Little Sister of the Poor. Her simple profession was made on Valentine's day, 1925, but none of her family could attend. Some of Bella's religious sisters attended and told her that Margaret looked extremely happy. A childhood friend reported, "she looked at the tabernacle with a glance which was not of this world."

In her resolutions for 1925 Margaret wrote, "I shall submit to everything, remembering my Lord and my God who submitted to St. Joseph and who was obedient even unto the death of the cross." How little she knew that in a short while God would call on her to submit to her own painful death. Less than a month after her profession, Margaret became sick and began to cough blood. She was diagnosed with tuberculosis of the throat and was sent to Marillac Sanitarium at Warley, which was directed by the Sisters of Charity of St. Vincent de Paul. Margaret cried all the way, but through her tears she whispered continuously "It is God's holy will."

God had accepted her resolution of submission and she performed it in heroic degree. She had left her home and loved ones, her beloved convent which she called "the sweetest place imaginable", and she ended her life with a painful disease in strange surroundings. The nurses who cared for her soon recognized the extraordinary quality of the new patient. In spite of her terrible sufferings from the disease, Margaret kept her serenity, her patience and her gaiety.

One day a new patient, a Sister Clare, came in while Sister Mary Frances was sitting with the other nuns. Teasingly, Sister Mary Frances announced, "She is the only lady among you." In answer to their astonished looks, she explained, "You are all Bernards, Johns, or Columbas!" (She was referring to their masculine religious names.) Another day while gasping for breath she swallowed a wasp that stung her in her already tortured throat. When asked if she was okay, she smiled through her tears and told the nurse, "It is just another wee splinter of the cross."

Margaret's illness dragged on for seven months with increasing weakness and sleeplessness. Her childhood confessor, Father Agius, went to see her and she told him that Our Lord was always with her and that she had no fears and no problems. She said that she had seen Our Lord and Our Lady, not with the eyes of the body, but as interior lights. Her confessor said, "It seemed as if her whole soul was poured out in the whispered 'I want to see Him.'" Still death kept her waiting and she suffered patiently. One day she told the nurse with a sweet smile, "Oh, Sister, this has been a great day. A day of great suffering. If I could only gain one soul for Jesus it would be worth it all."

Margaret went to her eternal reward on November 24, 1925, shortly after looking out of the window and saying, "great things are coming to Warley, great things." Her last words were the prayer "Jesus,

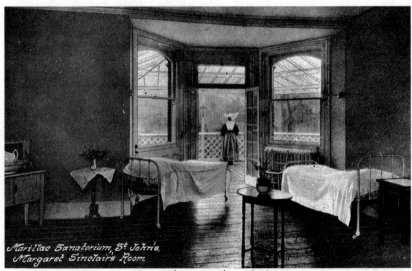

Margaret's room at the sanitarium

Mary and Joseph, I give you my heart and my soul." Her body was taken back to the Poor Clare Convent for the funeral and she was buried in Kensal Green in northwest London, under a soft blanket of snow. As the reports of favors attributed to her intercession began to spread, her remains were transferred to Mount Vernon Cemetery, Liberton, Edinburgh. She was declared Venerable by Pope Paul VI in 1978. His Eminence Cardinal Gordon Gray, Archbishop of St. Andrews and Edinburgh said, "We can still admire the heroism of the early martyrs, but the unlikelihood of our being thrown to the lions makes these first Christian saints somewhat remote and shadowy figures. Margaret Sinclair may well be one of the first to achieve the title of Saint from the factory floor." ☦

19

Visitandine Martyrs of Spain

During the bitter bloodbath of the Spanish Civil War (1936-1939), 7,937 bishops, priests and religious were slaughtered for the "crime" of being Catholic religious who would not give up their faith. Causes for many of these have been entered, and in recent years Pope John Paul II has beatified a large number of these saintly heroes and heroines of Christ the King. Within the scope of this volume it is impossible to do other than highlight the lives of a mere handful of these martyrs.

Seven Visitandine Sisters of Madrid

Mother Maria Gabriela: July 24, 1872–November 18, 1936
(Amparo de Hinojosa)
Sister Teresa Maria: July 30, 1888–November 18, 1936
(Laura Cavestany)
Sister Josefa Maria: May 23, 1881–November 18, 1936
(Carmina Barrera)
Sister Maria Inez: January 28, 1900–November 18, 1936
(Inez Zudaire Galdeano)
Sister Maria Cecilia Cendova: January 10, 1910–November 23, 1936
(Maria Feli Cendova)
Sister Maria Angela: November 12, 1893–November 18, 1936
(Martina Olaizola)
Sister Maria Engracia: July 12, 1898–November 18, 1936
(Josefa Joaquina Lecuona)

November 17, 1936, a rough group of anarchists swarmed through the apartments on Claudio Coello Street. Their curses and indecent gestures accompanied their thorough search for anything that might mark one of the occupants as a religious. Evacuees who had found refuge there were expelled. Finally they left, announcing loudly that they would return the following day. From the tone of their words, their intent was clear. Seven sisters of the Visitation who had been living in one of the apartments since July realized that their time was close and spent the night in prayer. These sisters had been left in Madrid to watch over the monastery property while the rest of the community had taken shelter in Oronoz (Navarre). Since July, it had become too dangerous to stay in the monastery itself, so the little group moved to the apartments. Although they had been given several opportunities to leave, they felt bound by obedience to stay at their appointed place.

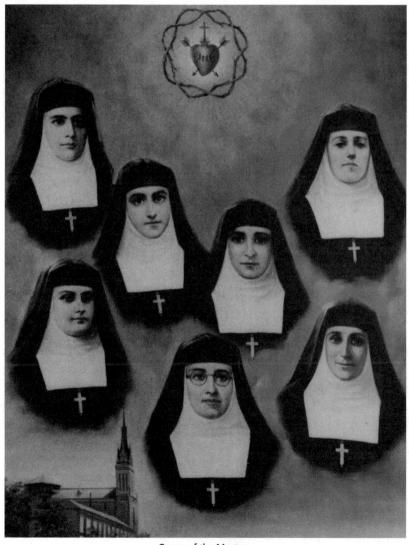

Group of the Martyrs
PHOTOS COURTESY OF THE VISITATION OF TOLEDO, OHIO

On the morning of the eighteenth, Manuela Gomez-Ugalde, a friend, paid the sisters a final visit. They greeted her at the door with the words, "For the love of God, don't stay here. Any minute now, we are expecting them to come to get us; if they find you here, they'll take you too!" Sister Theresa Marie ushered her out, giving her a treasured little medal and promising to ask Our Lady to keep her safe amid the dangers. The stalwart Isaias de la Fuente, the caretaker who had been secretly bringing them provisions arrived to make a final attempt to save them. Solicitously Sister Teresa Maria told him that he, himself, should attempt to escape and not put himself in further danger by helping them. "Please don't be concerned about us any longer; we are full of joy to be going to heaven." That afternoon, Carmen Arnaiz, another of their helpful caretakers, brought up some milk and the change from the money the sisters had given her for the weeks' supply. They told her to keep both the milk and the change. Teresa Maria added, "Now we have no need of anything; you must have the milk and the 100 pesetas too. These are the last we have; our accounts are already closed. We are going to our Lord. What a grace — to attain the palm of martyrdom." As the faithful Carmen left, Sister Maria Gabriela, the head of the little group, told her that she had offered the sisters the chance to return to the safety of their families but that all preferred to stay. The sisters had searched their hearts and believed it was the will of God that they lay down their lives.

About seven that evening, the faithful caretaker returned just at the time that eighteen anarchists arrived to make a fourth house search and to arrest the sisters. Just as he had during the previous house searches, the caretaker entered the apartment with the anarchists. Sister Maria Ines was in bed with a high fever and the soldiers roughly told her to get up. The caretaker protested but the soldiers turned on him and told him "If you don't shut up, you will be first in the line-up." Valiantly he responded that at least they should leave the room while she arose and ushered them out of the room. Staggering, the sick nun joined her sisters. As they left the apartment, one of the sisters wanted to return to get a blanket for her. Roughly one of the men replied, "It won't be necessary. This fever is going to be over very quickly."

Serenely, the sisters boarded the truck that had come to fetch them. Without speaking as they entered, each of them courageously made the sign of the cross. Their tranquillity contrasted greatly with the agitation of those who had gathered to watch. A voice from the crowd called out that they should be killed immediately for making the defiant sign of their faith.

The truck began to move but the trip was short and it stopped at an empty lot on a nearby street. The sisters had barely set foot to the ground when a rain of bullets stilled six valiant hearts. Sister Maria Cecilia was holding the hand of Sister Maria Gabriela, and as she felt her companion fall, instinctively she ran. Oddly, no one followed her.

In her own words, she testified, "I began to run, run. I did not know what I was doing. I ran along many iron fences, many fences. I do not know Madrid. They caught me. I said I am a religious." In a moment of terror, this shy, timid twenty-six year old fled, distraught and hardly realizing what she was doing. In spite of this, she retained the courage to declare openly that she was a religious, proving that she did not hesitate to accept martyrdom. By the strange and wondrous way of God, she was able to tell her fellow prisoners in jail of the martyrdom of the other six and to encourage them in their own trials. After her capture, she was offered escape but refused. Two of these fellow prisoners were freed and later told Sister Cecilia's story. Although Sister Cecilia considered herself unfaithful for having run away, her love was not extinguished until her final offering. The two lay women who shared her prison cell were so impressed with her humility, her patience and her union with the divine will that they stated they had the certitude that she was a saint.

At the end of the war, one of these kind women, Isabel Becerro, went to the monastery of the Visitation in San Sebastian to tell Sister Cecelia's story which was relayed to the sisters in Madrid. The Madrid superior went to the police station and was able to find the record card for Sister Cecilia, along with a document signed by her. An address written on the document was that of those destined to be executed, but although the superior asked at that prison, she was unable to obtain any further information.

For nearly five years, the community was saddened by not knowing the eventual fate of Sister Cecilia. Daily they begged the Virgin to allow them to obtain some details about their little sister. With a strange twist of fate, Divine Providence at last shed light on her story.

Young Amalia Lopez came to the monastery in Madrid to ask for admission. She was accompanied by her aunt, Araceli Sanchez Pelaez.

The superior and the mistress of novices went to the parlor to greet the applicant and when Araceli saw them wearing the black habit with its distinctive cross hanging from their necks she exclaimed, "I saw a cross like yours at the court of Pont de Vallecas when I was looking for the bodies of my husband and brother. It had been pierced by a gunshot."

Araceli accompanied the sisters to the court where they were given some small objects that Sister Maria Cecilia had on her person: her pocket rosary, a small crucifix, a little cloth case with a prayer to our Lady and other little papers in her novice mistress's handwriting, and identification marks from her clothing. The greatest treasure was her profession cross which had been pierced by a bullet. They were told that she was shot in front of the wall of the Vallecas Cemetery at dawn on November 23, making her death official. Araceli made further inquiries and learned that her husband and brother were executed on the same day as Sister Cecilia and that they were buried without caskets in a common grave, along with eleven or twelve other victims. In 1959, the remains of these martyrs were transferred to the Valley of the Fallen where they rest in peace. Much to the regret of the community, Sister Cecilia's remains were not brought back to the Monastery.

The community of Madrid was a large one numbering eighty-three nuns. A group of sisters had formed a new foundation in León, Mexico, in 1903, but when the persecution of the Church in that country broke out, the sisters returned to Spain. They also gave shelter to the nuns from the three monasteries of Portugal who fled the revolution there, and to others from the Third Monastery of Madrid[1] that was under construction. For some years they also welcomed groups of Benedictines and Carmelites, living the spirit of charity and love established by their founders, St. Francis de Sales and St. Jane de Chantal.

As a consequence of the events of 1931, the Madrid community dispersed, leaving the monastery empty and taking shelter with their relatives and friends. A few days later, they recalled a few of the sisters to keep watch over the monastery. Then, they were offered a refuge in Catholic Navarre where the majority of the sisters could continue with their community life. After a time, they returned to Madrid when the situation got better, but they were forced to leave again in 1936. This time, a group of seven sisters was left in charge of the monastery, with plans for rotation of these caretakers. Also, the superior rented a small basement apartment for use in case matters became too difficult for the sisters to stay in the monastery. They moved into the apartment on July 18.

Mother Maria Gabriela

The leader of the little group was Mother Maria Gabriela (Amparo de Hinojosa), who had been superior of the monastery at the time of the 1931 dispersion. A naturally timid and indecisive person, her responsibilities proved the hidden metal of her soul. She was born in Andalusa, the eighth child and only girl of devout Christian parents. Her father died when she was only eight years old and her mother became ill with a fatal disease. After her death, Amparo was raised by her brother

Amparo de Hinojosa

Edward who treated her as if she were one of his own daughters. She went as a boarding student to the Second Monastery of the Visitation in Madrid and from the moment she arrived she felt "like a fish in water." When her brothers asked if she weren't tired of being shut up all the time she responded joyously, "no where else have I felt so happy." An affectionate child with a merry and joyous character, she spent pleasant summers with her family. When she was fifteen, on a family trip to Lourdes, she first felt the call of a religious vocation. At sixteen she mentioned her desire to her brother who told her she was too young and withdrew her from boarding school. At last her guardian granted her permission and she entered the First Monastery of the Visitation in Madrid in June of 1892 at the age of nineteen. She pronounced her vows at the age of twenty-two. Although all her personal notes were destroyed with the repeated burning of the monastery, the other sisters remember her as one who loved her institute enthusiastically and who became a "living rule" for the edification of the other sisters.

Blessed Maria Gabriela de Hinojosa

As a child, Amparo had suffered severe stomach ailments and her health remained delicate. In the last few months, her health had seriously deteriorated. It was not her own health, however, that she wrote about in these lines from a letter to the community at Oronoz. Full of peace and abandonment, she wrote in innuendo of the situation of her beloved country: "The invalid is not getting better at all; since she became ill, she has never been in such a bad state and we fear a very sad end. But be tranquil; God, our Lord, in Whose hands we find ourselves will do all that is good for us." And three days later, "We are at peace in the hands of God, sure of Him."

Sister Teresa Maria

Laura Cavestany was born July 30, 1888, the fourth of fourteen children of Juan Antonio and Margarita Anduaga Cavestany. Her father was a man of letters and a gifted poet; her mother ably performed the duties of a Christian housewife and mother. The day of her First Communion she awoke with a high fever, but she begged to be allowed to go to Mass anyway. They sat her at the edge of the chapel and she was carried, seated on a chair, to the altar for communion. Attractive and likable as an adolescent, she enjoyed parties and recreations with her friends and her loving brothers and sisters. At last, inclined to the religious life, she applied for entrance to Carmel, but the community thought that she could not tolerate the austerity. At the age of twenty six she

Laura Cavestany y Anduaga

entered the Visitation. She was endowed with an independent character and it was not easy for her to overcome her old self. On the first day she was so tempted to go back that when night came she said to herself, "Tomorrow I am leaving." In the struggle between nature and grace, God won, and she completed her novitiate and took the name Teresa Maria. She developed an intense spiritual life and wrote a number of poems of which only a single example addressed to her sister remains. Although she served in all the offices of the house, she is remembered best for her charity and abnegation while serving as the community infirmarian. Taking after her father in her literate manner of expression, she wrote many letters to her sister and to a Visitandine religious which have been preserved. The text of these letters gives a glimpse into her spirituality and shows her insatiable thirst for God alone. In addition to loving advice to her sister, she constantly exhorts her to live joyfully. In 1935, she was stricken with cancer and her breast was removed. Four months after her operation she wrote to a friend, "I feel, thank God, very well and I can work almost as I did before; since it happened on the left side, that helped very much. I was still too green to be united with my God." The terrible illness appeared again the following year and without doubt she would have suffered a slow martyrdom had God not chosen her for another one. Six months before her death, she wrote to her sister,

Blessed Teresa M. Cavestany

"Amalita, in this little corner, where everything speaks of Him, desires for heaven have taken on alarming proportions, while being always ready to do His most holy will." On her arrival in Madrid to take her place as one of the guardians of the monastery, she was met by two of her sisters whose fear showed on their faces. In a resolute tone she asked them, "What is the matter? The Lord wants generous souls, and we must give Him everything with joy." Gently and joyfully this generous soul gave Him her everything.

Sister Josefa Maria

Sister Josefa Maria was thirty-seven before she followed her vocation to the cloister. Carmina Barrera was born May 23, 1881, the oldest child and only daughter of a naval captain, Emilio, and his wife Maria Izaguirre. She was born in Galicia, but lived most of her young days in Andalusia where her father was stationed. Carmina was a kind, tranquil and very docile child who told the sisters she was also lazy and a sleepy head. Even as a young child she felt a call to the cloister and dreamed of being a Carmelite. As a teenager, she became a bit of a coquette, vain, loving adornments and moody. Then, sorrow appeared in her life. Two of her young brothers and her beloved father died. Her older brothers had left home, and

Carmina Barrera Izaguirre

when her mother fell ill, Carmina nursed
her with loving care until her death.
Carmina was then free to pursue her vocation and applied to the Carmelites but
her spiritual director suggested the idea
of the Visitation. Docile as always, she
accepted his advice and entered the First
Monastery in Madrid in 1918. Good na-
tured, pleasant, and warm, she remained
humble and simple, giving herself without reserve to the community. She exerted
herself to correct her faults, in particular
her slowness and failings in punctuality
at community exercises. She told her nov-

Blessed Josefa M. Barrera

ice mistress "All I want is to go to Heaven as soon as possible." The
mistress responded, "For that it is indispensable to suffer much." In
her humility, Sister Josefa Maria said, "I don't have the necessary tim-
ber for martyrdom," but events would prove otherwise. She made her
solemn vows in 1923. Although she was in charge of the oratories and
shrines of the house for a time, cleaning and decorating them lovingly, she spent most of her religious life as the community infirmarian.
Here she is remembered as affectionate and accommodating. Although
she felt it a sacrifice, she embraced with generosity the assignment as
one to remain in Madrid to care for the monastery. In a letter she
wrote, ". . . but I am happy, because I believe I am accomplishing the
will of God." The face of Sister Josefa Maria, which in life was so
tranquil and serene, was completely destroyed by the bullets that completed her final, unconditional surrender to God's will. The superior
whose job it was to identify the bodies of the martyrs could not swear
that the body presented as that of Sister Josefa Maria, and so her relics
remained in the cemetery of the Almudena.

Sister Maria Inez

Inez Zudaire Galdeano was born in Navarre in 1900, one of six
children of a pious laborer named Valentin and his wife, Maria. There
is little extant data about her childhood and her few writings which
have been preserved are a few phrases directed to the Blessed Virgin.
She entered the monastery of Madrid at the age of nineteen and pro-

nounced her solemn vows at the age of twenty-three. She was devoted to the labor of domestic duties, active, respect-ful, and always at the service of the others. She worked in the kitchen until a species of eczema on her face caused her transfer to other work. When the sisters left for their second retreat to Oronoz, Sister Inez was one of those designated to stay. She was frightened and told one of the sisters who was leaving, "Pray very much for us; we could be put to death." Although the stay in the apartment brought with it sufferings and house searches, there was also a great peace,

Inez Zudaire Galdeano

surrender to the will of God, and the hope of martyrdom, all of which Sister Inez shared with the others. A friend who had visited the sisters almost daily before escaping to Belgium wrote the superior in Oronoz, "they were always happy, waiting for news and praying with great fervor for Spain. They were able to have the Blessed Sacrament much of the time, although sometimes it was more prudent not to keep it. . . . They were true saints, capable of every sacrifice."

Sister Martinez Lopez, R.A., one of the biographers of the Visitandine Blesseds interviewed the surviving sisters. One of them showed her two photographs of Sister Inez, which made a deep impression on her. The first, taken in life, shows her with a round face and an expressive, somewhat serious gaze. The other, taken after her

death, depicts her with blood running down her face, eyes open as if gazing at Heaven, and a card with the number 6 suspended around her neck. White Relief, a lay association, had washed the bodies, photographed them, and then interred them in the cemetery of the Almudena, taking great care to make certain that the photograph and the number matched in order to make later identification possible. When the bodies of the martyrs were transferred to the crypt of the Monastery, in 1940, Sister Maria Inez's hand was still

Blessed Maria Inez Zudaire

flexible, with skin and flesh as if ready to give a final blessing to her sisters.

Sister Maria Cecilia

Maria Feli was born January 10, 1910, in Azepeitia. She was the third daughter of Antonio and Isabel Araquistain Cendoya, Christian parents who considered the religious formation of their children of prime importance and who inculcated in them a deep love of God. As a child, she had a loving personality, and was tran-quil, silent, and timid in contrast to her lively tem-perament. She developed a great love of the Eucharist, becoming a "Maria of the Tablernacles," an organization founded by Bishop Manuel Gonzalez. In addition to daily Mass and Communion, she made frequent visits to the Blessed Sacrament and assisted her parish priest in caring for the church. She also had a great love for the Virgin Mary and was frequently heard sing-ing in her honor, both at home and at her place of work. By the age of fourteen, Maria Feli had be-

Felicitas Cendova
Araquistain

gun working in a textile mill in order to help her family. Her fellow workers remember her as straightforward. They say she never spoke ill of anyone and she constantly sang. When she felt the call of a voca-tion to the cloister, her spiritual director suggested the First Monas-

Blessed Maria Cecilia Cendova

tery of the Visitation in Madrid. Although her family protested that there were con-vents closer to home, her mind was made up. She would leave her country, her fam-ily, and would accept the difficulty of learn-ing to express herself in another language. She entered in 1930 at the age of twenty. Her natural sister Juanita tells us, "She was of a very happy disposition, but at the same time silent and reserved. She had a very quick temper and when she first told our mother that she wanted to become a nun, my mother told me later that she had said to her: 'You a nun, with that temper? You have to correct yourself if you want to become a nun.' " And correct herself she did, making her final profession in 1935. For this event, her sturdy Basque family traveled to Madrid and her mother asked her "What is it that has cost you most in the monastery?" They all laughed when Sister Cecilia replied, "to walk slowly."

Sister Cecilia had been in the monastery only a few months before the first retreat and noticing her fear her novice mistress asked her if she would prefer to return home. Her spirited reply in her poor Castillian was "No, dear Sister; I would rather have my head cut off." Later, in her prison cell, she bore her crucifix on her breast and said, "I will not hide it that I am a religious, because I want to die like my sisters."

Sister Maria Angela

Martina Olaizola was born in Garin, in the Onate valley. She was the eighth child of José Ignacio and Justa Garagarza. The family was poor but very devout. Although she attended the rural school near her home, she went to work as a servant at an early age in order to better her family's condition. She worked first for a Christian pharmacist where she was loved by the family for her great patience and her charity. When a member of the family developed tuberculosis, she nursed him with tender care. Her family, afraid of contagion, called her back; she left in tears at abandoning the dear invalid. Her dominant qualities were her serious character, her desire to make herself useful, and to make others happy. At twenty-five she left to enter the Monastery of the Visitation and her

Martina Olaizola Garagarza

family and those whom she worked for saw her leave with great regret. She did not speak any Castilian and the language was difficult for her. At recreation the sisters would tease her and mimic her expressions, but she joined in the joking mood and her efforts and good nature endeared her to the others. She was a good and capable outsister,[2] prudent and painstaking. She had a love for silence and recollection and asked the superior for the life of the enclosure but with unconditional obedience remained in her place, saying, "I want to submit to the will of God and make His will my own." Talented in the shoemaker's art, she put together shoes for the nuns which all said were the most comfortable they had ever worn. She made her Oblation[3] in the community in 1922 and was later allowed to pronounce perpetual vows. In 1931 she was among the group who stayed in Madrid. Her young nephew visited her and advised her to come home to safety. She replied, "The loving designs of God are that I remain where obedience appoints me. I am ready to follow the will of God, wherever He wishes." Again remaining in Madrid in 1936, she wrote to the sisters in Oronoz,

Blessed M. Angela Olaizola

". . . we are very content, and understand better every day that that is what God asks of us. I believe that He asks all these sacrifices as a remedy for all the evil, and there is so much of it!" In life, this humble sister had always wanted to remain hidden. She remained so even after her death because the bullets that pierced her face so disfigured her that it was impossible to identify her. Her mortal remains rest anonymously in the cemetery of the Almudena.

Sister Maria Engracia

Josefa Joaquina was born in the province of Guipuzcoa in 1898, one of fourteen children of Pedro and Matilde Aramburu Lecuona. She never attended school, although her mother taught her to read and write and gave her lessons in catechism. As a young child, Josefa was noted for her intelligence, her sense of responsibility, and for trying to make all the members of her family happy with her lively, unselfish nature. She was also known for her great devotion to the Virgin Mary. The family was poor and Josefa went to work at thirteen, caring for the children of a family that lived close by. She returned home briefly when she was fifteen but the following year she began working as a servant in a family in San Sebastian. The mother was ill and Josefa had the care of six children

Josefa Lecuona

under ten. Later she worked for two years for another family in Renteria until a high fever made her resign her post. She visited the Monastery of the Visitation in San Sebastian where she learned that the monastery in Madrid needed another extern sister. With total honesty and simplicity she admitted that her health was delicate and was overjoyed to learn that that was not an obstacle to her vocation. She entered at the age of twenty-seven and from her first days was happy and content with her vocation. In one of her letters she wrote, "The fact is that from the moment I rise until night, I have the feeling that my heart is in Heaven. How could I not be happy and content if I am in the house of God, where He wants me?" She made her perpetual Oblation in 1930, and took perpetual vows in 1934, the year her sister joined her in the Visitation. Although her health always remained delicate, she managed to joke about it. She wrote, "I always maintain 'that fasting look' as they tell me here." "Others go around saying, 'that sister has one foot in the grave and the other in the portress's quarters.' " "I am stronger, but always look like a stalk of asparagus."

Blessed Maria Engracia Lecuona

In her response to fidelity there was much joy. "They tell me that I always have 'an Easter face.' It is just that our Lord grants me many graces at this season, and because of this I am always so filled with joy that the slightest little thing makes me laugh." Through her years in the monastery, Sister Maria Engracia seemed always to be thinking of others. She continued this trait to the end. The monastery gardener, Mariano Duque, took the sisters food as often as he could until a few days before their deaths when they advised him not to come back. Sister Maria Engracia told him, "Now, Mariano, since we do not know what is going to become of us, if you escape alive . . . when the other sisters return, tell them to be very grateful to the caretakers who were so very good to us." She also retained her joy and her happiness, even in the face of martyrdom, telling the caretakers that it would be sad not to profit from such an extraordinary opportunity of going to Heaven. ✝

Notes

1. There are three monasteries of the Visitation in Madrid and they are called in order of their founding, the First, Second, and Third Monastery of the Visitation.

2. Some sisters remained outside the enclosure to carry on the work of the monastery. This work required contact with the public.

3. At this time, extern sisters made an oblation but the regulations were later changed and they were also admitted to perpetual profession.

20

Michael Joseph McGivney
United States, 1852-1890

A Knight Ahead of His Times

When we say that someone is "ahead of his times," we mean that his ideas were not limited to those of his peers, but instead had far-reaching results that are more in line with the ideas of later times. A young priest of the Hartford Diocese in Connecticut, Father Michael J. McGivney, lived more than a hundred years ago. His ideas of the role of the laity and the sacredness of Christian family life, however, seem to anticipate the sentiments and teachings of Pope John Paul II in our own day.

Father McGivney presumed that the role of the laity was central to the life and mission of the Church. In a very real sense, he anticipated and acted on the principles underlying the Papacy's call for Catholic Action. He pursued the layman into the paths of his everyday social life and animated him there with Catholic principle. His message is timeless, and he is in many ways a model for today's parish priest in his collaboration with the laity, his attention to contemporary social ills and injustices, and in his zeal for a life of union with God through prayer and the sacraments.

His major work, founded from the impulse of his priestly heart full of compassion and concern for the young Catholic families of his day, lives on in the largest Catholic men's organization in the world — the Knights of Columbus. In establishing the Knights, Father McGivney began an institution that would nurture and protect the faith of its members, provide for the needs of their families, and challenge them to the generous service of their neighbors. Father McGivney was convinced that the key to the betterment of family life was the strengthening of the faith and vocation of husbands and fathers. In addition, the heart of this young priest wanted to be God's instrument in the work of salvation, bringing souls to Christ and his Church. Today, the Knights make an extremely wide diversity of charitable contributions to Church and community. In addition, they have an ongoing commitment to fostering vocations to the priesthood and religious life, continuing Father McGivney's own efforts in this regard.

Michael Joseph McGivney was born in Waterbury, Connecticut, on August 12, 1852. He was the oldest of the seven surviving children of Patrick and Mary Lynch McGivney, first-generation Irish immigrants from County Cavan. The McGivneys had left Ireland in the wake of the disastrous potato famine, seeking a better life, like so many other Irish immigrants to our shores. They were married in Waterbury in 1850.

Michael was baptized at St. Peter's Church (later re-named Immaculate Conception), the only Catholic church in Waterbury at the time. Although the McGivney family was never destitute as were many of the Irish immigrant families, they struggled for the daily bread to feed so many mouths. Patrick worked under harsh conditions at a brass foundry. Young Michael learned the tenants of his faith at home, and witnessed the death of six of his young brothers and sisters. He learned early lessons about the nearness of death and the struggles of poverty.

At the age of seven, he was admitted to what would today be considered the third grade. At school, he was noted for excellent deportment and proficiency in his studies. At thirteen, Michael had finished his first schooling and he worked in the spoon department of Holmes, Booth and Haydens, a manufacturing firm in Waterbury for the next three years.

Michael's pastor, Father Thomas Hendricken, took a strong interest in the boy. In 1868 he accompanied him to the College of St. Hyacinth in Quebec, Canada, where Michael spent two years preparing to enter the seminary. Here he won the prize of excellence in English and honorable mention in Latin translation and grammar. From 1870-1872, he studied philosophy at Our Lady of the Angels Seminary attached to Niagara University in New York. He received honorable mention for Algebra, Greek and Latin. Although no records have been found to substantiate it, there is an oral tradition that he studied in 1872 and 1873 at St. Mary's Seminary in Montreal.

Michael's father died in June of 1873 and the family was left without sufficient funds for him to continue his priestly education. Bishop Francis P. MacFarland of Hartford paid his seminary expenses and, at the bishop's request, Michael entered St. Mary's Seminary in Baltimore, Maryland, in the fall of 1873. Here he was appointed sacristan, a position reserved for a seminarian of deep piety. A note from his Sulpician rector reads, "Mr. McGivney is a very good and pious young man, with good and attractive manners, and much address and industry, exceedingly sensitive *usque ad lacrymas* (even unto tears)."

Michael McGivney was ordained to the holy priesthood on December 22, 1877, by Archbishop (later Cardinal) James Gibbons. He celebrated his first Mass at his home parish in Waterbury. What a delightful Christmas present for his mother! Then, he moved immediately to New Haven where he was assigned as curate of St. Mary's Church.

A contemporary described the young priest: "Father McGivney was a man of simple character, pleasant, light-hearted and [one who] delighted in the companionship of children; although rather retiring in his disposition, he possessed an indomitable will and never was discouraged no matter what obstacles might come his way."

As the curate of a sprawling parish, which encompassed the burgeoning Irish-American neighborhoods in New Haven, Father McGivney was constantly busy with his parish work. His strength of character combined with his gentleness and compassion made him beloved by the people. He did what all priests do: he celebrated Mass, heard confessions, baptized, witnessed marriages, catechized the children, visited the sick and brought the comfort of the sacraments to them. The records show that every three or four days there were multiple baptisms, marriages and funerals. Not favored with today's computer-aided record keeping, Father McGivney, in his strong and legible handwriting, carefully recorded all the details of the giving of the sacraments in the parish ledgers. Concerned to be a good confessor for his people, Father McGivney read and kept St. Alphonsus Liguori's handbook for confessors. On his death, the book

Father McGivney as a young priest
PHOTOS COURTESY OF THE KNIGHTS OF COLUMBUS

was passed on to his younger brother, Patrick who was also a priest. In addition to his other duties, he was the leader of the St. Joseph's Young Men of New Haven, a total abstinence society at St. Mary's. The group advocated complete teetotalism and also embraced a program of life taken from the Gospel.

The pastor of the parish, Father P. A. Murphy, was often sick, which left Father McGivney "pulling a double load" in parish work. In October of 1878, the young curate wrote to a former professor "I have not had time for even one day's vacation since I left St. Mary's." In spite of his poor health, Father Murphy was a man with zeal and determination and was a good influence on the inexperienced young priest. Shortly before his own early death, Father Murphy became involved in an important battle for prayer in public schools and his activism in the fearless defense of Catholic principles could not help but impress the young McGivney, who learned much from his ailing pastor, particularly the need to defend the rights of the poor and the young.

After Father Murphy's death, Father McGivney received a pleasant surprise in the appointment of the new pastor, Father Patrick P. Lawlor. Father Lawlor's brother was married to Father McGivney's next youngest sister, Mary Anne. It was Father Lawlor who listened attentively to Father McGivney's ideas of forming a fraternal order for Catholic men and who encouraged these plans. Father Lawlor eventually became the first priest member of the Knights of Columbus after Father McGivney.

In addition to his parish duties, Father McGivney was also responsible for the pastoral care of the inmates of the New Haven jail. He was such a frequent visitor that even years after his death the jail guards still circulated stories of his warmth, humor and genuine concern for the prisoners.

In 1881, a young man, twenty-one years old, named James "Chip" Smith got drunk and shot and killed a policeman who was attempting to arrest him for being disorderly. He was tried for first-degree murder and sentenced to be hanged in spite of the arguments of his attorney who said the crime was not premeditated. The condemned man was held for several months before he was hanged and Father McGivney visited him daily, spending hours counseling him and giving him spiritual guidance. In the death cell before the march to the scaffold, James told Father McGivney, "Father, your saintly ministrations have enabled me to meet death without a tremor. Do not fear for me. I must not break down now." The reporter for the weekly Connecticut Catholic wrote that Smith "went bravely to his death and let it be said to the honor and credit of his spiritual advisor Rev. Father McGivney that he so braced him with the comforts of religion that Smith could not help but die as he did." The priest celebrated a requiem high Mass for Smith and "many tears were shed when the Reverend spoke of the unfortunate fate of the young man."

Always a peacemaker, Father McGivney was at a parish picnic in July of 1879 when a fight broke out between two young men vying for the affections of the same young lady. One of the men expressed a desire to kiss the girl who was dancing with the other at the time. The fight came to blows and Shea and Leahy were "on the ground in deadly combat" and others prepared to join in and support one side or the other. Father McGivney came along and broke up the fight, telling the combatants to "shake and make up." One witness said that had it not been for the priest's intervention it would have been a worse fight than it was.

Father McGivney lived during one of the most anti-Catholic times in America. St. Mary's was located on one of the most prominent streets of the city and the presence of the immigrant Catholics seemed a slap in the face to the dominant Protestant social class. A headline in the New York Times clearly indicated the social tensions in New Haven: "Roman Catholic Troubles in New Haven — How an Aristocratic Avenue Was Blemished by a Roman Church Edifice." Although the reporter focused on the church as an architectural eyesore, he also mentions it as "a source of annoyance and injury to neighboring residents as it invaded the most exclusive homes of wealth and culture."

Father McGivney's charm and his soul of immense sympathy attracted many Protestants, some of whom later converted. The daughter of a prominent Episcopalian minister frequently accompanied the family's maid to Mass at St. Mary's. The maid's devotion to her faith and her pious lifestyle greatly attracted the minister's daughter, who became fatally ill. She told the maid that she wanted to die a Catholic and asked her to bring Father McGivney to see her. This was a very delicate situation because the girl's father was the minister of the richest Protestant church in the city. Father McGivney fearlessly but kindly called on the minister. The father, a true Christian, told Father

McGivney, "If my daughter wishes to embrace the Catholic faith and die in that faith, she shall have her wish with my full consent." Father McGivney then received the girl into the faith and prepared her for death with all the customary rites of the Catholic Church. Another convert due to God's grace through Father McGivney was a student at Yale, David Buell, who later became a Jesuit priest. Buell served for a short time as president of Georgetown University in Washington, D.C. Father McGivney's reputation as a catechist for converts was well known, and shortly before his death two other converts who had entered the priesthood were frequent visitors to the dying priest.

Father McGivney's pastoral concerns prompted him to explore the formation of a fraternal society that would prevent young Catholics from entering the secret societies such as the Masons, which were very popular in his day. In an 1884 encyclical on the evils of Freemasonry, Pope Leo XIII encouraged the bishops and priests to work closely with the laity to deter the faithful from the attractions of secret societies. This Pope of the working man had written: "By uniting the efforts of both clergy and laity, strive . . . to make men thoroughly know and love the Church, for the greater their knowledge and love of the Church the more will they turn away from clandestine societies."

In addition, the formation of such a group would help to combat other social evils of the day. Young men were naturally attracted to the amiable and approachable young priest and often sought him out for counseling. He wanted to form them into good husbands and fathers, in order to strengthen young Catholic families. Having experienced poverty first hand as a child, and having seen the struggles of his widowed mother, Father McGivney wanted to instill within Catholic men a sense of moral responsibility for the financial integrity of the family especially in the unexpected death of the breadwinner. In working to this aim, he had to counteract the Irish repugnance at the thought of insurance.

In Irish village society, the ties of kinship provided for social security, but in America's urban and industrial society, insurance was rapidly becoming a necessity. Breaking down the remnant of the superstitious attitudes of the Old World Irish village was a slow process. Traditional Irish folk wisdom viewed any attempt to prepare for death as a fool's desire to outwit "Mr. Death," and thought that such folly would only bring on an early demise.

The society that Father McGivney envisioned would naturally foster an appreciation of the truths of the Faith. In order to work against the anti-Catholic prejudices of the day, he also wanted to engender true pride in the American Catholic heritage. For this reason, he thought of naming the group the Sons of Columbus, but one of the early organizers successfully argued for the use of the word "Knights" to better symbolize the ritualistic character of the order. By adopting Columbus as their patron, they affirmed the discovery of America as a Catholic event that pre-dated the Puritan landing at Plymouth Rock.

He began to explore his ideas with a group of laymen. Serious and optimistic about the success of these ideas, he finally called a meeting on Sunday, October 2, 1881,which was held in the basement of St. Mary's Church and which was attended by about eighty men from a number of parishes. Although Father McGivney called the meeting, he deferred to lay leadership from the very beginning. He retained the role of organizer and catalyst. He wrote letters to other pastors to gain support for the idea and visited Boston and New York to speak with representatives of the Massachusetts Catholic Order of Foresters and The Catholic Benevolent Legion to discover what he could about these societies. Eventually, plans were made to draw up a constitution and by-laws for a completely new organization, which was incorporated March 29, 1882.

At first, the new group met with severe criticism, and its members experienced disillusionment and doubt of the value of their efforts. Some critics referred to the Knights as the "Catholic Masons." No one could have predicted the eventual, remarkable expansion of the order. A far more sensible prediction would have been its early demise. But Father McGivney worked with persistence and optimism to carry the order through its infancy. Due to illness he was absent for much of January and February 1883, and he later wrote, "the Order I was endeavoring to establish fell back almost lifeless, but not dead." The lack of initial interest was discouraging and Father McGivney wrote to a friend in the Massachusetts Catholic Order of Foresters, "Our beginning is extremely slow, but I think that when our by-laws are distributed we will advance more rapidly." He could hardly envision that within fifteen years of his death, the Knights would expand into every state of the Union, Canada, Mexico and the Philippines.

Father McGivney did not intend that his Knights would become a canonical lay society (legally) attached to the authority structure of the Church. The presence of a chaplain, appointed by the Bishop, signaled the Church's indirect approval of the fraternal organization. Father McGivney had earlier discussed his plans with Bishop Lawrence McMahon, and received his full approval. (Because the Knight's chaplains are elected, not appointed, the group has been considered from its foundation a society that Catholics are permitted to join in good faith.)

The ceremonials were established not as the ritualized mumbo-jumbo of secret societies, but to symbolize the fact that the Knights could be proud of their religious heritage and could additionally be patriotically loyal to their country.

The first council was established on May 15, 1882, with twenty-four members. They named the council San Salvador to commemorate the name of the island where Columbus first set foot in the New World. Father McGivney personally installed the officers of the fledgling group. He assisted with all the work necessary for the foundation, although he kept aloof from the social dimension of the order. Two of the original incorporators of the group later failed to join it, possibly in opposition to the fact that a priest was involved. However, Father McGivney was never known to hold the slightest feeling of resentment towards them or to anyone who differed with him. His charity in this respect was one of the marked features of his life. His inspiration of the Knights was not one of rhetoric, but rather was founded on his practical work as organizer and ambassador.

In November 1884, Father McGivney was assigned as pastor of St. Thomas' Church in Thomaston, Connecticut. In a final moving sermon at St. Mary's, he spoke of his transfer and asked forgiveness if he had ever seemed severe or austere. He prayed that they would all meet in Heaven "where there are no partings, and where no one is called upon to say good-bye." There were tears in the eyes of many in the congregation. Although he was sad to leave his beloved parish, the wishes of his Bishop were, for this obedient young priest, God's Will for him.

In his brief thirteen years of priesthood, first as curate at St. Mary's and then as pastor at St. Thomas, Father McGivney performed the customary duties: he celebrated Mass, heard confessions, baptized, witnessed marriages, visited the sick and brought the comfort of the sacraments to them. His manner was gentle yet firm. He was understanding but demanding, a friend to all but set aside as a man of God. He had a tender heart. The sick and elderly were close to his heart and he took time out from his busy schedule to visit them. Some of them even spoke of him as "a living saint." Faithfully he prayed the Divine Office daily, made private meditations and said his rosary. He examined his conscience and went to confession regularly. His ordinary life flowed from an extraordinary union with and love of God. One day, if this ordinary parish priest is raised to the honors of the altar, he may serve to inspire ordinary people to live their own vocations with the same optimism, courage and heroic virtue as he did.

In preparing for the great feasts of the liturgical year and on holidays, Father McGivney was energetic and creative. He took care to ensure that all events would bear spiritual fruit and provide good wholesome fun. The beauty of the Easter decorations and the repository for Holy Thursday at St. Mary's was commented on favorably in the secular press. Special dramatic presentations and musical revues were held to celebrate the annual St. Patrick's day observance and Father McGivney was always coming up with new ways to entertain the parishioners, especially the young men and women, at the annual fair. On one occasion while at St. Thomas, Father McGivney made a special trip to New York to obtain just the right costumes and props for a production of the play "Eileen Oge" on St. Patrick's day. At the parish picnic he made certain there were enough hired horses so the young who wanted a horse and buggy ride would not have to wait too long in line. His strength of character combined with his compassion made him well loved by his parishioners.

Father McGivney was a Marian soul, deeply devoted to Our Lady. He delivered a number of beautiful and touching sermons on the Blessed Virgin and bequeathed to his parishioners

Father McGivney in his rectory parlor

and to the Knights a tender devotion to her. In 1883 two hundred youngsters were received into the Children of Mary sodality through his encouragement. He took a personal interest in organizing the annual May devotions with the crowning of the image of Blessed Mother. Today, a standard part of the work of the Knights of Columbus is the distribution of Mary's rosary.

Another favorite devotion of Father McGivney was the Sacred Heart. He was educated by the Jesuits, Vincentians, and Sulpicians, all noted for their devotion to the hearts of Jesus and Mary. One of Father McGivney's few extant letters was signed, "In the Sacred Heart."

As pastor of St. Thomas, Father McGivney proved he was an able administrator. In 1885, a member of the parish wrote, "Improvements are constantly coming from his hand." He had steam heat, electric lights and a telephone installed in the parish and walkways around the church paved.

When laying some pipe one summer day in order to bring water to the parish cemetery, Father McGivney asked for help from some of his unemployed parishioners. With true concern, however, he reminded them, "Now, boys, don't work too hard this warm day." Later, he thanked them publicly at Mass on Sunday.

Father McGivney's new parish was closer to his hometown of Waterbury than New Haven, so he was able to visit his family more often. He proudly attended his brother John's high school graduation. John was a good student and valedictorian of his class. Later, this brother succeeded him as supreme chaplain of the Knights. In 1888, his beloved mother died.

Excitement and even adversity were also part of Father McGivney's time at St. Thomas. Just a few months after his arrival, there was an attempted robbery of the safe in the rectory's basement. The intruders, however, hadn't counted on the dog. A wise householder, Father McGivney had gotten a dog to "watch" the place. Everyone was awakened and the thieves fled before they were able to break into the safe.

Lightning struck the steeple of the mission church in Terryville that was also under Father McGivney's pastoral care. In 1889, the young priest was almost killed in a road accident, which caused the death of his horse and the destruction of his carriage.

Father McGivney had never been in robust health. Pneumonia struck him in January of 1890. There was an epidemic raging in many of the New England states at this time. Two doctors were called in consultation, but this was the beginning of the end. For the next seven months his condition gradually worsened. In early March, Father McGivney traveled to Virginia, out of the area of contagion, for a period of rest in hopes of a complete recovery. He stopped in New York where he was treated by an "eminent medical staff." He cut his rest short and returned to Thomaston in time for Holy Week and the local paper reported that he was "much improved in health." He continued to improve until June and kept on with his heavy schedule of work as long as he could. He suffered a relapse in July and was confined to bed. By early August his condition was critical. He died at the age of 38 on August 14, the vigil of the Assumption, officially of tuberculosis. Before his death he visited with his sisters and many friends. His obituary remarked, "having done his work so thoroughly, his greatest regret was that he could not live to see his two brothers ordained." In his will, he showed his loving concern for the welfare of these two brothers, Patrick and John, who were both just a few years from priestly ordination.

Always unassuming, the priest had his love of simplicity carried out at his funeral, where there were no flowers at his own request. The custom at this time was for extremely elaborate floral decorations at funerals, to the point that many of the clergy preached against this. All businesses in Thomaston were closed and there were more than fifty priests at the service and the church was overflowing with mourners. A special train accommodated the Waterbury friends of Father McGivney and more than 250 Knights from nearly all of the fifty-six councils in Connecticut were in attendance. The funeral procession was the largest ever seen in Waterbury and nearly every horse-drawn taxi in town, and in the nearby towns, was rented for the day. The cortege ended at St. Joseph's Cemetery where Father McGivney was buried in his family's plot.

The young priest's cedar casket was put in a brick vault and sealed with two slate slabs. In December of 1981, his remains were transferred to St. Mary's Church in New Haven. His mortal remains and even his burial vestments were preserved in remarkably good condition, more than ninety-one years after his death. The cause for canonization of the Servant of God Father Michael J. McGivney was formally opened in December 1997. ✢

21

Rogelio "Francisco" Gonzalez-Corzo
Cuba, 1932-1961

"Viva Cuba, Viva Cristo Rey, Viva la Agru . . . !"

The young man known in the clandestine Cuban resistance forces as Francisco did not deceive himself about his chances of survival. He was experienced enough to understand that no one could operate in the underground forever and that sooner or later there would be a fateful moment in which the fish would not be able to evade the dragnet. Still, he strove to serve as much and as long as possible. Recently he had grown a mustache and dyed his hair. On a trip to Miami, he visited a friend late at night. While there, he woke up one of his friend's small daughters and asked her, "Who am I?" The little girl barely opened her eyes and drowsily muttered, "Francisco." The young revolutionary turned to his friend and softly said," I am doomed." In fact, within a few weeks of his return to Cuba, Castro's police finally trapped him.

His captors knew that there was a clandestine leader called "Francisco" who commanded great respect because of his courage, discretion, and resourcefulness. One of the most important men of the underground, he was a prime target of Cuban intelligence, which recognized his prowess and ability. According to official documents, he was "a well-known and extremely dangerous counter-revolutionary who had taken part in the organization of armed uprisings in many places in the country and was responsible for innumerable acts of terrorism and sabotage." In effect, "Francisco" had directed the underground's assault against cities and towns and wreaked havoc in the countryside. The young agronomist engineer organized rendezvous positions to receive weapons, explosives, and other supplies by sea, and had supported the infiltration units of the brigade. He was a leader of the M.R.R. — Movimiento de Recuperación Revolucionaria (Revolutionary Recovery Movement) — the group that maintained the closest contact with the United States government, specifically with the Central Intelligence Agency. In addition, he was an active member of the Cuban Catholic lay association of students and young professionals, the Agrupacion Catolica Universitaria. Castro's security people knew all this, but when they surprised a meeting of the underground chiefs and arrested all those present, Rogelio Gonzalez Corzo's youthful looks misled them, and they were unaware that they had at last captured the notorious "Francisco." Instead, they believed that their net had drawn up an obscure fish named Harold Bove Castillo.

Frantically, Cuban exiles in Miami did all they could to make it appear that "Francisco" was in the United States taking a special training course. The Miami Herald cooperated by publishing the picture of a hooded man taken while in the middle of some sort of military drill. According to the caption of the photograph, the man was "Francisco." Other friends tried to plan a way of escape for him. Their plans failed. Within a few days, police interrogators accumulated enough information to discern the true identity of Harold Bove Castillo, and the death sentence was imposed.

Rogelio Gonzalez-Corzo was born in Havana on September 16, 1932 to Spanish Catholic parents, Manuel Gonzalez and Gloria Corzo. He had two older brothers, Isidro and Manuel.

He attended the Colegio San Francisco de Sales for his primary school studies, after which he attended the Jesuit Colegio (High School) of Belen. He continued his education at the University of Havana, graduating in Agronomy. Later he took a post-graduate course in the United States, in Baton Rouge, Louisiana, studying rice production. In all his studies, he proved to be an outstanding student.

At the University, Rogelio became an active member of the Agrupacion Catolica Universitaria. Devout in his religion, he was a daily communicant. He prayed the rosary daily and took an active part in the Saturday afternoon Honor Guards through which the ACU

Rogelio Gonzalez-Corzo
PHOTOS COURTESY OF JOSÉ M. HERNANDEZ

manifested its devotion to the Virgin Mary in a special way. Rogelio was deeply concerned with the problem of poverty in Cuba and helped to establish a number of cooperatives throughout Cuba that would loan money to the poor. Once he deposited all of his savings in the account of a newly organized credit union just to set an example and allay the fears of a group of distrustful workers.

Soft-spoken and smooth-faced, at age twenty-eight Rogelio still had the looks of a freshman student. This impression was accentuated by the friendly smile, which usually illuminated his handsome countenance. At the ACU, he was always the first to volunteer for even the most unpretentious jobs such as painting a room or apartment or organizing a jaunt to the countryside. His happy and outgoing nature often cloaked the depth of his spiritual strength and nature.

In 1957, Rogelio attended a play in the Auditorium Theatre in Havana, presented by the Agrupacion Catolica. He was seated next to Miss Dulce Carrera Justiz, the daughter of a local lawyer and statesman. They were introduced at intermission and when he returned from Louisiana in 1958 they began dating. Eventually, they became engaged to marry.

In 1959, when Castro came to power, Rogelio became the Director of Agriculture under the minister Humberto Sori Marin. He soon became disillusioned by Castro's redirection of the Revolution. He realized that the government was marching swiftly toward Communism. Previously, his fiancée's father had warned him that many of the new government appointees were members of the Communist party, but Rogelio had responded that they would be weeded out, little by little. Gloomily, Mr. Carrera predicted that the Communists would take over the country.

When the Cuban episcopate realized that what they were seeing under the new regime was an ill-disguised attempt to transform Cuba into a totalitarian Communist state, it did not hesitate to denounce the warping of the revolutionary process. It made it clear that it rejected communism and the majority of Catholics began to actively oppose the enthronement of the communists. One of the Agrupacion members, Manolo Artime, attended a meeting in the fall of 1959 with Castro, Che Guevara, and other government officials and realized that Castro's real purpose was to destroy the institution of private property in the country, give no compensation whatsoever to the dispossessed landlords, and make the state the sole owner of the land. The young lieutenant immediately resigned his commission in the rebel army and published a letter about the meeting, which was widely distributed throughout the country.

Eventually the ACU became the focal point of a specifically Catholic and religiously motivated anti-Castro underground. In October of 1959, Monsignor Eduardo Boza Masvidal, Auxiliary Bishop of Havana and an active ACU member, explained why Castro's revolution could not be styled as Christian in an article published in La Quincena. In the article, he gave six reasons why he had arrived at his conclusion: 1) Castro's revolution was not based on a spiritual conceptualization of life and man; 2) it had no room for love, only for the hatred and resentment implicit in the class struggle; 3) it failed to recognize the dignity of the human person and its inherent freedom as God's creature; 4) it negated private property, the cornerstone of individual liberty; 5) it sanctioned the indiscriminate use of slander and character assassination for the pursuance of its goals; 6) its ties with the Soviet Union and the Soviet-block countries went far beyond what was advisable and reasonable. The bishop concluded, "I might have missed something; however, what I have said suffices to show that it is foolish to keep talking about the 'ghost' of communism unless of course we persuade ourselves to believe in ghosts." By December of that year, Catholic resistance was formally constituted as the M.R.R., so named because it originated from Castro's own revolutionary ranks. Along with Artime, Rogelio was among its founding members. The pro-Communist government had hardened its attitude toward religion and embarked on an increasingly strident and aggressive campaign against the Church. Many young Catholic intellectuals and students believed that the time for armed resistance had finally arrived, and began to plot against the government.

Rogelio dreamed of a Cuba where Christian social justice would be in practice, and where the principles of the Church would improve the lives of the people. He was totally convinced that only through the strength of a liberated Cuba could this dream come true. He offered himself totally to the effort to eradicate Communism in order to recover for God his beloved homeland. With his natural leadership abilities, he became the M.R.R.'s National Coordinator and the head of the underground in Cuba. In the underground, he became known simply as "Francisco." Fearful of the danger because of his position, he sent his parents and his brothers to Spain. He wanted Dulce to leave the country also, but she refused.

Since Dulce had refused to leave Cuba, Rogelio told her that they would pretend to break up. Later, he would call her under a different name, and he would send flowers the same way. Several times they were able to meet. To this day, she does not know where the meetings were because she would be picked up by others and taken to see him in safe houses. The meetings were brief, usually less than half an hour. From time to time, he hid out in houses that belonged to Dulce's family. Once he called her and said, "Hello, how are you? Fine? Oh, I'm sorry I have the wrong number." She understood that the call was only to let her hear his voice and to reassure her that he was okay. Another time he called her from the United States. Once, returning from the States, he brought her a few souvenirs.

Rogelio lived through six months of the fighting, minute-by-minute, never resting, to provide the resistance that he felt God had prepared him for. His spiritual depth and stature came to the fore during these darkest of times. In many respects he had to set himself apart from the world in which he had previously lived. He was away

Rogelio as "Francisco"

from his family, his beloved fiancée, his work and his companions in the ACU. He did not, however, forsake the practices on which his piety rested. Constantly being hunted by government agents, he had to move frequently, but he invariably found time to receive Holy Communion, sometimes standing on a sidewalk, sitting on a parked car, or in the house in which he happened to be hiding at the time. Never a man given to grumbling or lamenting, with unfailing courage and the strength of the ultimate rationale of his actions, he continued with imperturbable tenacity to serve as much and as long as possible.

Rogelio was arrested on the afternoon of Saturday March 18, 1961. A number of leaders of the underground were meeting in a supposedly "safe house" to discuss plans to intensify the sabotage campaign that had been rocking the country since the previous fall when they were surrounded by Castro's heavily armed agents.

Dulce's sister Elvira learned of Rogelio's capture the following day. She felt immediately that his captors would find out who he was in spite of his false identification. She spent two weeks without telling her sister; she says she felt as if she were dying inside. Eventually, one day in the family garage, Elvira began crying and Dulce guessed, "They caught Rogelio." Later, standing in front of her house she saw two military cars passing. Rogelio was looking at her from one of them. That was the last time she ever saw him. She wasn't allowed to attend his funeral. The last time the young couple had spoken, they had named a date for their wedding, but the careful preparations Dulce had made were never to be completed.

Rogelio Gonzalez-Corzo spent his last hours in a secluded section of La Cabana known as the "chapel." Here an eyewitness has reported that he spent his time giving Christ's comfort and strength to the other six prisoners also condemned to death. Here, too, he wrote a final, moving letter to his parents and brothers. Full of concern for them, he wrote:

"I am fully aware of what it will mean for all of you to learn about my death where you are, so far away from where I am. But this is what I have always prayed for to God. I sincerely believe that your moral and even physical suffering would have been far greater had you been here and lived through the intervening time between my detention and my death — a total of thirty-two days. I hope that my imprisonment and my execution will not embarrass you under any circumstances. On the contrary, you should be proud of your son, who knew how to rise to the occasion and assume the right attitude when God and the fatherland asked him to sacrifice himself. I want you to know that such was the only attitude that your son could assume given the situation that the fatherland is going through at the present moment.

"I am writing this letter at 2:00 am on the morning of 20 April. I am in a cell that is called capilla [chapel], and I will be dead in a matter of minutes. It is my wish to let you know by means of this letter that my last thoughts on this earth have been for you and my dear brothers.

"Parents, brothers: I have only one truly serious concern at this moment, but since this is my last will I trust that this source of anxiety will become the origin of great joy. I am talking of your spiritual life, your religious life. You know that to be a good Catholic and to obey God's will has always been of great importance to me. Right now I am sure that I am conducting myself in the way that God wants, and I wish that my death, of which you should be proud, serves the purpose of making you two, mom and dad, promise me that you will attend Mass every Sunday, go to confession, receive Holy Communion, and do so regularly. I also want my brothers, Manolito and Isidro, to make the Spiritual Exercises every year, go to confession and receive Holy Communion every month and attend Mass every Sunday. They should do their best to be good husbands, which should not be difficult since they have two gems for wives, Laurita and Fifi. I ask both of them to improve their spiritual lives, too. As to my nephew, Carlos Manuel, please tell him that he had an uncle who loved him dearly and who died so that later on he could live in a reputable and Catholic Cuba. And please send him to a Catholic school, because it is more important to save the soul than to learn English. Many kisses for my godson and my two nieces. Send them too to Catholic schools, so that they may grow to be good sons and daughters.

"Death is already knocking at my door, but as all my companions I have great peace of mind, because cost what it may it will show me the way to heaven and eternal happiness. Besides, it will take me to my grandparents' side, wherefrom I will be waiting for all of you when the time comes.

"Fix it in your minds, lamentations are uncalled-for. This is the best thing that could happen to me. Remember, I will be waiting for you in heaven. Be strong as I am strong even at this moment. And never forget that I am leaving this world worrying only about one thing: your spiritual life. Please do not neglect it for any reason. Under no circumstances my fate should be a motive for the weakening of your faith in God. Quite to the contrary, it should strengthen it. I have nothing more to say. Waiting for you in heaven, I remain your son who will never forget you, and together with [my] grandparents will be looking forward to see you again."

The morning of April 20, Rogelio was executed in la Cabana, after a summary and secret trial. His last words were "*Viva Cuba, Viva Cristo Rey!*" ("Long live Cuba! Long live Christ the King!"). He began a final Viva to the Agrupacion Catolica Universitaria, but the discharge of bullets interrupted that Viva and ended his earthly life.

Thirty-three days after Rogelio's arrest, just after the Bay of Pigs invasion, he was executed in the fortress of La Cabana on the morning of April 20. As his last words paid tribute to Christ the King, those who knew Rogelio Gonzalez-Corzo believe he now attends at the court of Christ, his King.

There were a number of other devout young Catholics who were also executed in La Cabana including Virgilio Campanería and AlbertoTapia. In September 1999, a group of Cubans living in exile petitioned Pope John Paul II to open the cause for beatification for Gonzalez-Corzo, Campaneria, and Tapia. ✢

22

Satoko Kitahara
Japan, 1929-1958

Ari no Machi no Maria — Mary of Ants Town

Yase Gaman: "Grow Thinner to Endure!" The slogan was posted throughout Tokyo. Sixteen-year-old Satoko Kitahara was thoroughly sick of her new staple diet — sweet potatoes — but she endured and worked hard at the lathe in the Nakajima Aeroplane Factory. Since September 1943, the military government, worried about the U.S. advance northwards had decreed all-out airplane production and Satoko worked long shifts to double her production. She began to show signs of lung trouble; some of her school friends had already died of tuberculosis. Satoko worked hard this freezing winter, but she missed the colorful kimonos, music and stage plays that as a member of the upper class she had been accustomed to. She uttered no complaint, however, for that would be unpatriotic and treason to the soldiers risking their lives in the war.

Tokyo, a city built of wood, lived in terror of fire and now its citizens awaited the delivery of "Flowers of Washington," the napalm flowers that the B-29s would deliver in aluminum vases. Satoko and her friends had begun regular bamboo spear practice, in readiness for the invasion. She had knelt before the family altar and vowed to her ancestors and the Shinto gods that she would fight and willingly give her life for her sacred homeland, her sole request that the others in her family be spared.

By the summer of 1945 the last Japanese rifle on Okinawa was silenced. The Americans had paid with 12,500 dead and 30,000 casualties. 110,000 Japanese soldiers and 75,000 Okinawa citizens had died. Half of the city of Tokyo, 56 square miles, was destroyed. 13 million Japanese people were homeless. August 6th and 9th, B-29s devastated Hiroshima and Nagasaki with a powerful new bomb. August 15, 1945, the Emperor broadcast to the nation for the first time. Japan was stunned to hear the voice from the Chrysanthemum Throne telling them to "bear the unbearable." Unconditional surrender!

Forty-six percent of the citizens of Tokyo had lost their homes and tens of thousands lived like rats in lean-tos made of scorched beams and pieces of tin. The food ration was less than two small cups of rice a day. Morale slumped and discipline cracked. In May 1946, 28 Japanese military leaders were put on trial for war crimes. Satoko saw her beloved country put on trial by a world court and found guilty. She felt betrayed. She had believed the Militarists' propaganda, believed her heroes had died for a noble cause. Instead, it was for a lie foisted on the people by the generals. Three million Japanese had died for a lie. She longed to discuss it with her brilliant professor father, but she did not want to burden him with her dark questions.

In 1947 or 1948, Satoko visited a friend in Yokohama, a girl with whom she often discussed weighty thoughts on the meaning of life. They took a walk through the western area of the city and came to the Church of the Sacred Heart. Noticing a Japanese entering, the girls decided to look inside. Neither had ever been inside a Christian church before. Here they saw a statue of Our Lady of Lourdes, made of plaster and hardly a work of art. Yet the lady touched something deep inside of Satoko and moved her as no other statue had ever done. Later she wrote, "This was the very first time I had seen a statue of the Blessed Mother. Drawn, I know not why, to enter that church, I gazed on the statue, sensing the presence of a very attractive force that I could not explain." As is the case for many others, the Virgin seemed to call Satoko Kitahara. The loving mother tugged at her daughter, pulling her ever deeper into the love of Christ.

Satoko Kitahara was born August 22, 1929, two years before her father was awarded his third doctorate degree and began a highly successful career as a university professor. The family lived in a beautiful two-story house in the western suburb of Tokyo. In 1935 she began her primary school and one day on the way to school, she was hit by a bus. The driver rushed into her house carrying the small

Satoko as a young girl
PHOTOS COURTESY OF THE ANTONIAN

girl in his arms. She did not seem badly hurt, but from that day a limousine took her to and from school.

One of Satoko's two older sisters began to teach her kanji, the beautiful and difficult Chinese calligraphic lettering, before she was in school. When that sister died, a sad little Satoko took her copy book and practiced the ideographs before her sisters' black lacquered mortuary tablet on the family altar. After Satoko entered school, her parents had a teacher come to the house to teach her special writing lessons. Satoko's father chose the ideograph for her name, which meant "love of law and order." For the professor, this was the foundation of wisdom. The words that make up her name stand for "child of enlightenment."

After six years of perfect attendance at primary school, Satoko attended one of Japan's best private girls' schools. The Kitaharas were wealthy but not ostentatious. They used their money wisely, and expended it lavishly on their children's education. When Satoko was ten, they bought a German piano and Satoko began lessons. She loved music and dreamed of becoming a concert pianist.

In February of 1946 in order to honor her older brother who had died of pneumonia, Satoko determined to enter the medical field. She passed the exams and began her university studies at the Showa Women's Pharmaceutical University. In 1949 she graduated as a qualified pharmacist. She was offered two good jobs but declined both, telling her parents she was not ready to choose a career yet. Her father told her that he and her mother agreed, "I don't mind what you do in life. We will never oppose the path you choose, so long as you walk it well." How often later the professor must have regretted this bold, uncompromising statement!

A new school run by a Spanish order of nuns, the Mercedarians, was opened in Koenji and Satoko's

Satoko with her sisters just before college

parents enrolled their youngest daughter, Choko, there. When Satoko accompanied her mother and sister to a ceremony there, she was impressed by the principal's speech. Two months later, she walked her sister to Mass at the church and as she left Choko there, Satoko realized that she didn't know what her path in life was to be. She spent the next few weeks attending the movies five or six times a week, dressing in her beautiful kimonos, and rejecting the marriage proposal from a young doctor. The diversions didn't help; Satoko still had no peace of heart.

One day in July she marched off to her sister's school and asked to speak with a sister. Hesitantly, Satoko explained her restlessness to Mother Angeles Aguirre and asked her the troublesome question about the meaning of life. Mother Angeles replied, "Well, why don't you sit down and hear what we Christians think is the answer." Daily Satoko returned to the convent for more lessons, and in October she asked for Baptism. She said, "I was convinced I had found the truth and asked to be baptized. . . . I was baptized Elizabeth on Sunday, the 30th of October, which that year was the feast day of Christ the King. Two days later I was confirmed, taking the confirmation name of Jesus' mother, Mary." Satoko's par-

Satoko with Mother Angeles on her Baptism day

ents were opposed to her baptism but in the end agreed she was free to choose for herself. Although she wanted to become a Mercedarian, she was not able to do so for health reasons.

In the freezing winter of 1950, the Polish Franciscan Brother Zeno visited Tokyo on a fact-finding tour of the city's most destitute areas. A friend and co-worker of St. Maximilian Kolbe, he had come with Kolbe to establish a Conventual Franciscan foundation in Japan and to begin their publishing apostolate here in 1930. Although Kolbe returned to Poland and a heroic death in a Nazi prison camp, Zeno remained in Japan and did much for the orphans and the destitute after the war.

One cold December day, Brother Zeno was passing the Takagi Footwear Wholesalers owned by Satoko's brother-in-law when a shop attendant greeted him and invited him to have a cup of tea, telling him the shop owner's sister was a Catholic. The assistant then went upstairs and told Satoko that she had a visitor who "looks like Santa Claus." Satoko wrote that she was startled by "his extraordinarily penetrating yet gentle eyes. I had the sensation that here was someone who could see into the depths of my heart." Zeno gave Satoko a pamphlet, asked her to pray for the pitiful poor on the streets and left, promising to return. Satoko read the little booklet on how a Father Kolbe once worked in Nagasaki and later gave his life to save a fellow inmate in Auschwitz.

That same day, Zeno came across a settlement of bataya, ragpickers, on the bank of the Sumida. The settlement had been begun by a man named Ozawa whom the people called "The Boss." A construction worker in Manchuria, he returned to Tokyo after the war and was horrified at the numbers of people homeless with no prospect of a job. A shrewd businessman, he moved into an abandoned building in the public park and began employing the homeless people to bring scrap, which he sold for recycling. He was joined in the work by Tooru Matsui, a young writer turned attorney, who helped Ozawa establish the ragpickers as a legal entity that they named Ants Town because "ants work hard, anywhere at all, and gain strength from community." Matsui had been turned off by a Christianity where he felt the "Gospel Christ would feel a stranger," but recognized in Zeno one who might help Ants Town gain needed good publicity. Quickly, without consulting the Franciscan, Matsui phoned a local newspaper and announced, "the famous Father Zeno is here in Ants Town where we are going to build a church. I can hold him here for another 20 minutes if you are interested in interviewing him." A quick reporter responded and that evening's paper carried an article and photo of the men discussing the new church and the plight of the homeless ragpickers who lived in bare huts.

Satoko read the article with interest. A few days later she spotted Brother Zeno in the street and followed him to Ants Town. He introduced the wealthy young woman in the beautiful kimono to the Boss and then took her on a strange sightseeing tour in the rain. He left her at home and promised to call again.

Satoko wrote, "I lay down in bed but could not get to sleep. Br. Zeno, a man without formal education, unable to read Japanese, had bridged a chasm separating two nations and two cultures. He had discovered a part of Japan I did not know existed, where thousands lived in unbelievable destitution. Many of them lived less than a kilometer from my home! I had lived in the pampered, educated ignorance of an over-sophisticated world while this unlettered foreigner worked without thought of self in the world of painful reality. . . . I lived surrounded by carpets and gas stoves while he went without even an umbrella into the terrible twilight world of destitution." She had been led to the world of the Gospels and she had been trying hard to live them, but chapters like Matthew 25 disturbed her. For months she had been uneasy and had prayed for guidance. Were the things she saw on Brother Zeno's tour God's answer to her prayers?

A few days later Brother Zeno appeared again, this time bringing Matsui with a request that Satoko help them arrange a Christmas show for the children of Ants Town. Her grandmother who recognized Matsui as a former famous playwright thought it was a worthwhile request, so Satoko went that afternoon to begin, seeing Ants Town for the first time by the light of day. She was both repelled and attracted by this place, home to a hundred people. She began trying to teach a group of children to sing but soon realized they had no concept of music. So she took them home to her beautiful, wealthy home, to sing with them by the piano. She couldn't believe their joy at being allowed in such a lovely place, and when she asked them about school, they told her they didn't attend because the other children were hateful to them about their raggedy clothes. When they were fortunate enough to have a new pencil box, the others accused them of stealing it and so they hated school.

"Suddenly I felt an urge to hug these pitiful little children. They were beautiful, beautiful! Hot anger surged through me as I listened to the unadorned tales of injustice and segregation. Somehow someone must

Satoko with some of her "ants"

find a way out of this ugly maze to give them hope for the future. I became absolutely determined to make at least their Christmas Eve a really good one."

The Christmas program was indeed a good one. The ragpickers had made a cardboard stable and Santa Claus and the children's clear voices touched the heart of all. Brother Zeno was delighted with the manger scene and fell to his knees with his rosary. The Ants Town people also knelt, even the caustic Matsui who later wrote that he could accept this impoverished holy family surrounded by the likes of the Ants Town people, it was just religionists he could not stand. Satoko had brought some cardboard puppets to tell the story of Christmas to the children, but a power outage caused them to cluster around her, calling her Sensei (teacher). She told them ghost stories as they all burrowed closer in around her. By the time she left, their dirty smell and sleeves used to wipe runny noses no longer bothered her.

At home, her horrified mother fixed her tea and, noticing her scratching her hair, she rushed Satoko to the bathroom and washed her with Lysol and warm water to remove the lice.

Soon afterwards, Satoko wrote to a friend expecting a child, "It has become a real joy spending time with these little disadvantaged ones. My heart swells with special joy for your child because I too have come to know the joys of motherhood ... thanks to my children in Ants Town." She went with Brother Zeno to a shantytown built in a cemetery where the people resorted to drawing drinking water from the hand basin of the public toilets. She helped the illiterate Brother by writing notes to send to the Franciscans, and was startled to find that these people were not insane, just homeless and jobless. The problem of the poor of Tokyo became a consuming passion for her. She went daily to help the youngest children at Ants Town and in the afternoon brought a few of the older ones home. She planned to tutor them until they were caught up in their studies and then get them all back in school. In spite of complaints of the neighbors, her parents allowed her to continue although her mother insisted that she daily delouse and fumigate the piano room used by the children.

One day, burning with a high fever, Satoko met with the cynical Matsui who bluntly poured out his feelings and told her that Catholic charity was nothing but a sad charade. He said, "Were they genuine followers of Christ they would be poor and share the painful life of the poor. . . . Surely you don't imagine you are followers of Christ just because you give the poor what you don't need at Christmas and Eastertime. You people use Christ's beautiful life. . . . You in your fine two-story house, you wouldn't have a clue about the misery of people who have to live in destitution 365 days a year!" Then he challenged her "As you know, there has been talk of putting up a church in Ants Town. If you people still want to do that there is a condition. You'll find that condition in 2 Corinthians 8:9."

Satoko later wrote that his words left her speechless. "It seemed that Jesus had just spoken to Elizabeth Satoko through this man who was an unbeliever, exposing my Pharisaic pride." Dizzy and hurt, Satoko struggled home where she was immediately put to bed and the doctor called. For weeks she lay in her bed, suffering from the first stages of tuberculosis. Matsui's challenge remained constantly with her: "Remember how generous the Lord Jesus was; though rich, he became poor to make you rich through his poverty." Through her crucible of suffering, she began to understand the gospel ideal and with blind trust she put everything in God's hands.

Satoko checking the scales at Ants Town

After a month, Satoko was finally allowed to get up and take a walk outside. In the beauty of spring she began to think. "With a start of realization, I stood up. In my pride and insensitivity I had not seen what God was trying to show me. I had thought I was a great Christian because I condescended to dole out some free time, helping Ants children with their homework! To save us, God sent His only Son to be one of us. . . . He really became one of us! It hit me now. There was only one way to help those ragpicker children: become a ragpicker like them! At precisely the moment that truth took possession of me a child's voice shouted 'Kitahara Sensei!'" It was one of her favorites of the teenagers who told her that it was his last day of ragpicking as he and his father were leaving Ants Town. She helped him collect a large load of scrap and begged him to allow her to pull the cart back to Ants Town. There she helped him sort the scrap and told the Boss, "I'm now one of the ragpickers." Matsui passed by and asked her if she had read 2 Corinthians. She answered in the affirmative so he responded with a bow and a gracious "Arigato" (thank you) and disappeared. Only a few days later a new building appeared in Ants Town — a church with a cross on top.

Satoko began teaching classes to the children. Then she helped with planning a diet and proper meals in a community refectory. Finally, she brought up the matter of a bathhouse at least for the children. Satoko convinced the Boss to build a small bathhouse. A gasoline drum cut in half made two baths, which were laid sideways and heated on a wood fire. Satoko organized bath times for the children, bathing the littlest ones herself. When older children misbehaved in the bathhouse, she established order with well-aimed buckets of cold water. There was a lot of sickness in Ants Town and Satoko spent a great deal of time visiting the sick and the aging.

Responding to the idea of one of the children who wanted to collect scrap in order to pay for real desks rather than their fruit box makeshift ones, Satoko, too, began pulling a cart and collecting scrap. She changed her fastidious ideas about collecting scrap. It not only provided a living for people with no work but also helped the country by saving precious and scarce materials. The first time, when a neighbor spotted her, she became embarrassed and instinctively cried out

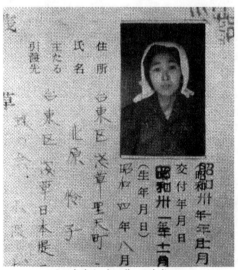

Satoko's junk collector's license

to the Virgin, "Maria-sama, help me!" In that instant of prayer she was freed of false human respect, and Mary's words came to her: "Behold the handmaid of the Lord. Be it done unto me according to your word." Truly at one with her beloved poor, Satoko resisted any temptation to ask for financial help from her family. She felt the only way to help the children was to teach them self-reliance.

The children's summer assignments were to do essays and projects about the mountains and the sea — but they had never seen such beautiful things. Satoko helped them earn the huge sum of 6000 yen for transportation and a friend of Matsui allowed them the use of a summer home. The children had a wonderful vacation and were able to complete their assignments well. In order to teach the children charity and unselfishness, she led them in a drive to collect scrap and raise funds for a community drive for the needy. How proud they were when they had an appointment with the governor of Tokyo and delivered the improbable sum of 12,000 yen.

A reporter had heard of the work Satoko was doing in Ants Town and when he interviewed people about her he heard of her great devotion to Mary. When his article appeared, he called Satoko Ari no Machi no Maria, Mary of Ants Town.

Satoko was working a fierce schedule. She arrived before five in the morning to plan for the day and finish sorting the scrap from the day before. Then she led the children in calisthenics and morning prayers. After breakfast, she helped them with their homework and made certain they got off to school. Then she visited the sick and the old. After school, she went with the children to collect scrap. Afterward they would sort, weigh and tally their day's haul and often it was nearly midnight when she returned home. Although they had been sworn to secrecy, Matsui got word of a story from one of the children that worried him. One afternoon collecting scrap, Satoko had fallen and the children felt she looked sick. In November the doctor was called and ordered her to rest. In spite of a long vacation, her health continued to decline.

In August of 1952, shortly before her twenty-third birthday, Satoko was praying and trying to conjure up her normal image of Mary, but all she could see was Our Lady of Sorrows. She wrote, "It would be a precious grace if God asked me to offer myself so that I could make our Mother, Our Lady, smile. . . . I feel my path to Heaven will be a long and painful one. I do not intend to work just for my own eternal salvation, closing my eyes to the people around me. No, I want to offer God many beautiful sacrifices so that I may help others avoid the pains of hell and reach Him in Heaven. If my sufferings can help achieve that, what a joy! Then let me embrace suffering!... May the saints in Heaven help me discover joy in suffering. . . . What I must do is ask the Lord for the grace to abandon myself totally to His Divine Providence. Most sacred Heart of Jesus, I trust in You."

In Ants Town, both the Boss and the cynic Matsui realized that Satoko had spent her health and possibly her life for their people in true Christian charity. Both decided to request baptism, then went to cheer up Satoko with their news. The doctor was drinking tea with

Shortly before her death

her parents when they arrived and told them that Satoko was steadily getting worse. They began to discuss how much she had meant to Ants Town and her parents told how much Ants Town had meant to her. The doctor, knowing psychological factors are important to T.B. patients made a startling suggestion. "Let her go and live there as she wanted." Her mother's face flooded with tears as she said, "Even if Satoko died in a car on the way, she'd die happy!" Matsui ran up the stairs to tell

her the plan but she demurred saying she would be too much trouble. The former cynic said, "We don't want you to do a thing when you come. Just be with us, just be Ari no Machi no Maria, with your beautiful heart." In response, Satoko kissed the crucifix on her rosary.

They partitioned the storage shed and made her a small room about nine feet by nine feet. She wore a mask when visitors entered and kept a strong disinfectant in her spittoon. She was given a controversial new medicine and the crisis passed. Soon she was able to walk about. When she protested that she was not pulling her weight, Matsui told her, "Your work is to pray, to pray for us all."

Matsui asked her to write a small book detailing her experience in Ants Town. He knew that she had good writing skills as she had helped the children begin a newspaper the previous year. He felt that such a book might help publicize the plight of the homeless. She did not like the idea but he kept after her and she asked one of the priests to give her advice. He convinced her and she began writing.

Her tuberculosis was stabilized by the new medicine but forbidden to do any heavy work, she began to visit the old people in Ants Town and to help Matsui in his work. She became his secretary and helped him collect and tabulate statistics about the homeless of Tokyo.

Both Matsui and Satoko felt that the only way to help the destitute was through profitable work that restored their dignity, which was close at hand and which required no special training. Together they wrote a pamphlet on selective garbage collecting. Thousands of copies were distributed by the ragpickers. About the same time that Ants Town began, the Parisian Abbé Pierre began his Emmaus movement based on the same ideas. Some years later Ants Town joined the Emmaus International group.

Matsui's wife became a Jehovah's Witness, developed an intense hatred of Catholicism, and began to accuse Matsui of illicit relations with Satoko. There was never any solid evidence of such a thing, only the angry accusations of a woman who had never even set foot in Ant's Town. Matsui said, "I loved Satoko, but in the chaste way St. Francis loved St. Clare — if you will excuse the exaggeration of comparing me with St. Francis."

While Satoko was bedridden at Ants Town, Matsui managed to copy some entries from her diary. One of them reveals the source and spirit of all that she did. "It is difficult to be still while others are out working. Rest, they tell me! . . .There is nothing I can do except renounce my self-will. And love Jesus! . . . I have offered the Lord all I possess, and I am with Him. Not my will but His be done. If I never forget that His Providence watches over all things that happen, my heart will always be at peace. Anyhow, why should I complain about my humbling sickness and suffering? Didn't Jesus carry a cross? Elizabeth Maria, it is good for you to suffer, it is good for you to meditate alone in your bed. As long as it is for God's Glory, accept pain, make it your gift to Him. Then you can truly be the handmaid of the Lord. May His will be accomplished in me."

A young French priest of the Paris Foreign Mission Society, Robert Vallade, read about Satoko and visited her at Ants Town. She advised him, "Japanese don't like being beggars. If you want to be accepted and help them, show them how to make an honest living by setting up a ragpickers' group like us here at Ants Town." Then she invited him to stay a while to learn more about the project. He stayed and with Matsui and Satoko agreed that the poor were best helped when their dignity was respected. After his internship, he began to carry the Ants Town concept to other parts of Japan.

When the government announced its intention to burn the ragpickers of Ants Town out, Satoko prayed a great deal and reached the decision to announce her intention of praying and fasting in front of the City Office, to death if necessary, unless the city fathers found an alternative site for them. Matsui delivered her written promise along with a copy of her book, "The Children of Ants Town." Impassioned he pleaded, "Help us to keep helping ourselves. Use your authority to find us a new site where we can continue making an honest living by collecting scrap. And send us your other homeless and we will teach them how to make a living, too!" The ploy worked and they were offered the chance to buy some land for the astounding price of twenty-five million yen.

In the meantime, Satoko's health began to decline again. She wrote the impossible sum on a strip of paper and pasted it on the wall of her room. Then she told Matsui their only hope was in prayer. Brother Zeno visited and agreed to join his prayers to theirs. A few days later the government officials called Matsui to come in and hear some new developments. The price had been dropped by half, several organizations including the Archdiocese of Tokyo would contribute and the department handling the sale had agreed to payment terms that Ants Town could meet! Overjoyed, Matsui went to tell Satoko. Then he told her to pray for the recovery of her health so that she could help

Satoko's funeral Mass

with the building of the new Ants Town. She refused. Later, her mother and the doctor who had been in the room at the time discussed it with Matsui. All seemed to feel that she had offered her life to God for the Ants Town community.

The next day, about eight in the morning, Satoko slipped into a coma and within minutes stopped breathing. A priest arrived and gave her the last anointing and the doctor verified her death of a nephritis infection presumably tubercular in origin.

Satoko's funeral Mass was held in front of the Lourdes grotto in Ants Town and in spite of the bitter cold over six hundred people attended. She was buried beside her brother and sister in the Garden of Souls Cemetery in Tokyo. In 1975 Archbishop Shirayagi of Tokyo began the official investigation of her reputed holiness. ✝

23

Vincent Robert Capodanno, M.M.

United States, 1929-1967

The Grunt Padre

September 4, 1967, the static of a radio crackled in the Fifth Marine Combat Center, Quang Tin Province, Republic of Vietnam. A hollow voice announced, "Three — five, number twenty-one is KIA." Twenty-one is the numerical code for chaplain. The chaplain had been killed in action. The Fifth Regimental Commander, Colonel Stanley Davis, and Major Richard Alger, the Regimental Operations Officer, were together when Father Vincent Capodanno's death was announced. Both refused to believe the initial report and they asked the radio operator to repeat the message. The normally busy and noisy combat center became silent.

In the field, the Marines, officers and grunts (infantry soldiers) alike, openly wept for their fallen chaplain. This Catholic priest who so loved his men that he wanted to share their sufferings had died as he had lived: brave and impulsive, heroic and self-sacrificing. Chaplain Capodanno was with his men, giving comfort and courage by his presence, to the last.

The death of the courageous chaplain had a profound effect. Corporal James Harnfeldt said, "He gave his life. No one can do any more than that — that's what Christ did. . . . The only way I can justify it is that he did it because that is what he had to do, and if he is going to be a priest and a Christian there really can't be any other way. I know that but it still kills me. . . . Of all the deaths I saw and did, the greatest was his. I don't know if he knew the tremendous impact he had on me. I came back to Church because of Father Capodanno. In my life he is a saint."

On receiving notification of Capodanno's death, the whole Marine Corps in Vietnam seemed to mourn his death. Poetically, Chaplain Joseph Cloonan wrote of his death, "But every once in a while, like a flash of heat lightening, the self-giving of someone like Father Capodanno illuminates the mystery of nobility in an ignoble world."

The citation accompanying the Medal of Honor, awarded post-humously to Vincent Robert Capodanno, gives the circumstances of his death: "For conspicuous gallantry and intrepidity at the risk of his life above and beyond the call of duty as Chaplain of the 3rd Battalion, 5th Marines, 1st Marine Division (Rein), FMF, in connection with operations against enemy forces in Quang Tin Province, Republic of Vietnam of September 4, 1967. In response to reports that the 2nd Platoon of M Company was in danger of being overrun by a massed enemy assaulting force, Lieutenant Capodanno left the relative safety of the Company Command Post and ran through an open area raked with fire, directly to the beleaguered platoon. Disregarding the intense enemy small-arms, automatic-weapons, and mortar fire, he moved about the battlefield administering last rites to the dying and giving medical aid to the wounded. When an exploding mortar round inflicted painful multiple wounds to his arms and legs, and severed a portion of his right hand, he steadfastly refused all medical aid. Instead, he directed the corpsmen to help their wounded comrades and, with calm vigor, continued to move about the battlefield as he provided encouragement by voice and example to the valiant Marines. Upon encountering a wounded corpsman in the direct line of fire of an enemy machine gunner positioned approximately fifteen yards away, Lieutenant Capodanno rushed forward in a daring attempt to aid and assist the mortally wounded corpsman. At that instant, only inches from his goal, he was struck down by a burst of machine-gun fire. By his heroic conduct on the battlefield and his inspiring example, Lieutenant Capodanno upheld the finest traditions of the United States Naval Service. He gallantly gave his life for the cause of freedom."

Chaplain Eli Takesian flew into Da Nang to deliver the eulogy at the formal memorial service at the 1st Marine Division Headquarters on September 13. Several other memorial services had already spontaneously been held in a number of areas in the field. His first request was to drive to the Army mortuary where all of the bodies of the men killed in action were taken. He wanted to see and identify for himself the body of his friend. He said, "We counted 27 gunshot wounds . . . saw the shrapnel embedded in his shoulder . . . and some fingers missing from his hand. The shot that killed him entered his head from the back of his neck. Most of the gunshot wounds were in the back. Usually we looked down upon anyone with a wound in his back because it was a sign of running away . . . in Capodanno's case it verified what eyewitnesses had said. Capodanno, having seen an NVA machine gunner aim his weapon at a cluster of Marines, ran and deliberately shielded one of them with his own body, back turned to the NVA. Whether he was praying at the time is cloudy. Some said he was . . . others said he wasn't. . . . Whatever the case, his action was a profound prayer itself."

Vincent Robert Capodanno was born February 13, 1929, the youngest of nine surviving children of Vincent and Rachel Capodanno. He was born in the family home in Elm Park, Staten Island, New York. The father was an Italian immigrant who worked as a day laborer in the shipyards while Rachel handled the management of the

family's small vegetable store. The family was devoutly Catholic and young Vincent was baptized at St. Michael's Church in Mariners Harbor. Here, too, he made his First Communion and later received Confirmation. The family home was always bustling with the activities of nine children and an assortment of relatives. The children enjoyed playing simple games, listening to the radio, and roughhousing with the family sheep dog, Dawny. Vincent inevitably got tagged with the nickname,

Little Vin Capodanno, age 3, enjoys a pony ride with his older brothers Albert and Philip
PHOTOS (EXCEPT PAGE 257) COURTESY OF JIM CAPODANNO

"Junior." Although he grew up in the traditions of a profoundly religious culture, young Vincent gave no outward sign to his family during his childhood or adolescence that he ever considered a religious vocation, but later told a high school friend that he had first thought of it while in grade school.

Vincent attended Public School 44 in the borough of Richmond where he earned average grades, struggling with arithmetic and penmanship. Tall and slender, he was always neat and well-dressed. He enjoyed swimming and riding his scooter.

In 1939, Vincent Sr. suffered a fatal cerebral hemorrhage while working on a barge. It was his youngest son's tenth birthday. The family waited in vain that evening for their father to come home to celebrate the big day. Finally, some co-workers on the barge notified the family of the tragedy. Following the sudden and unexpected death of her husband, Rachel struggled to provide for her large family. The children unselfishly worked to find ways to help her. That same year saw the beginning of World War II, and three of Vincent's older brothers joined the service: two in the Army and one in the Marines.

Vincent's eighth grade graduating class voted him best looking and best dressed. He wrote in his school autograph book that his favorite song was "The Star Spangled Banner" and his hero was General Douglas MacArthur. He also noted his plans to be a doctor and listed his motto as "Do a Good Turn Daily."

In 1943, he entered Curtis Public High School where his highest grades were in Latin. Here he was a class officer, a member of the Biology Honor Society, and a counselor in the CYO (Catholic Youth Organization). His social life was somewhat limited because of his after-school job in a local drug store. In the morning before school, he attended Mass at Our Lady of Good Counsel, carrying his breakfast, usually a boiled egg, in his pocket. After finishing high school, he began working as an underwriting clerk at the Pearl Insurance Company on Maiden Lane near the Wall Street District in New York City. He continued his education by attending night classes at the School of Education at Fordham University.

In the spring of 1949, Vincent made a retreat. During the retreat he confided to his friend William Richter his deep desire to became a priest, a desire he had kept silent for years and often dismissed. He mentioned that he thought William also had a vocation to the priesthood, which Richter at the time thought was "simply crazy." As it turned out, both boys not only became priests but also entered the same religious order — The Catholic Foreign Mission Society of America, better known as Maryknoll. Because of his solicitous concern and deep love for his mother, knowing his leaving would cause her pain and hardship, Vincent delayed his entry into the seminary. He was formally accepted by Maryknoll on May 17, 1949.

On his application to Maryknoll, Vincent was asked, "What is your idea of the life and work of a foreign missioner?" He wrote, "It will mean hard physical labor with and for a group of people I may never have even heard of before. I'll be separated from my family and friends, and all the things I'm now accustomed to, for indefinite lengths of time, during which all my efforts will be devoted to the people I'm serving. Their lives, both troubles and joys, will be my life. Any personal sacrifice I may have to make will be compensated for by the fact that I am serving God." These strong and noble sentiments written by the young seminarian found their truth in his subsequent life and actions.

His college days passed quickly, and he seemed to enjoy them. In the summer, he returned home to visit his family and work at the insurance company. He received his B.A. degree with a major in philosophy in the spring of 1953 and in the fall began his first year of theology at Maryknoll's major seminary in Ossining, New York. At the Maryknoll seminary, Vincent is remembered by fellow students as a "regular guy — not very athletic, neat and meticulous in manner and dress . . . one who enjoyed smoking during the few periods in the day when it was allowed. He also had the reputation of being quite an actor."

In the final years of his academic studies, he also advanced through the minor orders in the church and proceeded to the major orders. He was ordained deacon in June of 1957 and made his lifelong commitment to remain with Maryknoll. His last year of seminary was dif-

Vincent at age 8 (left) with his brother Albert and a friend

ficult because of his mother's failing health. She had broken her hip and Vincent was given both a loan and leave time to help out at home. At last on June 14, 1958, Vincent was ordained by Francis Cardinal Spellman, Archbishop of New York, at the main Maryknoll chapel in the presence of all his family. His mother attended the ceremony in her wheel chair.

The day after ordination, Vincent attended the traditional Maryknoll departure ceremony where he, along with the other young men in his class, would receive his first formal mission assignment. Here he received his mission crucifix and his assignment, to Formosa (Taiwan). Allowed to spend the next month at home with his family, the entire Cappadano family celebrated with parties and dinners and the gregarious Vincent was the life of the party. He also took the time to read the book *Radiating Christ, An Appeal to Militant Catholics* by Raoul Plus which had been given to him as a graduation gift by the Superior General, Father Comber. The book counsels a transformation by which a person loses his own identity in His, allowing Christ's light and image to radiate from within us. The book had a profound influence on Father Capodanno and its influence unfolded in his priestly life.

Vincent's assignment to Taiwan would last six years with no vacations and he was aware that this might be the last time he would see his mother. At Idlewild (now John F. Kennedy Airport), his sister Pauline remembers that he went into the restroom to cry before the family said their final, emotional good-byes.

August 4, 1958, in company with five other Maryknoll priests, Vincent boarded the S.S. Nadilee and set out from Los Angeles to the Orient. After fourteen days they arrived in Japan where they had to wait out a typhoon. On a taxi ride into Kyoto, Father Vincent was shocked at the filth and the fact that the driver relieved himself by the road. One of the most difficult adjustments for this neat and meticulous young priest would be to adapt to the physical conditions of the people and cultures he served. After the typhoon was over, the young missionaries flew on to Taipei, the capital of Formosa. Fathers Capodanno and Sheehan were sent to work with the Hakka-Chines living in the municipality of Miaoli, located on the west coast of Taiwan. Their first home was the language school in Miaoli where they would spend the next ten months learning the Hakka dialect and culture. In their leisure time, both would visit with one of the other Maryknoll priests, go to the theater in downtown Miaoli, and spend part of their thirty-dollar-a-month stipend on Winston cigarettes available on the black market. Curious children would come up to Father Vincent to run their hands over his hairy arms, an unusual sight in the Orient. They also enjoyed riding their bikes and motor scooters. They always laughed when they heard one of the Hakkas say a favorite expression: "A perfectly happy person lives in America, marries a Japanese wife, and eats Chinese food."

After ten months of study, the two young missioners were ready to begin work. Although Father Vincent had struggled with diligence, he never achieved the proficiency in the language that he wanted. However, this same failure that disappointed him may have contributed greatly to making him an attentive listener who was able to express his ideas in a simple manner. His listening ability is one thing remembered as outstanding by the many soldiers he later counseled. Father Vincent began his work "in the field" at a Hakka plains parish in the tiny village called Tunglo. His pastor, Father Maynard Murphy, and the young Capodanno were alike in their wish for cleanliness and order, and fit together quite well. In the little mountain village, Father Vincent's duties included distributing relief food and medicine, teaching native catechists, following up their teaching work, and celebrating the sacraments, especially baptism. The title "shen fu" meaning "spiritual father" was given to the missionaries.

Missionaries in other parts of mainland China under the Communist leader Mao Zedong were imprisoned, tortured and killed. Maryknoll Bishop James Walsh was sentenced to prison where he stayed from March of 1961 until July of 1970. Although all the missionaries were prepared for the worst, Taiwan was for the most part peaceful and the people were generally receptive to the Gospel message.

For Father Vincent, the poor and unsanitary conditions of his mountain village must have provided multiple opportunities for him to gain the true spirit of humility. Although only a few letters have survived from this period, he wrote frequently to his family and friends back home. In one letter he tells about the traditions of the Chinese New Year in the village. "Even Tunglo had a dragon parade! We contributed thirty TN (ninety U.S. cents) towards the making of the dragon and since that was the largest contribution in

Tunglo we got a special bow as the dragon went past last night." Before making the contribution, it had been Father Vincent's job to make certain the dragon didn't go first to the pagan temple to worship the idols.

In 1961 Vincent's mother died but following the policy of Maryknoll he did not go home for the funeral. A letter to his sister shows his deep love for his mother and his Christian thoughts on death. After pointing out that the family can be eventually reunited in Heaven he begs her, "The ignorance, fear and hopelessness with which pagans face death must indeed be a terrifying thing to have to go through life with. Keep them in your prayers that our work here . . . will bring them to a knowledge of God and ultimately to eternal happiness, such as we can have for the asking."

In the fall of 1961, Vincent was assigned to the mountain village of Ch'ng An as the director of a youth hostel for boys of high school age. The boys spent a year at the hostel preparing for the national college entrance exam. The pressure to do well and the intense competition very often led to extreme depression even to the point of suicide. It was Father Vincent's job to meet their spiritual needs, counsel them through the difficult examinations, and to try to instill Christian values. His gift of ministry to young men facing trials seemed to blossom here and he is remembered as soft-spoken, a good listener, and one who made the boys feel as if he were truly with them in their sufferings. After this assignment, he became the acting pastor in North Miaoli and later returned to Tunglo as associate pastor. His final assignment was as pastor of a parish in Ch'ng An.

After completing his six-year mission, he spent the traditional six-month furlough with a fellow Maryknoll classmate in a tour of the Holy Land and a visit back home where he stayed with his sister in New Jersey. On his return to the Orient, he discovered to his shock and dismay that he was to be transferred to a mission school in Hong Kong due to a lack of manpower there. He arrived there in March of 1965. Although some of his correspondence shows him focusing on the positive part of the transfer, he requested to be re-assigned to his original mission territory. A turbulent restlessness within himself called for change and he continued to explore alternatives, but he lived out this time of discernment without ever defying his superiors. In early July, he sent his bishop a cablegram requesting to be allowed to join the Navy chaplains. In a letter to the Chief of Chaplains he asked about the possibility of serving specifically with the Marines and of volunteering for service in Vietnam. In August of 1965, Bishop Comber consented to Father Vincent's request and allowed him to transfer to Hawaii and begin the process of military induction.

In 1966 a reporter in Vietnam asked Father Capodanno why he became a chaplain, and he answered, "I joined the Chaplain Corps when the Vietnam War broke out because I think I'm needed here as are many more chaplains. I'm glad to help in the way I can."

The word for chaplain comes from the Latin word for cloak. It is the cloak of St. Martin of Tours that became the symbol of brotherly love of the men who serve as chaplains. In putting on the cloak of his chaplaincy, Father Vincent was inspired by a renewed sense of purpose and pastoral ministry in which his spirituality blossomed and forced him to go deeper as a priest and a missionary. Christ's thirst for souls became his thirst. Christ's compassion was to be reflected in this priest who served among those who were in the deepest of the agonies of war. Vincent was sworn in as a Lieutenant in the Chaplain Corps on December 28, 1965, and reported for active duty in January at the Naval Chaplains School in Newport, Rhode Island. Here he went through a basic eight-week course, absorbing an endless list of Navy regulations — how to salute, wear his uniform and other matters pertaining to the military. Although it was unusual to assign a priest directly from chaplain's school to Vietnam without prior military experience, possibly Father Vincent's knowledge and experience in Asia added to his own request allowed for just such an assignment. After three weeks of training at the Field Medical Service School at Camp Pendleton, California, Vince was sent to Vietnam during Holy Week of 1966. Vincent described his training at Camp Pendleton in a letter to his brother, "About half the group had never had any military service before and in the beginning, the drill classes looked something like the Marx brothers running around."

On Easter Sunday, just a few days after his arrival in DaNang, Vince went with a fellow chaplain to the front lines south of the city, his first trip into a hostile area. His companion and friend Chaplain Stanley Beach, a Baptist minister, recalled, "We spent Easter Sunday morning ministering to those men. It made a deep impression on both of us and those moments of looking into the eyes of Marines who were experienced with death gave us a greater appreciation of the hope of the Resurrection in Jesus Christ. Vin and I talked about that. He had tears in his eyes when he shared that experience." With an acute spiritual instinct, Father Vincent seemed to understand that he would sanctify men more by suffering with them than he would by preaching.

Chaplain Capodanno was sent to the 7th Marine Regiment south of Da Nang. Regimental headquarters was close to Chu Lai, and there were about four thousand Marines organized into three battalions posted near the Chu Lai airfield. Father Vincent was specifically assigned to the 1st Battalion, but he served all the battalions because he was the only Catholic chaplain in the regiment. His ministry covered a wide area and he was constantly on the move. At home base he stayed in a tent known as a "hootch." During one move he was left without a tent and one of the majors suggested he bunk with him and a lieutenant. The lieutenant did not like the idea of a chaplain bunking with him and tacked up nude photos all around Father Vince's cot to test him. Father never said a word and after a few days the lieutenant became embarrassed and took them down.

Father Vincent's future work was to be with the Marine grunts. This term refers to the enlisted infantrymen, and the term reminds them of the seriousness of their training: sweat in peace saves lives in war. Most of these infantrymen in Vietnam were very young, usually eighteen or nineteen years old, and just out of high school. What set Father Capodanno apart was the way he lived out his ministry. He lived as they did and where they went, he went. He was available night or day and he was approachable. His identity with the men enhanced and made obvious the genuineness of his loving care and concern for them. Soon he was respectfully and affectionately dubbed "The Grunt Padre."

Father Vincent attracted people and there are numerous stories recalled of his personal assistance to his men. One young man had feet too large to fit standard marine boots, so he was restricted to base while his buddies were out on the line. This led to depression, feeling he was letting his unit down. Father Vincent stepped in and had the young man sent on leave to Hong Kong where he was able to have a pair of boots tailor-made.

As part of his duty, Father spent endless hours with wounded and dying soldiers. Then he wrote letters of condolence and information to their parents and families. Most of his few spare hours were filled with this merciful mission of correspondence. He also wrote letters to friends and organizations, asking for gifts for his Marines and wrote again with thanks for their response. There were occasions for formal religious training since some of the young men made the decision to enter the Church. And there are countless stories of Father Vincent's comfort and compassion in the face of death.

After a battalion move across the Tra Bong River, Father Vincent received permission to pick the site for a new chapel and to supervise its construction from native materials. With his typical quiet humor he wrote home about their new location, "It is here that I live and here that we have a bamboo and coconut-thatch chapel. Incidentally, coconut tree branches form a more waterproof thatch than does straw . . . just in case you are ever required to make the choice." Father was proud of the new chapel, which was usually full to overflowing during services. He had a prodigious work schedule and routinely said a minimum of fifteen Masses each week. He went on as many operations as possible with his men in order to be, as he put it, "available in the event anything serious occurs; to learn firsthand the problems of the men, and to give them moral support, to comfort them with my presence." Very often, blood joined the sweat, mud and tears of this battlefield priest. The fastidious young missionary of Taiwan had evolved into a "mud Marine."

A friend teased him about wearing a flak jacket, telling him that it wasn't a very good advertisement for his faith. Laughing, Father Capodanno replied, "I know it, but it's protective coloration so I blend in with the men. In addition, I understand their trials better if I accept the same burdens they do, such as wearing the jacket and carrying a pack."

Father Vincent loved the orient and grew to have a special love for the Vietnamese people. He joined in the Marines' social programs and often assisted and visited in the villages. He was sometimes called on to give lectures on Asian culture to other chaplains and officers. A fellow officer recalled his compassion not only for the Marines but also for the Vietnamese citizens. He treated them with compassion and comforted them on every opportunity.

For their part, the Marines loved and valued their "Grunt Padre" and went out of their way to help him in many ways. One sergeant managed to routinely supply Father Vincent with ice for his personal use. Those who have never been in an excessively hot and humid climate can hardly realize what a wonderful gift this was. Completely unselfish and always thoughtful of others, the padre usually gave the ice away. Knowing that this ability gave the padre much pleasure, the sergeant never let on that he knew his gift was being distributed to others and continued to get ice for the chaplain. Stories about Capodanno's generosity are numerous. He gave away his personal towel, his books, and once even his seat in the dry cab of a truck. He let two tired young grunts sit in the cab while he got soaking wet in the back of the truck. During one operation, he took off his rain suit and gave it to a wounded Marine, spending the remainder of the operation without suitable rain clothing. Wherever he was and whatever he had he gave to ease and elevate the lives of others.

On election day in 1966, the battalion was assigned to the village of Van I Ia to supervise the national elections which the Viet Cong tried to disrupt and to protect several tons of rice from falling into enemy hands. From a hillside, Father Vincent and others were watching the Vietnamese vote with amazing perseverance in spite of constant shelling from the Viet Cong. Laughingly, Father Vincent remarked that he had only thought that Staten Island was a tough place to vote. Then he ardently noted that Americans back home had forgotten what a cherished thing freedom is and what it meant to fight for it.

On operations, by his own request, Father Vincent would deploy with the assault companies because he knew he would be most needed there. In a recommendation for the Bronze Star award, Major Edward Fitzgerald wrote, "Father Capodanno was particularly adept in putting men in the proper frame of mind before and during battle. He had the confidence and deep respect of the men and healed the scars, which the loss of a friend frequently cause in those who survive. He eliminated bitterness from the hearts and instilled Christian determination and morals to be drawn against in future battles. He encouraged the men of all faiths to do more for their God, our Country, their corps and themselves." For his efforts during six combat operations, Father Capodanno received the Vietnamese Cross of Gallantry with Silver Star and the Navy Bronze Star. Modest and humble, he did not even mention these awards to his family.

In 1966, Father Capodanno was transferred to work in the medical field hospital near Chu Lai. Here, the Medical Corps treated over a million South Vietnamese civilians as well as nearly seven thousand wounded Marines and sailors. Many Marines died in his caring arms. His duties alternated between receiving the wounded and visiting patients in the ward. He rarely got more than four hours sleep a night with his draining and hectic schedule. A Navy doctor commented about him, ". . . never had I ever seen such dedication and selflessness, not as a sticky 'piety' but as a 'way.' For the hundreds of cigarettes he held for the wounded, many of whom could no longer reach their hands to their lips, and for the hundreds of letters he wrote and helped to write for his men, the Marines will never forget that he was one of them, this priest of God is a hero."

A young corpsman was brought in with such severe burns that he knew from his own training that he was dying. Capodanno heard his confession and asked if there was anything he wanted. When the corpsman requested a beer, Father brought it from the officers' club at once and then stayed with him, holding him until he died.

A final homily written for a memorial service was found scribbled in Father Vincent's pocket calendar. In part it reads, "... our minds groan amid the tragedies and complexities of life looking for an answer. It is with hesitation that we accept the fact: there is no easy answer, . . . Somehow these events have a meaning that somehow they work for the good of the persons involved. We cannot fully comprehend how but only that they do."

In January of 1967, Father Vincent completed the necessary paperwork to extend his tour in Vietnam for six months. He made a brief retreat in Manila, then visited friends in Taiwan and Honolulu and went home to visit his family. This visit was a rather somber one because the anti-war climate he found at home and the growing lack of support for the brave men he knew at the battlefront depressed him. For Father Vincent, the United States' involvement in Vietnam was a justified and ethical undertaking and he believed that the war was fought in order to free the Vietnamese from Communist oppression. Partially his beliefs were influenced by his having seen first-hand, and understanding the tragedy, of Communist rule in China. He felt that the war opponents just didn't understand what was going on and that they were being misled.

Father Vincent returned to Vietnam in July of 1967, assigned to the 1st Battalion, 5th Marines in one of the fiercest combat zones, the

Que Son Valley. The entire valley was the scene of violent fighting throughout the summer.

Lieutenant Frederick Smith remembers meeting Father Capodanno at a late night card game and remembers him not only as a good player but also says, "He was a man who had the courage of a lion and the faith of a martyr."

Father Vincent loved his Marines and wanted to stay with them, especially during the holiday season, which is always the most difficult time

Lt. Vince Capodanno, U.S.N.
PHOTO COURTESY OF CHAPLAIN WILLIAM E. TAYLOR, U.S.N. (RET.)

for a young man to be away from home. Although they were denied, he put in requests to remain even past the one-allowed six-month extension.

Father Vincent never committed any act of aggression for his was a spiritual battle. However, because he went into the field he was ordered to wear a gun which at first he allowed to rust as he knew he would never use it. At last, one of the soldiers told him it was a shame to let the pistol rust, which made him realize that it might be recycled to one of the soldiers when he finished with it and it might be needed. Therefore he cleaned it perfectly and for the rest of the time he had the cleanest, shiniest pistol in the unit. Once his division chaplain asked what he did when he was out with the troops and Capodanno replied, "I am just there with them. I walk with them and sit with them; I eat with them and sleep in the holes with them, and I talk with them but only when they are ready to talk. It takes time but I never rush them."

Chaplain Takesian's eulogy was a beautiful tribute to his friend and fellow soldier. He said, "Chaplain Vincent Robert Capodanno died in the manner in which he lived: unselfishly. He was ascetic, humble and thoughtful, a man imbued with the spirit of Christ. . . . Later, upon hearing the fatal news, a young Marine came to me and tearfully asked, "If life meant so much to Chaplain Capodanno, then why did he allow his own to be taken?" 'The answer is in your question,' I replied. 'It was precisely because he loved life — the lives of others — that he so freely gave his own.' Chaplain Takesian closed with these words: "For the life and Christian witness of Chaplain Vincent Robert Capodanno, thanks be to God. Amen." ✝

THANK YOU

Rev. Xavier Albo, S.J., La Paz, Bolivia.

Mons. Oscar Sanchez Barba, postulator of the Mexican diocesan causes, Rome, Italy.

Alejandro Bermudez, Lima, Peru.

Rev. John Boscoe, C.S.B., Tehuacan, Mexico

Janine M. Bruce, archives, St. Mary's Seminary, Baltimore, Maryland.

Rev. Blaine Burkey, O.F.M. Cap., Hays, Kansas.

Sister Rita Bussieres, R.J.M., Centre Dina Belanger, Quebec, Canada

Sister Marie de Chantal, V.H.M., Toledo, Ohio.

Rev. Jose de Vera, S.J., Jesuit Information Bureau, Rome, Italy.

Rev. Augustin Churruca, S.J., Veracruz, Mexico.

Discalced Carmelite Nuns, San Remo, Italy.

Rev. David Fernandez Davalos, S.J., Guadalajara, Mexico.

Professor Jean Duchesne, special adviser, Secretariat particulier du Cardinal, Archeveche de Paris, Paris, France.

Rev. Mateo Garau, S.J., La Paz, Bolivia.

Rev. Tomas de Hijar, Guadalajara, Mexico.

Sister Sharon Elizabeth, V.H.M., Toledo, Ohio.

Rev. Herondi Fernandes de Araujo, S.X., Wayne, New Jersey.

Rev. Richard Flores, Ft. Worth, Texas.

Sister Mary Frances, C.P., Ellisville, Missouri.

Rev. Francis Fukamizu, Archbishop's House, Tokyo, Japan.

Jim Gilboy, C.M.J., Marian Publishers, Oak Lawn, Illinois.

Sister Gabriel, Our Lady's Nurses for the Poor, Coogee, Australia.

Brother Hilary Gilmartin, f.s.c., Romeoville, Illinois.

The family Gonzalez Barros, Madrid, Spain.

Gonzalo Guimaraens, CubDest, São Paulo, Brazil.

Rev. Boniface Hanley, West Milford, New Jersey.

José Manuel Hernandez, Key Biscayne, Florida.

Rev. Paul Hu, SOLT, Corpus Christi, Texas.

Rev. Armando Llorente, S.J., Miami, Florida.

Friar Eugene Masaru Kawashimo, O.F.M. Conv., provincial, Tokyo, Japan.

Leo Knowles, Manchester, England.

Rev. Philip S. Kean, S.S., St. Mary's Seminary, Baltimore , Maryland.

Rev. Terence Kristofak, Passionist Historical Archives, Union City, New Jersey.

Sister Marcelle Lachance, R.J.M., Centre Dina-Belanger, Sillery, Quebec, Canada.

Rev. Campion Laly, O.F.M., Tokyo, Japan.

Guy Levac, director of communications, Archdiocese of Ottawa, Canada.

Anita Lewis, The Passionist Historical Archives, Union City, New Jersey.

Rev. Stephen McGrath, O.F.M., vice postulator for the cause of Margaret Sinclair, Edinburgh, Scotland.

Irma Magana, Dallas, Texas.

Brother Rodolfo Meoli, postulator general of the Christian Brothers, Rome, Italy.

Father Roger Mercurio, C.P., archivist, Passionist Research Center, Chicago, Illinois.

Rev. Daniel L. Mode, Arlington, Virginia.

Bill Moreau, Toronto, Canada.

Therese Mulhern, Oakdale, Minnesota.

Karin Murthough, Houston, Texas.

Rev. Gabriel B. O'Donnell, O.P., postulator, Michael J. McGivney Guild, New Haven, Connecticutt.

Rev. Alfonso Pedrajas, S.J., La Paz, Bolivia.

Sister Mary Carita Pendergast, S.C., Convent Station, New Jersey.

Rev. Luigi Peraboni, Milan, Italy.

Jan Petkov, Czech Republic.

Otto Perez, Houston, Texas.

Rev. Carl Quebedeaux, C.M.F., Chicago, Illinois.

Msgr. Roger Quesnel, P.H., Ottawa, Ontario, Canada.

Rev. John Render, C.P. Passionist Research Center, Chicago, Illinois.

Rev. Mario Riboldi, Milan, Italy.

Mary Alice Richard, Branch, Louisiana.

Rev. Enrique San Pedro, S.J. (deceased).

Rev. Ambrogio Sanna, O.F.M., Conv, postulator general, Rome, Italy.

Rev. Ignacio Segarra Baneres, Barcelona, Spain.

Rev. Munari Tiberio, Zapopan, Mexico.

Rev. Slawomir Trzasko, O.M.I., Our Lady Queen of Poland Church, Edmonton, Canada.

Rev. Redumptus Valabek, O.Carm., Rome, Italy.

Sharon Walsh, The Rev. Vincent Robrt Capodanno Foundation, Fairfax, Virginia.

Rev. Marcellus White, C.P., St. Joseph's Manor, Brockton, Massachusetts.

Johannes Zheng, Beijing, China.

Teresa Zheng, New York.

P. Giovanni Zubiani, C.P., postulator general, Rome, Italy.

SELECTED BIBLIOGRAPHY

Asociacion Causa Beatificacion Alexia. Noticias de Alexia. Madrid: 1989-2000.

Associacio pro Beatificacio d' Antoni Gaudi. *God's Architect*. Barcelona:

APBAG, undated.

Audette, Florestine, RJM, translator. *In Dina's Footsteps. Montreal: The Religious of Jesus and Mary*, 1994.

Ball, Ann. *Modern Saints: Their Lives and Faces*. Rockford, Illinois: TAN Books, 1983.

Ball, Ann. *The Persecuted Church*. Avon, New Jersey: Magnificat Press, 1990.

Barry, D.E. *Margaret Sinclair*. Edinburgh: Scottish Catholic International Aid Fund, 1979.

Belanger, Dina. *Chant d' Amour*. Sillery, Quebec: Sisters of Jesus and Mary, 1997.

Bermudez, Alejandro. "Some Homegrown Heavenly Help for the Young." Our Sunday Visitor, January 9, 2000, p. 14.

Bocos Merino, Fr. Aquilino, C.M.F. *Missionary Testament of Our Martyrs*.

Circular Letter by Fr. Superior General. Rome: Claretians, 1992.

Breton, P.E. *Blacksmith of God*. Toronto: Mission Press, 1960.

Bunson, Matthew, Margaret, and Stephen, *John Paul II's Book of Saints*. Huntington, Indiana: Our Sunday Visitor Publishing Division, 1999.

Coady, Mary Frances. "A Journey of the Heart." Canadian Catholic Review. October 1989, p. 324.

Coady, Mary Frances. *The Hidden Way: The Life and Influence of Almire Pichon*. Toronto: Novalis, 1999.

Corley, Feliz. "A Patron Saint for Cop Killers?" Our Sunday Visitor, October 1, 1995, p. 6.

Espinal, Luis, S.J. *Oraciones a Quemarropa*. Sucre, Bolivia: Qori Llama, 1987.

Fox, John. "Murder of a Polish Priest." The Reader's Digest. December, 1985, p. 66.

Garcia, Pedro, C.M.F. *Singing Into Life: Young 20th Century Martyrs*. Chicago: Miles Jesu Publications, undated.

Geddes, Diana. "Saint?" *National Catholic Register*: August 7, 1994, p. 3.

Gianopoulos, Janet. "The Story of Satoko Kitahara." Huntington, Indiana: Our Sunday Visitor, August 6, 1995.

Glynn, Paul. *The Smile of a Ragpicker*. Hunter's Hill, Australia: Marist Fathers Books, 1993.

Gonzalez, P. Norberto, C.P. *Hasta Dar la Vida*. Madrid: Ediciones Parionario, undated.

Gonzalez, Ramon. "Hundreds Celebrate Holy Brother Anthony." *The Western Catholic Reporter*. July 14, 1997, p. 3.

Hanley, Boniface, O.F.M. "All He Could Do Was Pray." *The Anthonian*, Vol 53, 1979.

Hanley, Boniface, O.F.M. *The Mary of Ant Town*. The Anthonian. Patterson, New Jersey: St. Anthony's Guild, Volume 60, 4th Quarter, 1986.

Hanley, Boniface, O.F.M. *With Minds of Their Own*. Notre Dame, Indiana: Ave Maria Press, 1991.

Hernandez, Jose M. *The ACU at the Threshold of the Third Millennium*. Miami: Agrupacion Catolica Universitaria, 1999.

Holbock, Ferdinand. *New Saints and Blesseds of the Catholic Church*. San Francisco: Ignatius Press, 2000.

Johnston, Francis. *Margaret Sinclair*. London: Incorporated Truth Society, 1979.

Kauffman, Christopher J. *Micheal J. McGivney*. A privately published paper, undated.

Kelley, Francis Clement. *Blood Drenched Altars*. Rockford, Illinois: TAN Books, 1987.

Klita, P.J. *Servant of God Brother Anthony Kowalczyk*. Edmonton, Canada: Accent Printing, 1982.

Knowles, Leo. *Candidates for Sainthood*. St. Paul: Carillon Books, 1978.

Lemonnier, Augustin-Michel. *Light Over the Scaffold and Cell 18*. New York: Alba House, 1996.

Lopez, Martine. *Et Elles Firent Don de Leurs Vies*. Madrid: Editorial Cor Jesu, undated.

McKinney, Br. Oswin. *A Remarkable LIfe*. Coogee, Australia: Our Lady's Nurses of the Poor, 1992.

McMahon, John F., MSC. *Eileen O'Connor and Our Lady's Nurses for the Poor*. Waverly, Australia: Society of Our Lady's Nurses for the Poor, 1988.

Miller, Michael J., trans. *New Saints and Blesseds of the Catholic Church*. San Francisco: Ignatius Press, 2000.

Mode, Rev. Daniel L. *The Grunt Padre: Father Vincent Robert Capodanno, Vietnam 1966-1967*. Oaklawn, Illinois: CMJ Marian Publishers, 2000.

Monet, Jacques, S.J. *A Man Who Walked With God*. Ottawa: Diocesan Life Publications, 1991.

Monge, Michael. *Alexia: A Story of Joy and Heroism in Suffering*. Manila: Sinag-tala Publications, 1994.

Munari, P. Tiberio. *Derramarron su Sangre por Cristo: Los Jaliscienses Siervos de Dios*. Guadalajara: Ediciones Xavierianas, 1998.

Munari, P. Tiberio. *Una Gloria de Arandas: Luis Magana Servin, Martir*. Guadalajara: Ediciones Xavierianas, 1998.

Naismith, Albert, press officer. *Margaret Sinclair*. Glasgow: Catholic Press Office, no date.

O'Donnell, Rev. Gabriel B., O.P. Father Michael J. McGivney Guild Newsletter, issues 1997-2000.

Parsons, Wilfred, S.J. *Mexican Martyrdom*. Rockford, Illinois: TAN Books, 1987.

Pedrajas, Alfonso, S.J. *¡Lucho Vive!* La Paz: Editorial Verbo Divino, 1999.

Pendergast, S.C., Sister Mary Carita. *Havoc in Hunan*. Morristown, New Jersey: College of St. Elizabeth Press, 1991.

Religious of Jesus and Mary of the Canadian Provinces. *Dina Belanger: The Fidelity of Love*. Paris: Editions Lambert-Laurent S.A., 1991.

Riboldi, Don Mario. *Un Vero Kalo*. Milan: La Voce, 1993 and 1997.

Salm, Luke, F.S.C. *The Martyrs of Turon and Tarragona*. Romeoville, Illinois: Christian Brothers Publications, 1990.

Segarra Baneres, Ignacio. *Gente Que Hizo Mucho.Barcelona*. Editorial Armonia, 1992.

Tuck, Jim. *The Holy War in Los Altos*. Tucson: University of Arizona Press, 1982.

Valabek, P. Redemptus. *Profiles in Holiness I*. Rome: Edizioni Carmelitane, 1996.

Vanier, Therese. "My Unforgettable Father." Readers Digest, May 1979, p. 212.

Villegas, Gabriel Campo, C.M.F. *The Claretian Martyrs of Barbastro*. May 20, 1992.

Villegas, Gabriel Campo, C.M.F. *The Claretian Martyrs of Barbastro*. Quezon City, Philippines: Claretian Publications, 1992.

Visitandines in the United States, trans. *And They Gave Their Lives*.

_____ Archival material, the Passionist Historical Archives, Union City, New Jersey.

_____ *Faithful . . . Even to Giving One's Life: Lasallian Martyrology*. Rome: Generalate FSC, 1998.

_____ *Sanguis Martyrum Semen: Galeria de Martires Mexicanos*. San Antonio: Imprenta Universal, undated.

_____ *The Life and Legacy of Father Michael J. McGivney*. Knights of Columbus, undated.

_____ *The Oratory*. Special issue dedicated to Brother Andre. Montreal, May 1971.

_____ *Pasion de Cristo en Cuba*. Santiago de Chile: Departamento de Publicaciones del Secretariado de Difusion, 1962.

HOLY PERSONS IN THIS BOOK

GENERAL INDEX

Our Sunday Visitor . . .
Your Source for Discovering
the Riches of the Catholic Faith

Our Sunday Visitor has an extensive line of materials for young children, teens, and adults. Our books, Bibles, booklets, CD-ROMs, audios, and videos are available in bookstores worldwide.

To receive a FREE full-line catalog or for more information, call **Our Sunday Visitor** at **1-800-348-2440**. Or write, **Our Sunday Visitor** / 200 Noll Plaza / Huntington, IN 46750.

- -

Please send me: ___A catalog
Please send me materials on:
___Apologetics and catechetics   ___Reference works
___Prayer books   ___Heritage and the saints
___The family   ___The parish
Name_____
Address_____Apt._____
City_____State____Zip_____
Telephone (   ) _____

                                               A19BBABP

- -

Please send a friend: ___A catalog
Please send a friend materials on:
___Apologetics and catechetics   ___Reference works
___Prayer books   ___Heritage and the saints
___The family   ___The parish
Name_____
Address_____Apt._____
City_____State____Zip_____
Telephone (   ) _____

                                               A19BBABP

- -

Our Sunday Visitor
200 Noll Plaza
Huntington, IN 46750
Toll free: **1-800-348-2440**
E-mail: osvbooks@osv.com
Website: www.osv.com